D0394353

MINE EYES HAVE SEEN THE GLORY

MINE EYES HAVE

A Journey into the

NEW YORK • OXFORD

SEEN THE GLORY

Evangelical Subculture
in America

Randall Balmer

OXFORD UNIVERSITY PRESS • 1989

Oxford University Press

Oxford   New York   Toronto
Delhi   Bombay   Calcutta   Madras   Karachi
Petaling Jaya   Singapore   Hong Kong   Tokyo
Nairobi   Dar es Salaam   Cape Town
Melbourne   Auckland

and associated companies in
Berlin   Ibadan

Copyright © 1989 by Oxford University Press, Inc.

Published by Oxford University Press, Inc.,
200 Madison Avenue, New York, NY 10016

Oxford is a registered trademark of Oxford University Press

Library of Congress Cataloging-in-Publication Data
Balmer, Randall Herbert.
Mine eyes have seen the glory : a journey into the evangelical
subculture in America / Randall Balmer.
p. cm.
ISBN 0-19-505117-3
1. Evangelicalism—United States—History—20h century.
2. Fundamentalism—History—20th century. 3. Pentecostals—
United States—History—20th century. 4. United States—
Church history—20th century. I. Title.
BR1642.U5B35   1989
269'.2'0973—dc19   88–34315   CIP

1 2 3 4 5 6 7 8 9

Printed in the United States of America
on acid-free paper

*For Christian
who in time, I trust, will find his place
in the patchwork quilt of American evangelicalism*

ACKNOWLEDGMENTS

A NUMBER OF PEOPLE contributed to this book in myriad ways. John Wilson, Yoma Ullman, Albert Raboteau, Mark Noll, and Frederick Borsch all provided advice and encouragement at the formative stages of this project; Don Haymes, Marvin Bergman, Sue Anne Morrow, and Stephen Stein led me to believe I might be on to something. Several colleagues at Columbia—Robert Somerville, Wayne Proudfoot, and Jack Hawley—gave an early draft of the manuscript the benefit of their scrutiny, as did Grant Wacker and Elena Garella. Peter Awn got me thinking about the meaning of modernity to fundamentalists, and Harry Stout suggested several interpretations which I have tried to develop in various places. Stephen Warner, a true sociologist, corrected some of the mistaken notions that fell from the pen of a shade-tree sociologist. Jack Fitzmier is both a good friend and a trenchant critic, and he manages somehow to keep one role from compromising the other.

Others contributed in ways less tangible but no less important. Countless late-night conversations with Jerome and Kay Iverson over the years have helped me understand the psychology of growing up fundamentalist. Also, I owe a debt of gratitude to my parents, whose gentleness, faith, and piety I have always deemed worthy of emulation, even as I fell so abysmally short of those standards.

I know that many of the people I've just named will disagree with some, much, and perhaps all of this book, so I hasten to add the following disclaimer: I alone bear responsibility for what follows. Far too often in their history evangelicals have judged people guilty by association. That verdict, I emphasize, should not be rendered in this case.

Several others made possible the completion of this volume. A grant-in-aid from the American Council of Learned Societies helped to defray the costs of travel. The Columbia University Council for Research in the Humanities also provided a stipend, for which I am most grateful. Paul Schlotthauer and Cynthia Read made this a better manuscript than it would have been without their steady editorial hands.

The most timely encouragement, however, came from this latter source. After several fruitless approaches to foundations and publishers, I had virtually given up on my quixotic idea to travel around America and write about popular evangelicalism. Then an envelope arrived from Cynthia Read, religion editor at Oxford University Press. Responding to a letter I had written in the *New York Times*, she asked if I was working on any projects that Oxford might find interesting. Figuring I had nothing to lose, I dusted off an old prospectus, and soon thereafter, armed with a contract and fueled by a modest advance, I set off to explore the evangelical subculture in America.

Kathryn, my wife, bore patiently with those travels, especially since my absence as half-time homemaker necessitated other, more complicated arrangements for the care of Christian and Andrew. On the morning of one of my final trips, I informed Christian, not yet three years old, that I would be leaving again for several days. "You know what, Daddy?" he said. "You sure do leave a lot."

Well, son, after two years of airports, rental cars, cheap motel rooms, and enough bad sermons to last a lifetime, I'm home.

New York   R. B.
March 1989

A WORD ABOUT WORDS

FOR OUR PURPOSES, any discussion of the terms *evangelical, fundamentalist, charismatic,* and *pentecostal* should steer a middle course between an extended, technical treatment and the kind of dismissive description suggested by Potter Stewart's attempt to define pornography a few years back. "I can't define it," the Supreme Court justice acknowledged, "but I know it when I see it."

The term *evangelical* has been bandied about a lot in recent years. The *Oxford English Dictionary* defines it simply: "Of or pertaining to the Gospel" of the New Testament, especially the gospels of Matthew, Mark, Luke, and John.[1] Historically, the term often refers to the theology of the Protestant Reformation in the sixteenth century, when Martin Luther "rediscovered the gospel" after its eclipse in the scholastic theology of the Middle Ages. Luther believed that Roman Catholic theology, particularly the thought of St. Thomas Aquinas, had compromised the *evangel* or gospel, the "good news" of the New Testament, by substituting a theology of works (the notion that you effectively earn your salvation by good works, avoiding sin, and remaining in communion with the Church) for the New Testament theology of grace (God, through Jesus Christ, bestows a

saving grace without regard to human merit). For Luther, this discovery, based on his study of St. Paul's letters to the Galatians and
to the Romans, liberated him from responsibility for his own
salvation.

Ostensibly at least, modern-day evangelicals still subscribe to the
rudiments of Luther's theology, although they rejected his ideas
about polity and worship as too formal and "papist," and their theology emphasizes human volition in salvation far more than Luther
would have countenanced. *Evangelical* has picked up other connotations in the four-and-one-half centuries since Luther challenged
the papacy and launched the Protestant Reformation. Evangelicals
generally believe that a spiritual rebirth, a "born-again" experience
(which they derive from John 3) during which one acknowledges
personal sinfulness and Christ's atonement, is necessary for salvation. While Luther certainly took the Scriptures seriously—they
formed the basis for his attacks on Roman Catholic accretions to
Christian theology—many successive evangelicals have insisted on
a literalistic hermeneutic for understanding the Bible. In the nineteenth century, amidst challenges from Darwinism and the discipline of higher criticism emanating from Germany, this insistence
on literalism led to an emphasis on the inerrancy of the Scriptures.
Evangelicalism has also been characterized by a proselytizing zeal
that, at various points in its history, particularly in the eighteenth
and nineteenth centuries, has erupted into large-scale revivals or
spiritual awakenings.

Part of what defines an evangelical, however, transcends mere
doctrine or belief; in greater or lesser degrees, evangelicals place a
good deal of emphasis on spiritual piety. On May 24, 1738, John
Wesley attended a religious gathering on Aldersgate Street in Lon-
don. There, as someone read Luther's preface to his commentary
on the book of Romans, Wesley felt his heart "strangely warmed"
and felt an assurance that Christ "had taken away *my* sins, even
mine, and saved *me* from the law of sin and death."[2] Wesley's evangelical experience has served as a model for many American evangelicals. They, like him, point to some sudden, instantaneous,
datable experience of grace, and they aspire to the kind of warm-
hearted piety so characteristic of Wesley's spiritual life.

In the years since the Iranian Revolution, the term *fundamentalist* has been applied to many religions to denote literalistic, moralistic, pietistic, and even militant impulses within the larger tradition. However, the word has its origins in American evangelicalism and derives from a series of pamphlets entitled *The Fundamentals*, published early in the twentieth century to turn back the theological challenges of Protestant liberals or "modernists." These pamphlets, financed by California tycoons Lyman and Milton Stewart of Union Oil, set forth a series of doctrines their authors regarded as essential to evangelical Christianity. Those who subscribed to these doctrines, which included belief in the virgin birth of Jesus, the infallibility of the Bible, and Christ's imminent return to earth, became known as *fundamentalists*. Many within the fundamentalist camp, moreover, chose to separate from denominations that harbored modernist ideas, and their general suspicion of "worldliness" issued in strict codes of personal morality and taboos against such worldly evils as cosmetics, card-playing, dancing, movies, and alcohol.

Pentecostals, members of such denominations as the Church of God in Christ, the Assemblies of God, and Aimee Semple McPherson's International Church of the Foursquare Gospel, comprise another camp of evangelicals. Rising out of the holiness movement in the nineteenth century and the pentecostal revivals in the early years of the twentieth century, pentecostals believe that the spiritual gifts bestowed upon the early church in the book of Acts are available to modern-day believers. Pentecostals insist that a spiritual experience of baptism or filling by the Holy Spirit, often marked by *glossolalia* or "speaking in tongues," constitutes the mark of a true Christian. Other spiritual gifts include the word of knowledge (an ability to discern the needs and spiritual condition of another) and divine healing.

Like pentecostals, *charismatics* believe in the spiritual gifts (*charismata*), but this term generally refers to those affiliated with non-pentecostal denominations. Pat Robertson, a charismatic, is a member of the Southern Baptist Convention, a denomination that generally shies away from dramatic, emotive outpourings of the Holy Spirit. Charismatics, moreover, have been active among the Episcopalians since 1959, and since the mid-1960s the charismatic movement has taken root within Roman Catholicism and other denominations.

If all this sounds neat and compartmentalized, it isn't. Southern Baptists, for instance, squirm in the face of attempts to force them into categories. For years, evangelicals and fundamentalists have looked askance at pentecostals and charismatics. Many evangelicals resist the label fundamentalist. Jerry Falwell, on the other hand, styles himself a fundamentalist, not an evangelical, although he pulled off a minor miracle in the late 1970s and early 1980s by uniting hitherto diverse elements of American evangelicalism under the political banner of Moral Majority. I can think of several people in the pages that follow who would be embarrassed, even outraged, to appear in the same book as some of the others treated here.

Such is the unwieldly nature of evangelicalism in America. But its breadth and diversity, I think, only add to its allure. All of the terms above appear in the following pages; the context should make the meaning clear. Moreover, I shall use the word *evangelical* as an umbrella term to refer broadly to conservative Protestants—including fundamentalists, evangelicals, pentecostals, and charismatics—who insist on some sort of spiritual rebirth as a criterion for entering the kingdom of heaven, who often impose exacting behavioral standards on the faithful, and whose beliefs, institutions, and folkways comprise the evangelical subculture in America.[3]

NOTES

1. *Oxford English Dictionary* (1971), s.v. "Evangelical."

2. Quoted in Hugh T. Kerr and John M. Mulder, eds., *Conversions* (Grand Rapids: Wm. B. Eerdmans, 1983), p. 59.

3. I'd like to add here a parenthetical note about pronunciation. Almost everywhere I traveled, evangelicals pronounced the word *evangelical* with a short "e" (the first two syllables rhyme with "leaven" or, perhaps more appropriately, "heaven"). Almost all the people I encountered who could *not* be described as evangelicals pronounced the first syllable with a long "e" (ee-van-gel-i-cal; similar to the way Britons pronounce *economic*).

CONTENTS

MINE EYES HAVE SEEN THE GLORY

Upon my arrival in the United States, the religious aspect of the country was the first thing that struck my attention.

ALEXIS DE TOCQUEVILLE, 1835

... I can see no reason, but the most deceitful one, for calling the religion of this land Christianity. I look upon it as the climax of all misnomers, the boldest of all frauds, and the grossest of all libels. ... I am filled with unutterable loathing when I contemplate the religious pomp and show, together with the horrible inconsistencies, which every where surround me.

FREDERICK DOUGLASS, 1845

Heave an egg out of a Pullman window and you will hit a Fundamentalist almost anywhere in the United States today.

H. L. MENCKEN, 1925

Glibness is the great danger in answering people's questions about religion.

FLANNERY O'CONNOR, 1958

Prologue

IN BAY CITY MICHIGAN, on a rainy day during my childhood, I finally mustered the courage to "witness" to Stanley Strelecki, my next-door neighbor and playmate. Though not yet in my teens, hundreds of hours of sermons, Sunday school lessons, revival meetings, and Bible study had prepared me for this moment.

"Stanley," I began, my voice quavering. "Are you a Christian?" There. The opening gambit, everyone said, was the toughest. After that initial exchange, I had been promised, witnessing would get easier.

"Yes," he answered.

None of the coaching, none of the role-playing in church youth meetings or pep talks at Bible camp, had prepared me for that response. I was ready with reasoned arguments about the existence of God, the sinfulness of humanity, and every person's need to accept Christ as his or her savior. But how do you deal with someone who lies about his spiritual condition? Stanley, I knew, was a Roman Catholic, not a Christian, a plight in some respects worse than outright paganism, I had been told, because it lulled followers into

3

a deadly complacency. But *Christian?* Certainly no Catholic, no matter how benighted, would dare call himself a Christian.

"Are you sure?" I asked meekly, beating a hasty retreat.

He was sure. Once the rain cleared, we resumed playing catch and fantasizing about our futures in professional baseball.

I've long since lost track of Stanley Strelecki, although I know he never became a pitcher for the Detroit Tigers. I never became a second baseman for the Tigers, nor did I follow my father's footsteps and become the preacher and evangelist that my parents so fervently wanted.

It would be years beyond college before I realized why that exchange with Stanley Strelecki was so peculiar, why I as an evangelical, a fundamentalist, simply spoke a different language from Stanley. *Christian,* in the vernacular of my evangelical subculture, was an exclusive, elitist term reserved for someone who had "prayed the prayer," had acknowledged personal sinfulness and the need for salvation, and "accepted Jesus into his heart."*

Christian also meant a good deal more. It meant immersing oneself in the evangelical subculture, affiliating with a local church (not just any church, but a church that "preached the Bible"), eschewing "worldliness" in its many insidious forms, hewing to strict codes of personal morality, sending the kids off to Sunday school, youth meetings, Bible camps, and, eventually, to a Bible school or a Christian college. It meant establishing a daily "quiet time," a period of personal devotions characterized by reading the Bible, meditation, and prayer. Being a *Christian* meant witnessing, "sharing your faith" with non-Christians—that is, anyone who did not fit this definition.

It also meant feeling very guilty if you failed to do any of the above, or if you failed to do it with sufficient rigor or enthusiasm, for there were always spiritual athletes around to shame you—pastors, traveling evangelists, godly matriarchs in any congregation

---

* Semantics are quite important on this issue. Some evangelicals draw a careful distinction between being (merely) Christian and being *a* Christian; therein lies the difference between hell and heaven. Most evangelicals, moreover, bristle at being called *religious* because identifying their faith as a *religion* implies that there may be other, equally valid faiths, a concession most evangelicals are reluctant to grant.

whose personal piety served both as examples worthy of emulation and implicit rebukes to your own spiritual lethargy.

This is a book about popular evangelicalism, a kind of travelogue into the evangelical subculture in America, a subculture that encompasses fundamentalists, charismatics, and pentecostals. It was born of the suspicion that many Americans, and certainly the media, really did not have much of a clue about who evangelicals were, what they believed, or what motivated their recent forays into the political arena. The sudden surge of evangelicals into national prominence in the mid-1970s was treated as a kind of curiosity, with little acknowledgement of evangelicalism's history or its broad—and growing—popularity. The media relied far too heavily on the shopworn stereotypes that Sinclair Lewis and H. L. Mencken perpetrated in the 1920s, caricatures that depicted evangelicals as country bumpkins and their leaders as venal, disingenuous opportunists. As both a student of American religious history and a product of the evangelical subculture, I knew better.

But what began as an exploration of the variegated forms of American evangelicalism quickly turned into a personal odyssey of sorts. Although I was reared within the subculture, a series of personal circumstances, including impatience with a political agenda that I found (now, as then) reprehensible, prompted my withdrawal from the evangelical subculture in the late 1970s, a distancing born not so much of a resolve to reject my past, but as a curiosity about what lay beyond the citadel of evangelicalism, which I found more and more confining. After more than twenty years within the protective cocoon of this subculture, it was time for a breather, time to escape the censoriousness I had known much of my life.

I found in the ensuing years the joy of friendships uncluttered with the guilt and repressiveness that often comes with growing up fundamentalist. I discovered the beauty of worship in a liturgical, "high-church" setting. I found that many of the theological liberals I had been taught to despise had a good deal to teach me about tolerance and compassion, even as I became convinced anew of the theological bankruptcy of Protestant liberalism. To the extent that

I thought about evangelicals at all in those years, I regarded their theological quarrels as silly and churlish, if not irrelevant. The strict parietal rules they placed on children struck me as petty and mistrustful.

My subsequent forays into the evangelical subculture, then, provided a fresh look at a phenomenon I had all but ignored for the better part of a decade. My travels quickly triggered a personal agenda that included attempts to come to terms with what it meant to grow up fundamentalist, to sort out the many ways that the evangelical subculture had shaped me and continues to define who I am. After years of self-conscious withdrawal from evangelicalism, I also became interested in reacquainting myself with the revolutionary force of the evangelical gospel, those kernels of truth and insight into the human condition that had, in my judgment, become lost in the ephemera of modern evangelicalism and squandered in a kind of Faustian bargain by evangelicalism's assimilation to contemporary American culture, even as it purported to maintain a critical distance from "worldliness."

My purpose in undertaking this project, however, was neither to vilify nor to vindicate American evangelicalism, and the reader will early on detect my own ambivalence toward the subculture and all it represents. On the one hand, I felt something of a compulsion to defend evangelicalism against its many detractors who dismiss it without troubling themselves to understand it. On the other hand, I could not readily disguise my own discomfiture with all the nonsense that parades as the New Testament gospel of Jesus Christ.

What puzzled me even more was how much of my own reflections I should integrate into the narratives. No historian worthy of the name can claim utter objectivity, but in the early version of this manuscript I sought to maintain a scholarly detachment. After I had drafted a few chapters and sent them to my editor and to trusted advisers, however, I received a nearly unanimous response: "All well and good, but what do *you* think?" I stammered out some answer or another, but the question of how much (or how little) of myself I had invested in the narrative continued to haunt me. I have become convinced in recent years that one of the birthrights of Midwesterners is a sense that your opinions don't really matter, so I found it difficult to believe that anyone would truly be interested in my views or my reactions to the various phenomena I had described. Half of the blood that courses through my veins, moreover, is Swedish, and we Scandinavians are rather chary about tipping our hands. Finally, one of the things that has irked me over the years is the tendency of evangelicals to pontificate on anything from codes of behavior to politics to eschatology. They define *their* position as "Christian" or "biblical," and every other view as somehow less so. I am not a theologian, either by training or by temperament, and I emphatically did not want simply to dispense gratuitous judgments.

One day near the end of the project, an imaginary interlocuter appeared in the chair on the other side of my desk. "Why did you write this thing in the first place?" he asked.

"I was pretty sure that the press had missed the story, that they had bunched all evangelicals together and failed to appreciate the spectrum of evangelicalism in America."

"What else?"

"Well, I wanted to say something about the evangelical subculture that defines and nurtures and sometimes suffocates those who consider themselves born-again Christians."

"Anything else?" The interlocuter's eyes bore down on me.

"Well, I suppose I wanted to exorcise a few demons of my own."

"Aha!" he said. "I figured as much. Besides," he added wryly, "those demons need exercise. Tell us what *you* make of all this."

From that point onward, I began extemporizing. I wasn't always comfortable with this feet-on-the-desk analysis, but whenever I lapsed into the reportorial mode, my interlocutor turned me back to the task.

Some of what follows, then, is self-disclosure; I abandoned the detached and dispassionate analysis I had originally envisioned. But it is not autobiography. I have tried as much as possible in this ethnographic study to allow people to tell their own stories and thereby render a portrait—or at least a collage—of evangelicalism, America's folk religion, in all its variation and diversity. Whereas sociologists try to find commonalities among apparently disparate phenomena, I wanted to show variations within a subculture generally regarded as monolithic.

As a historian who holds an appointment in a research university, this project entailed other, professional perils beyond the risk of self-disclosure. I have tried to produce a book that might appeal both to scholars interested in popular religion in America and to the public in general—including, certainly, evangelicals themselves—curious about a phenomenon that has received a good deal of attention in the past decade.

At an early planning stage, I decided that this book would not be about the powerful evangelical bigwigs—Jerry Falwell, Billy Graham, Jimmy Swaggart, and locally renowned pastors—who exert such a large influence over popular evangelicalism. That is not to say that these people are not important, although I do think that their influence is overrated. I've long believed, in fact, that evangelicalism in America, lacking the confessional emphasis and liturgical rubrics that bind other religious groups, has been susceptible to the cult of personality, a weakness only magnified in recent years by the widespread use of television.

Several factors loomed in my decision to avoid these stars. First and most important, I wanted to write a book about *popular* evangelicalism, to examine the ways evangelical theology and morality shaped individuals within the movement, how their participation in the evangelical subculture defined who they were and shaped the way they viewed the world. As a cultural historian, I was curious to see how evangelical theology functioned in various social contexts. Whatever contemporary evangelicalism has to commend it lies not in its media stars but in the sincerity and ingenuousness of the ordinary folk who consider themselves evangelicals.

I remain convinced, moreover, that the attention paid to the televangelists is disproportionate to their influence within the evangelical subculture. There are good reasons for this, of course. For nonevangelicals, the televangelists are the most conspicuous element of evangelicalism, and their bizarre antics in recent years make for good copy and tantalizing footage on the six o'clock news. But for many evangelicals themselves, the televangelists are more of a nuisance and an embarrassment than a substantive influence (even though many local churches have imitated their style). I confess to no little amusement at the media's coverage of recent scandals, because the formula was always the same. After a lead-in about the scandal itself, a reporter would ambush an unsuspecting churchgoer at some Baptist church in Tennessee to ask whether Jimmy Swaggart's latest indiscretion would affect his or her faith. For anyone familiar with evangelicalism, that question misses the point. The faith of American evangelicals is shaped by many forces—their own reading of the Scriptures (which in turn is affected by what translation or study Bible they choose), their local church and pastor, the kinds of devotional materials they use, and, perhaps least of all, by Jimmy Swaggart or Jim Bakker or Oral Roberts.

Finally, I had another, more personal reason for steering clear of well-known evangelical leaders. As a product of the evangelical subculture, I knew that such people are especially adept at that parlance of piety known as "God talk," and I suspected it would be very tedious, perhaps impossible, to penetrate this verbal veil in order to tease out useful answers.

"How, Reverend Jones, do you account for the success of your church?"

"It's just the work of the Lord. I can't explain it any other way. The Lord has blessed our ministry here."

There's nothing wrong with such answers, I suppose, and I have no reason to question the sincerity of those responses. It's just that I have the same reaction to them as I have to weather forecasters on television. No matter how firmly I resolve to hear them out, my eyes glaze over after about twenty seconds.

I heard my share of platitudes from the people I talked with during my travels. But I found that if I pressed a bit further, repeated the question in a slightly different way, or simply allowed people to elaborate, they often gave more satisfying answers. Such comments form the core of this book.

The travel motif seemed especially appropriate, not only because of its discursive possibilities and because evangelicalism in America extends to every region of the country, but also because Americans themselves have always been on the move, migrating from one place to another in search of economic opportunity, personal fulfillment, and even religious contentment. Frequently, moreover, the genre of American travel literature has included observations about reli-

gion. Captain John Smith's comments on the natives of colonial
Virginia come to mind, as do Alexis de Tocqueville's assertions about
the relationship between American religiosity and the function of
democratic institutions, Charles Nordhoff's examination of nineteenth-century utopian experiments, and Robert Pirsig's tortuous
spiritual journey, *Zen and the Art of Motorcycle Maintenance.*
America's persistent religiosity has elicited comment in other travel
narratives as well: John Steinbeck's *Travels with Charley*, Jonathan
Raban's *Old Glory: An American Voyage*, and *Blue Highways: A
Journey into America* by William Least Heat Moon.

All these pilgrims discovered religion of one sort or another in
the purlieus and beyond the back roads of America. I did too.

Charting the pilgrimage was, in some respects, as perilous as the
journey itself. Several criteria came into play: geographical balance,
a thematic approach to various chapters, and a desire to portray the
spectrum of evangelicalism. It would have been easy (and, I confess,
a good bit of fun) to confine myself to the strange-and-wacky world
of American evangelicalism, but I was more interested in reaching
the heart of the subculture rather than perpetuating common stereotypes. Accordingly, then, I gave up on fire-breathing evangelists
and the born-again motorcycle gang down in Arkansas; those with
a taste for the bizarre will have to content themselves with Neal
Frisby, the "Phoenix Prophet," who will not disappoint.

At Calvary Chapel in southern California I wanted to assess the
maturation of a church that had its genesis in the Jesus movement
of the early 1970s. In Mississippi I found several groups of people
struggling against both the entrenched racism of the old Confederacy
and the social apathy that still grips American evangelicals. Word
of Life Island in the Adirondacks evoked in me the memories of
summers long past and showed me anew the quandary that evangelical parents face in trying to ensure that their children claim the
evangelical faith for their own. Dallas Theological Seminary provided a look at the theology that undergirds much of American
fundamentalism, but it also offered a glimpse of the sexism that
persists within the evangelical subculture.

If there is any one thing that has brought evangelicalism to the attention of the broader public in recent years, I suspect it would be the fundamentalist involvement in politics, beginning in the mid-1970s. I knew that over the long range of American history there was nothing novel about evangelicals asserting themselves in the political sphere, but I wasn't certain why such passion had been invested in a certain, rather narrow range of issues. So I headed off to Iowa for the precinct caucuses and then to New Hampshire prior to the first primary of the 1988 presidential campaign. I was interested to see how evangelicals, especially evangelical women, were learning the political process, and I came away convinced that they will be a force for many campaigns to come.

My search for an old-fashioned revival reminiscent of the holiness camp meetings of the nineteenth century took me to St. Petersburg, Florida, but I might just as easily have ended up in Arkansas or Ohio or Virginia. In the Dakotas I found a marked contrast in the mission strategies of different Protestant groups. Donald Thompson, an evangelical filmmaker whose best-known movies depict life on earth during the apocalypse, is also an extraordinary individual whose unblinking optimism and faith in God represents the kind of piety that many evangelicals aspire to. My editor suggested attending the annual convention of the Christian Booksellers Association, which turned out to be a huge, bewildering bazaar of Bibles, video, music, books, and kitsch.

I think I first heard the term *subculture* applied to evangelicalism from Douglas Frank when I was a college student in the mid-1970s. A visit with him in Oregon gave me the excuse to rekindle an old friendship, catch up on his thinking, and try to unravel the contradictions that afflict twentieth-century evangelicalism.

Such are the contours of my pilgrimage into the evangelical subculture in America. But the most arresting dimensions of any journey are the detours, the wrong turns, the unexpected vistas along the way. In many cases, what I saw and heard by chance or indirection was more interesting than what I'd expected to find.

Herewith, then, the journey.

1

California Kickback

I'VE ALWAYS SUSPECTED that you can tell a lot about a church (or any voluntary association, for that matter) by looking at the automobiles in its parking lot. In car-crazed southern California, that suspicion seems almost axiomatic. Herewith a sampling of bumper stickers, license-plate frames, and other paraphernalia on cars in the parking lot of Calvary Chapel in Santa Ana, California:

PEACE RULES WHERE GOD REIGNS

JESUS

I ♥ JESUS

I ♥ GOD

INVITE JESUS INTO YOUR ♥

PRAISE THE LORD

ROBERTSON '88

DONT BE CAUGHT DEAD WITHOUT JESUS

GET BACK TO BASICS. READ THE BIBLE

I'M INTO GOD

JESUS TAKES GOOD CARE OF ME

HAPPINESS IS BEING BORN AGAIN

HAPPINESS IS BEING SINGLE

JESUS LIVES

MY HEART BELONGS TO JESUS

GOD WILL BLESS AMERICA WHEN AMERICA BLESSES GOD

SMILE, JESUS LOVES YOU

GOD ALREADY MADE MY DAY!

TO KNOW ME IS TO LOVE ME

BEGIN YOUR DAY WITH NUTRITION. READ THE BIBLE

JESUS ON BOARD

BEAM ME UP, JESUS!

JESUS IS AWESOME

Some of the automobiles sport vanity plates. One California tag reads ADONAI, a Hebrew name for God. Another: DIED 4U2, presumably a reference to Jesus. Another: COM LORD. A car in the space reserved for the pastor reads CALVARY. The vehicles themselves range from a Rolls Royce, several Mercedes Benzes, Lincoln Continentals, and Cadillac Eldorados to old Ford Mavericks, motor scooters, and Volkswagen vans stuffed with junk, so dilapidated as to appear unroadworthy.

Inside on this Sunday morning, a quintessentially California crowd gathers, wearing anything from three-piece suits to beachwear—and everything in between: knit polo shirts, denims, madras, miniskirts, tee-shirts. Hairstyles range from the meticulous and coiffed to the insouciant and sun-bleached. Outside the auditorium, some worshippers lounge on the grass in lawn chairs, listening to the service on speakers located at various points around the grounds. Some listen from their automobiles as security guards on ten-speed bicycles patrol the parking lot. Virtually everyone totes a large Bible with some sort of casing—suede, hand-tooled leather, homemade quilting, vinyl with pictures of a cross and a dove. The woman in front of me carries one with PARTNER EDITION PTL CLUB emblazoned on the cover.

By eleven-fifteen, starting time for the third worship service of

the morning, the huge auditorium is full, and four men file onto
the stage beneath a stylized rendering of a dove to begin the service.
A large man in a light-colored suit comes to the pulpit. "It's good
to be back," he begins. I quickly surmise that this cheerful, avun-
cular man just short of his sixtieth birthday is Chuck Smith, founder
and pastor of Calvary Chapel and known to his large congregation
as "Pastor Chuck."[1] As his bald, evenly bronzed head indicates,
Smith has just returned from a two-week vacation in Hawaii. "It
was total kickback," he said. "God brought the surf up. It was really
great." He recounts days of golf and swimming and surfing and
concludes, "We thank the Lord for the privilege of just total kickback
for a couple of weeks."

The service itself at Calvary Chapel is simple, even spartan. After
an opening prayer, Smith leads the congregation in singing "Holy!
Holy! Holy! Lord, God Almighty." Another man on the platform
comes to announce some of the many activities available throughout
the week. A second congregational hymn follows the offering, which
is followed in turn by special music from five women, members of
the Joyful Life Bible Study. Smith then returns to the pulpit, reads
the morning's Scripture text, and begins his sermon.

Smith projects an air of competence in his preaching, but the
style itself won't make anyone forget Jimmy Swaggart, Billy Graham,
or even Chuck Swindoll, who preaches in nearby Fullerton. He
demonstrates a good deal of knowledge and dexterity, moving easily
from one text to another. On this Mother's Day, he talks about
"children in rebellion" and extols the value of "persistent and prevailing prayer." At the end of the sermon, the congregation stands
as Smith recites—from memory—a poem that concludes, "The hand
that rocks the cradle / Is the hand that rules the world." As the
congregation sings the benediction, Smith walks down the center
aisle and out the rear of the auditorium.

Calvary Chapel, a large, sprawling complex of buildings surrounded on all sides by a huge parking lot, lies at the corner of
Fairview and Sunflower in Santa Ana, just beyond the limits of Costa
Mesa. The architecture loosely resembles the Spanish mission style
ubiquitous in southern California, and its modest scale contrasts
with the ostentation of Robert Schuller's Crystal Cathedral down

the road in Garden Grove. The rear of the auditorium opens out into a courtyard surrounded by other buildings, which house the fellowship hall (complete with huge closed-circuit television screens to serve overflow crowds), various church offices, and a warren of classrooms used for Sunday school and throughout the week for Calvary Chapel's grammar school, Maranatha Christian Academy. When the services end, thousands of people spill into the courtyard and the adjacent parking lots. Amidst this flurry of activity, church-goers socialize. From a table in the courtyard, a girls' youth group sells sweatshirts to raise money, and young parents (of which there are many) retrieve their children from nurseries or Sunday school classrooms. In the parking lot just outside one of the exits, a gray pickup truck containing two large bins of avocados sports a hand-painted sign that reads:

CALVARY CHAPEL FARM

THIS IS YOUR FARM! PLEASE HELP YOUR SELF.

IF YOU CAN, LEAVE A DONATION. THANK YOU FOR YOUR SUPPORT!

Pastor Chuck had announced earlier, in what seemed to me at the time a spontaneous gesture, that each mother in the congregation could grab an avocado in celebration of Mother's Day, instead of the usual carnation offered by other churches. Avocados are moving briskly.

The Sunday evening service is even more casual. Once again, the auditorium, which seats about twenty-three hundred, is filled. After a brief opening prayer, a large group of people—mostly young, but not all—leave their seats and come to the platform. They sing several songs, each separated by only a few guitar chords. The congregation joins in freely, without prompting. The music alternates between lively and joyful on the one hand and solemn and devotional, almost lugubrious, on the other. The melodies are simple, rather folksy, and everyone seems to know the words.[2] After half an hour or more,

Pastor Chuck reappears and launches into a casual sermon, almost conversational in tone, about Second Samuel 3–5, an exposition that continues about ninety minutes.

Over most of his pastoral career, Smith has emphasized the systematic study of the Scriptures. And there on a Sunday evening in May, talking easily about one of the more recondite passages of the Bible, he is in his element, doing what he does best. For most preachers, Second Samuel is deadly, hardly the stuff of great oratory; yet Smith, in his workmanlike way, makes sense of the various Hebrew dynasties and the courtly intrigues, examining them as earnestly as a sports fan would study box scores. He digresses casually, calling on personal experience or, more often, other passages of Scripture (which he often recites from memory) to illustrate a point.

What is even more striking than Smith's deft handling of an obscure passage is his ability to hold this young audience's rapt attention for so long. Looking around the congregation, I find little evidence of impatience, and virtually the only sound is the rustling of pages. The auditors try in vain to keep up with Smith as he jumps from book to book, chapter to chapter, testament to testament.

Smith repeats the performance the following evening to another packed house with an exposition of Revelation 14 and again on Thursday night in his series on the Gospel of Luke. On Monday, after the obligatory half hour of singing led by several young people with guitars, Smith simply sits on the edge of the platform with a lapel microphone clipped to his pink polo shirt and talks extemporaneously about Revelation and the impending apocalypse. "We are living in the last days, when Satan is running amok in this world," he says at one point. "My heart goes out to you kids," he concludes. "In living for Christ today you have to go against the world." He exhorts them to a life of holiness and purity amidst a world careening toward God's judgment.

Many years ago, during revival meetings in Fairmont, Minnesota, I heard a pastor comment that Saturday evening was "the devil's night out." He explained that few churches conducted services on Saturday, and that gave the devil free reign to work his mischief, even among putative Christians.

If so, the devil doesn't have much of an opening among the faithful of Calvary Chapel. Pastors there estimate that up to twenty-five thousand people pass through their twenty-one acre campus every week, including a thousand students at Maranatha Christian Academy (kindergarten through eighth grade), Sunday school pupils, and worshippers at the three morning services on Sunday that fill the auditorium to capacity (the overflow for the latter two services also fills the seven-hundred–seat fellowship hall).[3] But that's just the beginning. A full range of other programs (or ministries, as the folks here prefer) round out the weekly schedule. Services and Bible studies are held for the deaf and in Korean, Spanish, and Arabic. The church sponsors ministries to high school and to junior high school youth. I counted fifty-one events scheduled for the week of my visit, including three prayer breakfasts and eleven Bible studies. The Working Women's Joyful Life Bible Study (not to be confused with the Women's Joyful Life Bible Study) meets on Monday evening, as does the Proverbs Class for Men, in addition to Smith's study of Revelation in the auditorium. A fellowship of ex-convicts meets on Friday night. Single parents gather on Wednesday night, singles on Friday, and the High School Mothers' Prayer Meeting convenes Tuesday afternoon. New Spirit, an alcohol and drug recovery program, meets Wednesday and Friday evenings. On Friday night, Calvary's Messianic Jewish Fellowship celebrated thirty-nine years of Israel's independence. Saturday evening, the Radical Street Ministry convenes opposite the Outreach Program, a weekly gathering for young people that features music by various Christian recording artists, a short devotional message, and an invitation to come forward and accept Jesus as savior.

In addition, the church runs a radio station, KWVE ("K-wave"), and a conference and retreat center in Twin Peaks, California. A tract of land near San Diego awaits development as another conference center. Through weekly gatherings for Bible study and prayer, thirty Home Fellowships scattered throughout the southern California area offer a more intimate sense of community than that available in larger assemblies at the church.

Some experts refer to a church like Calvary Chapel as a phenomenon or a "megachurch," a species that thrives here in southern

California.[4] But the success of Chuck Smith and Calvary Chapel is all the more remarkable because of its genesis in the mid-1960s as a congregation of twenty-five contentious people, and because of its identification with a larger cultural phenomenon, the Jesus movement.

In the early 1960s, Chuck Smith, a pastor in the International Church of the Foursquare Gospel, a pentecostal denomination begun by Aimee Semple McPherson in the 1920s, began to tire of church-growth schemes propagated by the denominational hierarchy. Typically, these notions (quite common in evangelical circles) involve dividing the congregation into two or more teams that compete against one another to rack up the most points for filling up their assigned pews or inviting the unsaved to church. Churches within a denomination then compete against one another for the largest growth during the contest period. When promotional materials for still another contest began arriving at his church, Smith discarded them. "I couldn't face another Blues against the Reds," he said, resolving instead simply to teach the Bible.[5] In compliance with the requirements of the contest, however, the church secretary filed periodic reports about attendance, and at the conclusion of the contest Smith received a letter congratulating him as the winner— the church with the greatest increase—and inviting him to a rally to collect his trophy, even though his congregation had known nothing about the contest.

Disillusioned with denominational officiousness, Smith soon accepted a call to a nondenominational congregation in Corona, California, where he enjoyed similar success by continuing his emphasis on Bible teaching. Then, in 1965, he received an invitation from Calvary Chapel in Costa Mesa, a congregation of twenty-five, deeply divided and on the verge of disbanding. Smith accepted, even though he was forced to supplement his income by cleaning carpets several days a week. Under his ministry, this tiny church, growing at a rate of five percent a week, soon had to look for new quarters.

The largest increase came from an unlikely source. At that time, the height of the counterculture movement, the beaches of southern California fairly swarmed with hippies, and Smith later confessed that "these long-haired, bearded, dirty kids going around the streets repulsed me." Still, he felt a calling to them: "My wife and I used to go over to Huntington Beach and park downtown to watch the kids and pray for them. We wanted somehow to reach them, but we didn't know how."[6]

Through the friends of his college-age daughter, Smith soon began to meet hippies, many of whom had discovered in Christianity an answer to their intellectual searchings, and a cure, sometimes instantaneous, to their drug dependencies. Smith's house became a "hippie pad," where "Jesus freaks," as they became known, found both physical shelter and, in Smith's teaching of the Bible, spiritual sustenance.

Oden Fong, now a staff member at Calvary Chapel, was an early convert. "I came out of mysticism. I used to study religions, and at the time I learned about Calvary Chapel I was living down in Laguna Beach where there was a different representative of every faith on just about every corner. You could walk down the street and talk to a Zen Buddhist, walk a bit further and see a Krishna, a little farther and see a Satanist. It was a real hodge-podge of different faiths. I spent years in metaphysics, trying to attain perfection— fasting and that type of stuff, eating nothing but pure foods, meditating for hours and days, sitting in the same position for days. When I was doing yoga and things like that, I was just trying to get perfect. And there was just no way. I studied under the hierarchy of Tibetan Buddhism, Krishna Consciousness. A lot of my friends had gone up to Calvary Chapel, and they invited me one day. I went, reluctantly, and it was just so real. It was so much more real than anything I had seen. I found compassion and love. There was a fullness in the hearts of the people I met—the Jesus people—and I wanted that, too." Fong found the answer to his searching in the grace of God. "There's no perfect man. By Jesus's simple act, we have the power to change and not to fall."[7]

Smith's message, his acceptance and compassion, caught on. L. E. Romaine, a retired military man and a longtime associate of Smith's, remembers that in the early 1970s "not more than five or ten percent of the crowd was over twenty-five. Everybody wore granny dresses and carried fur-covered Bibles and jeans and bib-overalls and tie-died shirts and long hair and beards," he said. "They were so wild it was scary. The news media couldn't understand it. Other churches couldn't understand it; some of them spoke against it."[8]

Fong remembers that when he first came to Calvary Chapel, it met in a small building down the street from its present location. "I think the most they could pack in there if they filled up all the seats and filled up all the aisles—which they did, it was standing room only in those days—was about three hundred people. We ripped down the walls, tore down the side walls, and had people sitting outside. Even in the rain people would be sitting out there. It was just a great, massive revival; there was a great movement of people into Christianity at the time. Every month or so, the church would double."[9]

To accommodate the crowds, the congregation bought a parcel of land at the intersection of Fairview and Sunflower (their present site), put in a parking lot, and purchased a big, second-hand circus tent as temporary quarters while they constructed an auditorium. The night before their first service in the tent, Smith and others set up sixteen hundred chairs and planned double services. "I looked out at that sea of folding chairs," Smith recalled. "I had never seen so many folding chairs in all my life!" He asked an associate: "How long do you suppose it will take the Lord to fill this place?" The associate looked at his watch and answered, "I'd say just about eleven hours."[10]

He was right. The next morning every seat was filled and people stood around the perimeter of the tent—for both services.

From all appearances, Chuck Smith seems like an improbable guru. What's the attraction? I put that question to many people during my visit to Calvary Chapel. Predictably, the answers ranged from the spiritualized to the philosophical.

Richard Cimino, an earnest young pastor at Calvary Chapel, waxed almost rhapsodic. "This balding, old guy taught the Word of God to the most bizarre hippies imaginable, and these people's lives were so changed by Jesus that they brought their friends, who brought their friends, who brought their friends. Now, people are here because they love to be taught the Word of God. They like coming to a place where they can wear Levi's, shorts, tennis shoes, bare feet, whatever, and sit and listen to some guy teach the Word of God in a way that they can understand it. I think Chuck Smith is Everyman's teacher. If I wanted to read a sermon, I'd probably read Chuck Swindoll's sermons before I'd read Chuck Smith's sermons. But there's a tremendous authority that God has given him in the pulpit, and yet it's something that everyone can understand. He's at ease. He's quick to confess his own faults. There are no pretenses about him. People respond to that. When they designed the church, he said 'I don't want anything big or flashy,' and as you can see it's major low profile. Everything about him is casual. He doesn't like structure. I just know that when I talk to him, I'm going to be a wiser man when I walk out."

More recent arrivals share similar impressions. When I checked into the motel in Costa Mesa and asked the woman at the desk if she could direct me to Calvary Chapel, she looked up and smiled. "That's my church," she said brightly. "Well, I've only been going there a little while. But I love it! I feel at home, and the people are really on fire for the Lord. There's good, solid Bible teaching there, and God has really been doing some radical things in my life since I started going to Calvary Chapel."

I met Tony when I sat in on the Single Parents Fellowship on Wednesday night. Tony moved to southern California from Brooklyn two years ago. "I just love it here," he said. "When I first started coming to Calvary Chapel I was struck by how real the place was, how real the people were. And I said, 'This is the place for me.' "

According to Oden Fong, the end of the 1960s found people "totally disillusioned with the counterculture revolution, the 'peace,' 'love,' 'flower power' movement, LSD, and so forth. All the heroes of that time—the musical heroes of the youth and political leaders of the youth—were all dying off, either by heroin overdoses or suicide or assasination. People were turning on one another, turning each other in. You had Timothy Leary turning state's evidence against the Black Panthers. It caused a lot of people to be extremely disillusioned with the counterculture revolution. But it was still a time of searching. The sixties was a time of looking inward and outward. We were trying to figure out who we were, what we were, where we were going as a human race.

"Just about that same time, there was a spiritual awakening in Christianity where the walls of the traditional churches that had not allowed certain elements of the society to enter—I'm thinking of the so-called hippies—began to crumble. Christians began to concern themselves with living for Jesus Christ on a day-to-day basis, rather than simply adhering to the dogmas of the Church. There were also incredible manifestations of spiritual power. I have seen people's legs grow out. I've seen blind and deaf people healed. These miracles added a lot of excitement to the movement, too. Calvary Chapel and Chuck Smith were just part of that broader movement. A lot of them, thousands of them, were hippies, people coming out of the drug culture. It was kind of like one hobo telling another where he can get a good meal. We got the name Jesus people or Jesus freaks from the media, primarily because of our baptisms."

Pirate's Cove at Corona del Mar State Beach lies at the entrance of Newport Bay, just across from the Balboa Peninsula. Protected from the waves by two jetties that guard the entrance to the channel, the sand in the cove slopes gently upward toward a large formation of rocks that fan out in a semicircle. Here in the early morning hours, at low tide beneath an overcast sky, the beach is empty save for a few seagulls and sandpipers. The surf thunders in the distance. A small fishing trawler sputters by. The mood is serene, peaceful.

But in the early 1970s a bit of history took place here, history involving Calvary Chapel and the baptism of Jesus people in the Pacific Ocean. On those occasions, Corona del Mar was anything but serene.

"Dope addicts, panhandlers, and just regular kids who were confused have come through here and accepted Christ," Smith explained to a reporter at the time. "Baptizing is the symbol of this acceptance."[11] Fong remembers the chaos. "You pushed and shoved to get either into the parking lot or somewhere above the beach area. You'd walk all the way down over the rocks. You'd see this mass of humanity, thousands of people sitting on the rocks and down on the beach and all around the outsides of the cove. And then down by the water itself would be the pastors and hundreds of people lined up to be baptized—usually three hundred or more."

Romaine, Smith's associate, also remembers the huge crowds. "The first big baptism down at Corona del Mar took place in 1970. We got down to Pirate's Cove on a Saturday around nine-thirty, ten o'clock, and there were thousands and thousands of people waiting there. These so-called Jesus freaks are climbing all over the rocks and into the adjacent residential area. They're knocking on doors and telling people about Jesus and hugging them. People were out there drinking iced tea in their swings, and these kids would just sit down and talk to them about the Lord. They had no pretenses whatsoever. They just loved the Lord, and if you'd sit still they'd tell you about the Lord.

"These kids are climbing all over the place, and the residents called the police; they thought it was another Woodstock or something. They're scared. They see two or three thousand young people, and they don't know what to think. So here come four or five police cars. The police got out, and these young people—I don't like to use the term hippies, but that's what they were—they were hugging the policemen and telling them about Jesus Christ. They wanted to know if the police would accept Jesus Christ. These policemen were scared to death. I watched them; I stood right there and watched their faces. Their eyes flew wide open. They looked as though someone had just stabbed them with a pin.

"When we started the baptisms, the kids sitting on the rocks surrounding the cove started singing. I'll tell you, I've never run into anything like that in my life. Four of us were baptizing people, and it took us two-and-a-half hours to baptize everyone who wanted to be baptized. I was so stupefied, I couldn't see straight. It was more than I could understand, more than I could handle."[12]

Baptisms in the Pacific took place about once a month. They're less frequent now, but still well attended. At the Monday night study of Revelation, Smith announced: "The next baptism will be

June 26 at Corona del Mar. A Friday night. We'll play volleyball,
eat some hot dogs, and then baptize anyone who wants to identify
with the death, burial, and resurrection of Jesus."

There is something comfortable, almost beguiling, about the services at Calvary Chapel. The mood is relaxed, the singing alternately
joyful and dolorous. There is also an appealing naiveté about Smith
and his approach to the Bible, an approach that might be characterized as, "Here is what it says, so this is what it means." When
Martin Luther posted his *Ninety-five Theses* on the cathedral door
at Wittenberg, he declared, in effect, that he would be guided by
his own understanding of the Bible and not by the teachings of the
Roman Catholic hierarchy. Luther's sentiments created a demand
for Scriptures in the vernacular, and Protestants ever since have
stubbornly insisted on interpreting the Bible for themselves, for-
getting most of the time that they come to the text with their own
set of cultural biases and personal agendas.

Underlying this insistence on individual interpretation is the as-
sumption (which received explicit sanction in the philosophy of
Common Sense Realism in the nineteenth century) that the plainest,
most evident reading of the text is the proper one. Everyone becomes his or her own theologian. There is no longer any need to
consult Augustine or Thomas Aquinas or Martin Luther about their
understanding of various passages when you yourself are the final
arbiter of what is the correct reading. This tendency, together with
the absence of any authority structure within Protestantism, has
created a kind of theological free-for-all, as various individuals or
groups insist that *their* reading of the Bible is the only possible
interpretation.

Chuck Smith clearly interprets Scripture literally and in its plainest sense, with the presumption of inerrancy, but he is remarkably
undogmatic by nature. In the past decade or so, virtually every
evangelical and fundamentalist congregation in America has had to
address the issue of the charismatic or pentecostal movement. Pentecostals believe in a "second blessing" of the Holy Spirit (after the
first, which is conversion) that makes the believer a "Spirit-filled"
Christian. This blessing is often accompanied by *glossolalia*, or

"speaking in tongues," where the believer, in a state of spiritual ecstasy, babbles in an unfamiliar language, just as the early Christians did on the original day of Pentecost.[13] Other "spiritual gifts" include the gift of healing and the gift of interpreting tongues. Many pentecostals (such as the Church of God or the Assemblies of God or the International Church of the Foursquare Gospel) regard this spiritual blessing as an essential mark of a true Christian. Fundamentalists and most evangelicals, on the other hand, acknowledge the spiritual gifts described in the New Testament, but they insist that these supernatural phenomena were confined to the first-century Christians and no longer apply to the modern Church.

This controversy, based on divergent interpretations of the Bible, has occasioned acrimonious battles among conservative Protestants in recent years, with many a congregation torn asunder over the validity of spiritual gifts. Pentecostal worship tends toward spiritual ecstasy and emotionalism, while fundamentalists emphasize teaching and preaching—a more rationalistic faith. Pentecostals value "the leading of the Spirit," and they are known for long meetings punctuated by healings, speaking in tongues, and by people lifting their hands in reverence or throwing up their arms in joyful abandon.[14]

During the services at Calvary Chapel, especially during the singing that opens the meetings, it's not uncommon to see some people close their eyes and lift up their hands in a gesture of worship and devotion (in fact, most people—leaders and congregation—close their eyes while singing). A few will even stand up and lift their arms high in the air. In some churches, such gestures would spark a theological controversy over spiritual gifts. But Smith seems unperturbed. Calvary Chapel's statement of faith reads, in part: "We believe worship of God should be Spiritual. Therefore we remain flexible and yielded to the leading of the Holy Spirit to direct our worship."

I asked Oden Fong to what extent pentecostal theology and practice influences Calvary Chapel. "We believe in the gifts of the Holy Spirit in this day—divine healing, prophecy, word of knowledge, speaking in tongues—but we differ from pentecostals in that we do not believe in emotionalism. In fact, we shy away from emotionalism. We believe that a faith grounded in emotions is rather shallow, that it will dissipate when the emotions disappear."

Chuck Smith's latitudinarianism, his unwillingness to engage in theological battles that he views as irrelevant, has defused many of the controversies that afflict other evangelical churches. Smith also retains his suspicion of denominations. "We are not a denominational church," the statement of faith reads, "nor are we opposed to denominations as such, only their overemphasis of the doctrinal differences that have led to the division of the Body of Christ." Still, Calvary Chapel of Costa Mesa has inspired others. There are over three hundred congregations around the country—and the world— that maintain a loose association or fellowship. These Calvary Chapels (some have different names) are all autonomous; they elect and ordain their own pastors. Typically, someone who has attended Calvary Chapel and then moves elsewhere will begin a Bible study in the new community. As this gathering expands, the congregation will contact Calvary Chapel for a pastor, whereupon Smith encourages one of his staff members to take the position. In this way, characteristically informal and uncalculated, Calvary Chapel has expanded its influence well beyond Costa Mesa.

Sociologists who study voluntary associations generally agree that a religious group goes through several phases in its development. During the first phase a group coalesces around a charismatic leader, who defines the group largely through the force of his personality. After a time, however, a process sociologists call "routinization" sets in as patterns of behavior and association become rationalized and institutionalized. This phase in the life of a religious group is generally associated with a dissipation of the religious fervor that characterized the organization in its formative period. I was eager to see how much routinization had affected Calvary Chapel in the last twenty years.

Saturday night was Outreach Night, geared especially toward the young people. From seven-thirty to nine-thirty this group, most of them in their early twenties, gathered in the auditorium to listen to a Christian recording artist and a sermon from a young preacher who earlier in the meeting had invited everyone in attendance to go down to Balboa Pier in Newport Beach afterwards for witnessing. "It's a heavy spiritual battle down there," he announced. All hands were needed.

As the meeting drew to a close, he repeated the announcement and offered some coaching. "When I begin preaching at the entrance to the pier," he said, "it's very important that you all pay close attention, that you look at me as if you've never seen me before. That's the key, because people walking by will look at the audience and see how interested they are before deciding whether or not to stop and listen." He advised the people to avoid arguments and confrontations. It's better, he said, "to just share the love of Jesus." Anyone interested in witnessing, he concluded, could pick up some tracts at the front of the auditorium. A good number, perhaps fifty or sixty, came forward after the service. One man in his late twenties or early thirties, who introduced himself as Mark, fidgeted nervously while paging through the tract he had collected. "I haven't done this for three or four years," he said. "I'm kinda out of practice."

The group reassembled in Newport Beach a little after ten o'clock, and for about an hour thereafter the entrance to the pier buzzed with activity. There was an almost palpable sense of expectation and excitement. People were milling about, floating in and out of conversations. "Jesus loves you. He's the only way to heaven." "He's real. I know He's real because I can feel Him in my heart." "Jesus delivered me from drugs, and He can do the same for you." Some spectators climbed atop cars in the adjacent parking lot to hear the preacher. Nearly everyone passing by stopped to listen, at least for a time; some of them took on an air of bemusement, others disgust, still others curiosity.

But the mood wasn't quite right—too contentious. Things got off on the wrong foot when a rather boisterous young man began taunting the "Jesus freaks," as he called them, and then, feeling surrounded, grew rather defensive and argumentative. "I don't need no God; I'm happy the way I am," he protested. That confrontational style spread as the eager evangelists circled their prey. One passerby, seeing all the commotion, said, "What's this, a brawl? Make a circle and let them go at it." When informed that they were talking about God, he elbowed his way in and joined the fray.

In all, there were too many graphic descriptions of the torments of hell. One woman complained: "I haven't even opened my mouth, and four people have told me I'm going to hell." Another woman was involved in Wicca, a kind of feminist neopaganism often associated, mistakenly, with Satan worship. "But Satan is the prince of lies!" one evangelist shouted in exasperation. The youth of Calvary Chapel had their hands full. Quite frequently, several of them would step aside and huddle in prayer over some prospect who was particularly obdurate. The young preacher had been right; the forces of righteousness were engaged in a "heavy spiritual battle" at Balboa Pier.

And yet, here, just a short distance from Pirate's Cove, the scene was strangely evocative of decades past: the briny scent of the ocean mixing with the smell of campfires on the beach, the restless waves— and, sure enough, a few people who looked for all the world like hippies, with long hair in pony tails, mutton-chop sideburns, denim shirts, necklaces made of turquoise, wide leather watchbands, sunglasses at eleven o'clock in the evening. One of them, sitting on a park bench at the periphery of the crowd, crouched over a guitar and belted out songs about Jesus in a throaty, insistent whine.

By eleven forty-five the crowd had dissipated and it was time to conduct a post-mortem. I asked Mark about the experience. "It went pretty well," he said. "I witnessed to a Catholic." I asked another woman, Carol, to assess the evening. "I'm really stoked," she said. "I ran into this guy I had talked to the last time we were out witnessing. He wanted me to meet his friends, and one of them said he wasn't sure whether he was a Christian or not. So we prayed, and when we finished tears were rolling down his face."

Not everyone reported successes, so it was important to close ranks and bolster sagging morale. "I had this guy so close, and then his friend came and pulled him away," one man said, shaking his head. "He didn't want to go either." Friends consoled him that a "seed had been planted," that "God's word does not return unto Him void."[15] Someone else opined that the people who resisted most vociferously were the ones most interested in the gospel. "Take my word for it," he said, "in six months they'll be Christians."

Toward the end of the evening, one man who appeared to be in his late twenties had launched into a long, desperate harangue. "Salvation is in every man's hand. Jesus loves you, man, He loves you with all his heart. And I love you. The truth is here. And people's lives have been changed: marriages coming together, alcoholics being renewed, drug addicts being changed. Man, this is the real stuff! And it's the Spirit of God, the Holy Ghost. God has changed my life. I walked as a heathen. I partied with the best of them.

"There's hope out here," he continued, his voice growing more forceful, his hands beating the air. "There really is hope. There really is a God, and you really are going to be accountable for your sins. I guarantee you'll be accountable for your sins. Receive the love of Christ. All you have to do is say, 'Yes, Lord, I know I've sinned against You, and I know I haven't walked with You, and I know I don't know You, man. But help me. Help Me!' All you have to do is be sincere, because God is merciful."

His cadence grew faster, his tone more plaintive. "It's getting worse in this world. There's people dabbling in mystics, man, and witchcraft, and they're loving it, man, they're pushing it. And it's going to get worse. I'm not going to contend with people about this and that, because I don't come to preach religion. I preach reality. Jesus is real, and He loves you. He loves you and He cares. He loves you so much that, like I said, if you come to Him with a sincere heart and tell Him, 'Hey, Lord, I've sinned against you,' He'll forgive you and square you away, I tell you, He'll square you away. He'll change your life around. You've got free will, man, you've got a choice. Repent, and your life will change; I guarantee your life will change."

Most of his auditors had drifted away. "I'm willing to put myself on the line right here. I'll pray with anyone who wants to accept Jesus."

No takers. When he learned later that many of the people he had preached to in the thinning crowd were from Calvary Chapel, he threw up his hands and chuckled at the incident. "Here I am preaching my heart out, and all these people are already Christians," he said in mock despair. "What a drag, man!"

"That's okay," someone assured him quietly as waves crashed in the distance. "The Spirit was moving."

NOTES

1. Everyone is casual here. I sat in on a seventh-grade algebra class at Maranatha Christian Academy (Calvary chapel's grammar school), where the students addressed their teacher, a man in his late thirties, as "Randy."

2. Singing is an important element in the worship at Calvary Chapel; every service or meeting I attended during my visit opened with a long period of congregational singing.

3. Estimates vary. One pastor quoted the figure at twenty thousand. A 1979 article in the *Los Angeles Times* put the number at twenty-five thousand; see Russell Chandler, "Cleric Finds Success Serving Hippie Needs," *Los Angeles Times*, 5 July 1979, pt. 2, pp. 1, 8.

4. Other examples: Robert Schuller's Crystal Cathedral in Garden grove, Vineyard Christian Fellowship in Anaheim, headed by John Wimber, and the First Evangelical Free Church in Fullerton, led by Chuck Swindoll.

5. Chuck Smith, *The History of Calvary Chapel* (Costa Mesa, Cal.: Word for Today, 1981), p. 3.

6. Ibid., p. 6. For a description of Calvary Chapel in its early years, see Ronald M. Enroth, Edward E. Ericson, Jr., and C. Breckinridge Peter, *The Jesus People: Old-Time Religion in the Age of Aquarius* (Grand Rapids: Wm. B. Eerdmans, 1972), ch. 4.

7. Oden Fong, interview, 11 May 1987.

8. L. E. Romaine, interview, 11 May 1987.

9. Fong interview.

10. Smith, *History of Calvary Chapel*, pp. 9–10.

11. Quoted in Richard Dalrymple, "Beach Baptism Helps Save the Young," *Los Angeles Herald-Examiner*, 24 October 1970, p. A–7.

12. Romaine interview.

13. See Acts 2.

14. These, I recognize, are generalizations. Pentecostals will protest that doctrine and theology are indeed quite important to them, while fundamentalists will insist that they value religious affections.

15. This is a reference to Isa. 55:11.

2

Dallas Orthodoxy

FLUSHED WITH OIL MONEY of the seventies and prompted in part by the arrival of Northerners to the Sun Belt, Dallas, Texas, has recast its skyline with a building boom that only now, in the unaccustomed austerity of the late 1980s, shows any sign of abating. The results are impressive: a passel of post-modernist structures that represents a wholesale assault on the canons of modernist and international-style architecture dominating much of the twentieth century.

The pleasant, well-manicured campus of Dallas Theological Seminary, just a couple of miles from the center city, will never win acclaim for architectural distinction, but the people of Dallas Seminary have sustained their own quarrel with a different sort of modernity for more than half a century. Since its founding in 1924 to combat the theological modernism then popular with American Protestants, Dallas Theological Seminary has, in its view, held down the fortress of evangelical and fundamentalist orthodoxy against the sundry assaults of twentieth-century theological liberalism. My visit to Dallas Seminary, then, was a kind of inspection tour of these doctrinal ramparts, or (to shift the metaphor) an examination of the

theological infrastructure of American evangelicalism. The intellectual case for evangelical theology, people here believe, rests to a
remarkable degree on the twin pillars of biblical inerrancy (the
conviction that the inspiration of the Holy Spirit rendered the Scriptures errorless in the original autographs) and a nineteenth-century
doctrine that goes by the rather ponderous name of dispensational
premillennialism.[1]

In the 1830s a British student of the Bible, John Nelson Darby,
came up with a novel interpretation of the Bible. All of human
history from creation through the present and into the coming millennium, Darby decided, could be divided into seven periods or
dispensations. These different ages also largely coincide with successive covenants between God and humanity. In the Noahic covenant, for instance, God had promised Noah that the world would
never again be destroyed by a flood. The covenant of works between
God and ancient Israel obligated the Hebrews to strict moral and
dietary standards. Since the day of Pentecost in the New Testament
book of Acts, Darby argued, humanity has lived in the covenant of
grace, under the terms of which Christ offers salvation and deliverance from the judgment of God to anyone who acknowledges Jesus
as savior.

Darby's ideas, grounded in a literalistic interpretation of Scripture, also led him to posit that we are living now in the sixth and
final dispensation before the return of Christ to take the true believers out of this world to their reward in heaven. The prophecies
of the Bible—principally the books of Daniel in the Old Testament
and Revelation in the New Testament—have been fulfilled and we
can look for this "second coming" at any moment. We are poised
at the end of human history, Darby believed, waiting for the apocalypse prophesied in the Bible. Although the notion of imminence
was not new in Christian theology, this doctrine, known as premillennialism, held that Christ would return to claim (or rapture)
His Church (the true believers) before the millennium, one thousand years of theocratic rule on earth predicted in Revelation 20.

Darby was not the first to predict the imminent end of human
history. Ever since Jesus admonished His followers that "this gen-

eration will not pass away" before the coming of the Son of Man, Christians have speculated about the future and taken a strong interest in eschatology, the doctrine of the end times. Enigmatic passages about the seventy weeks in the book of Daniel and the elaborate apocalyptic imagery in Revelation have fueled the imagination of everyone from St. Augustine in his classic *The City of God*, written in the fourth century, to Swedish filmmaker Ingmar Bergman, in his movie *The Seventh Seal*, released in 1957. The early Christians, taking Christ's words at face value, prepared for their immediate translation into heaven, while Martin Luther dismissed the book of Revelation as irrelevant to Christian life and theology and urged that it be excluded from the canon of Scripture.

Darby's interpretive scheme of seven ages or dispensations caught on in Great Britain, especially with the Plymouth Brethren (among whom Darby numbered himself), but his ideas found especially fertile soil among evangelicals in nineteenth-century America. When Darby came to the United States in 1862, he found that his premillennial views fit the evangelical temper perfectly. Although the New England Puritans had been decidedly premillennial in their theology—that is, they expected the return of Christ at any moment—most evangelical eschatology in the eighteenth and nineteenth centuries had veered toward postmillennialism, the belief that Christ was even now establishing His kingdom on earth and that He would return for His Church *after* the millennium.

Postmillennialism implied a certain optimism about the perfectibility and progress of both humanity and society. It inspired, for example, such diverse utopian communities as the Society of Believers in Christ's Second Appearing (better known as the Shakers) and the Oneida Community in western New York, John Humphrey Noyes's experiment in "complex marriage." The Second Great Awakening, an evangelical revival early in the nineteenth century that engulfed three geographical theaters of the new republic—New England, western New York, and the Cumberland Valley— prompted breathless predictions about the millennial age already under way in America. More important, this optimism about the amelioration of society energized countless evangelical reform movements—abolitionism, temperance, education, prison reform, the female seminary movement—all grounded in the conviction that Christ was even then, through the efforts of His people, constructing a millennial kingdom.

By the time John Nelson Darby arrived, however, much of this evangelical ebullience had dissipated. The sectional rivalries of the Civil War had fractured evangelical unity, and among Northerners the Emancipation Proclamation removed the one cause that, more than any other, had united them. The industrialization and urbanization of the latter half of the nineteenth century, moreover, together with the influx of immigrants (most of them Roman Catholic) engendered doubts about the progress of godly rule in America. Squalid tenements and rowdy taverns hardly resembled the precincts of Zion. Nineteenth-century evangelical orthodoxy also reeled from the assaults of two alien ideologies: The German discipline of higher criticism called into question the veracity of scriptural texts, and Charles Darwin's publication of *The Origin of Species* in 1859 challenged the Genesis account of creation and, pressed to its logical conclusions, undermined all literal interpretations of the Bible.

At the moment when evangelical leaders sensed the need for an adjustment to their theology, Darby arrived with his dispensational premillennialism. His claim to strict biblical literalism constituted part of Darby's appeal, but his elaborate schemata for understanding human history made even more sense. Darby convinced evangelicals that they had been mistaken to suppose the millennium already underway. In fact, such a supposition misconstrued biblical prophecies entirely, and he proceeded to recast the sequence of eschatology. The millennium would not begin before Christ returned for His Church. After this rapture, Darby said, a seven-year tribulation (predicted in Matthew 24) would occur, followed *then* by the millennium.

This premillennialism, the doctrine that Christ would return to rapture the Church before the millennium, had broad implications for the social ethics of evangelicals. Society, this new rubric insisted, was careening toward judgment; it could never be reclaimed for Christ, short of His return to establish the millennium. Despite the continuation of some evangelical reform efforts, this notion relieved evangelicals of the obligation to labor for the amelioration of social ills. Evangelicals increasingly stood in judgment of culture and awaited its destruction, which would follow their translation into heaven. "I don't find any place where God says the world is to grow better and better," evangelist Dwight L. Moody, a premillennialist, said in 1877. "I find that the earth is to grow worse and worse, and that at length there is going to be a separation." That separation of godliness from sinfulness, righteousness from worldliness, Moody believed, would take place at the rapture, when Christ came to translate the true believers out of this world.[2]

Historically, the adoption of this new eschatology coincided with the splintering of American Protestantism. At the same time that evangelicals began to neglect social reform efforts and exhorted anyone who would listen to prepare for the second coming by confessing faith in Jesus Christ, some of the more liberal theologians such as Washington Gladden and Walter Rauschenbusch articulated what they called the Social Gospel, a theology that sought first to understand the social conditions that lay behind the wretchedness of the urban dwellers and then worked toward their deliverance from the sinful social institutions that perpetuated their enslavement to poverty. As Protestant conservatives retreated to an otherworldly theology, liberals became convinced that the gospel mandated efforts to reform social institutions.

Even a century later, the twain still have not met. While evangelicals engage in internecine quarrels over eschatology—columns of the faithful have mustered over such issues as whether Christ will return before, during, or after the seven-year tribulation—mainline Protestants, for the most part, reject this dispensational scheme altogether. Grace Presbytery of Texas, for instance, whose bailiwick includes Dallas, has declared dispensationalism a heresy and "out of accord with the system of doctrine set forth in the Westminster Confession of Faith."[3]

Although John Nelson Darby formulated this dispensational premillennialism, a whole network of individuals and institutions disseminated these notions. Dispensationalism caught on with such evangelical preachers as Moody, Reuben A. Torrey, A. J. Gordon, James M. Gray, and A. C. Dixon, among many others. Those leaders, in turn, organized prophecy conferences to advance these views.

Schools such as Moody Bible Institute and the Bible Institute of Los Angeles (now Biola College) further promoted dispensationalism.

The one man responsible more than any other for popularizing this new gospel was Cyrus Ingerson Scofield, a Congregational minister from Dallas. Scofield sponsored a series of Bible institutes around the country and established the *Comprehensive Bible Correspondence Course*, the Scofield School of the Bible in New York City, and Philadelphia College of the Bible to propagate dispensational premillennialism.[4] His most enduring contribution to the evangelical subculture however, was the Scofield Reference Bible, an edition of the Scriptures, first published by Oxford University Press in 1909, that included elaborate glosses and cross-references to guide the reader in his or her understanding of dispensationalism. For generations of fundamentalists ever since, the Scofield Bible has served as a kind of template through which they read the Scriptures. Although superseded in many ways by the Ryrie Study Bible, compiled by a former member of the Dallas Seminary faculty, the Scofield Reference Bible continues to sell briskly.[5]

Scofield passed the mantle on to a protégé, Lewis Sperry Chafer, a graduate of Oberlin College and an evangelist who had met Scofield at Dwight Moody's Bible conference center in Northfield, Massachusetts. Chafer, who in 1923 succeeded Scofield as pastor of the First Congregational Church in Dallas (promptly renamed Scofield Memorial Church), began to explore the possibility of addressing what the World Christian Fundamentals Association called "one of the greatest needs of the hour," namely, "the establishment of a great evangelical premillennial seminary."[6] On October 1, 1924, thirteen students assembled for classes offered by the new Evangelical Theological College (later renamed Dallas Theological Seminary).

From the beginning, Chafer, president of the institution which now bills itself as "the largest independent evangelical seminary in the world," insisted that the curriculum emphasize the biblical languages, especially Greek and Hebrew.[7] At a time when theological liberalism (or modernism) and the Social Gospel prompted some of the older seminaries in the United States to abandon their emphasis on languages in favor of courses in psychology, philosophy, and sociology, Dallas held firm. Even today Dallas requires two years of Hebrew and three years of Greek, an exacting schedule that, coupled with all the other required courses, demands four years to complete, rather than the three years required for a divinity degree at most seminaries.[8]

My day in classes at Dallas Theological Seminary began early. A Protestant seminary is not supposed to be a monastery—the Reformation did away with that notion—but, at least by twentieth-century standards, the regimen here might draw grudging admiration even from St. Benedict, who required his charges to "rise at the eighth hour of the night" to engage in study, meditation, and prayer.[9] On Tuesday and Thursday mornings at seven forty-five, students choose among two sections of elementary Hebrew, two sections of elementary Greek, two sections of expository preaching, two sections called senior preaching, a course on pre-exilic and exilic prophets, and a course on eschatology.

I chose eschatology. Well in advance of seven forty-five, students toting briefcases and large, well-thumbed Bibles filed into the lecture hall. (The student population is overwhelmingly white, overwhelmingly male, and invariably dressed in jackets and ties, in compliance with the seminary's dress code. Despite an occasional lack of sartorial sophistication, students here look like they might be refugees from Wall Street: very clean, with closely cropped hair, conservative, very Republican.) When the professor, John A. Witmer, arrived, he grabbed a card from a lucite holder on the lectern and announced that today's prayer request concerned mission work in Bulgaria. Witmer said that, unfortunately, Bulgarian religion was overwhelmingly Eastern Orthodox, that the number of Protestants there was less than one-half of one percent. He asked for someone to "remember these missionaries in prayer." Even at this hour, it seemed, there was no shortage of volunteers. After choosing someone in the front row, Witmer asked, "Any special requests?" Yes, said a young man. He asked for prayer to help him locate a volleyball and volleyball net for the church youth gathering he was organizing for Saturday night. After some sympathetic moans from the class,

Witmer said, "Let's remember that youth meeting and the need for equipment." The man in the front row then prayed aloud for a volleyball and a net and asked God to "raise up the missionaries" in Bulgaria and to "send others to proclaim the Word."

The morning's lecture, midway through the semester, opened a section on "the imminent return of the Lord," an important tenet in dispensational theology. (Article XVIII of the seminary's doctrinal statement reads: "We believe that, according to the Word of God, the next great event in the fulfillment of prophecy will be the coming of the Lord in the air to receive to Himself into heaven both His own who are alive and remain unto His coming, and also all who have fallen asleep in Jesus, and that this event is the blessed hope set before us in the Scripture, and for this we should be constantly looking.")[10] This blessed hope, Witmer said, "is the next item on the prophetic agenda; it could take place at any time, without delay." He then recited a numbing litany of proof-texts that, he insisted, substantiate his view—and the view of the entire faculty here—that Christ will return at any moment and certainly before the tribulation. In the jargon of eschatology, this is pre-trib premillennialism, the belief that the rapture will precede the seven-year tribulation and the thousand-year millennium predicted in Revelation.

Perhaps it was the early hour or perhaps the soporific presentation, but the lecture prompted no dissent, just a friendly query from the back row: "Dr. Witmer, Christ spoke of the destruction of Jerusalem. How does that fit in?" "That does present a problem," the professor conceded. But it is a problem, his long, rambling answer implied, that can be finessed by juggling certain verb tenses and re-examining the context of the quotation.

A booklet published and distributed by the seminary insists that "Dispensationalism is an interpretive necessity," and that "Without this recognition of the different ways God has governed the world, consistent interpretation of the Bible becomes impossible."[11] Nevertheless, I found that many people at Dallas Seminary were eager to dispel the impression that dispensationalism was the most important tenet of the seminary's theology. "Some people have the idea that we live, think, and breathe dispensationalism around here," said Randy Gardner, a Master of Theology student who has also recruited students around the country for the past two years. He finds that dispensationalism is "the number one question I get from prospective students." Dispensationalism, Gardner acknowledged, is "an underlying philosophy" at Dallas, but what makes the seminary distinctive, he thinks, is a passion on the part of the faculty to "teach people to know and communicate the Scriptures." American evangelicalism, he said, has moved away from the Bible, and there's a need to reassert the importance of the Scriptures as the inerrant Word of God.

Norman Geisler, professor of systematic theology, agrees. "I think inerrancy is a test for evangelical consistency, for evangelical leadership, and it should be in our doctrinal statements. If you do not hold to inerrancy, that the Scriptures are errorless in the original autographs, you are not evangelical on that doctrine." How important is it? "I think it's crucial. It's a watershed. Almost everybody who is anybody in evangelicalism has affirmed this view."[12]

A greater attention to the dictates of Scripture, Geisler believes, would help evangelicals avoid the perils of what he calls experientialism, "an experiential test for truth." Accordingly, Geisler and others at Dallas Seminary take a dim view of even the modulated sort of pentecostalism at Calvary Chapel. Charismatics, Geisler said, are most culpable of relying on religious experience, but he sees other assaults on evangelical orthodoxy coming from Eastern or New Age spirituality, American pragmatism, and vestiges of existentialism. "All of these are experience-oriented epistemologies—it's true because you experience it—rather than a more rational, cognitive one," he said. "I think ultimately we could all drown in a cesspool of experientialism."[13]

This rationalistic approach to the Bible and theology, Geisler contends, implicitly refutes a neo-orthodox or Barthian view of Scripture. Karl Barth, an eminent twentieth-century Swiss theologian, believed that the Bible *becomes* the Word of God, an idea that lent dynamism to the reading of Scripture; the Bible, Barth argued, is not a static book meant to be treated as an ancient relic but is rather the *living* Word of God that, through the agency of the Holy Spirit, speaks afresh to the reader. But such a view, Geisler insists, undermines the whole process of hermeneutics or biblical interpretation. "When you finish your exegesis and you've found out, presumably, what the author meant—that's what exegesis is all about; what did the author mean?—you still have to ask the question, 'Hath God said?' You have to have an objective focal point that is hermeneutically determinable wherein rests divine authority."

One of the longtime fixtures on the faculty at Dallas is J. Dwight Pentecost, the redoubtable professor of Bible exposition, now retired. I sat in on an elective course he still offers on Thursdays called "The Biblical Covenant." Pentecost, a genial, white-haired man who drives to work in a Mercedes-Benz sports coupe, opened the class with prayer and then said, "I think we're somewhere in the Davidic Covenant." The notion of successive covenants, a distinctive characteristic of dispensational theology, asserts that God has adopted different strategies for dealing with humanity through the successive dispensations. According to Pentecost, the Davidic covenant— God's covenant with David, king of ancient Israel—came to a close when the Jews rejected Jesus as their messiah. That apparently signaled a kind of interregnum, also known to dispensationalists as the Church Age, between the Israelite kingdom of the Old Testament and the millennial kingdom predicted in Revelation. "The Davidic covenant was postponed," Pentecost said, "until Christ's return."

This covenantal understanding of the Bible has enormous implications for the relation of Christians and Jews. Pentecost and other dispensationalists believe that the Jews' rejection of Jesus as their messiah during His lifetime exempted them from God's favor and effectively transferred the Old Testament promises from the people of Israel to the Christian Church. Although the interests of Israel and the Church will be reconciled in the millennial kingdom, according to Pentecost, the very fact that we live now in the Church Age (or dispensation) implies that God has turned His back on the Jews for their rejection of His Son. "Israel is condemned by God," Pentecost said, "although individual Jews can escape judgment by acknowledging Christ and identifying themselves with the Church publicly, by baptism."

A student later elaborated this doctrine for me. "There's a future for Israel," he said, "but it's related to the messiah, to Christ. There's no salvation for Jews now, short of recognizing Jesus as the messiah." This conviction has prompted proselytization efforts (such as the organization called Jews for Jesus) among the Jews by fundamentalists. Although less rigid Christian theologians, following the lead of Reinhold Niebuhr in the late 1950s, have been willing to acknowledge that Jews, as God's chosen people, attain salvation through their own covenant, dispensationalists insist that Jews must become Christians in order to enter the kingdom of heaven.

But what does this interregnum between ancient Israel and the millennium mean for the present age or dispensation? The parables of the New Testament, Pentecost believes, reveal the essential features of "theocratic administration." In the present age God has assigned authority in four areas: in the civil realm, to magistrates to curb lawlessness; in employment, to the master or employer; in the Church, to elders; and in the family, to the husband and father. Moreover, according to Pentecost, "when God assigns authority, He demands submission to authority. So that in the civil realm, we are to be subject to rulers. The wife is subject, the children subject, to authority. The employee is subject to the authority of the employer." And finally, in the Church, "the younger are subject to the authority of the elders."

Perhaps unwittingly, Pentecost provided an illustration. At one point during the lecture a student, one of only seven women in a lecture hall of ninety-four students, admitted some confusion about the configuration of the covenants. Pentecost responded: "Can I ask you to hold that until I go a bit farther? Maybe a light will go on. Prayerfully. Hopefully." He paused. "If not, can I fall back on Paul's injunction? Ask your husband at home." The classroom erupted in loud, sustained laughter and guffaws. If the instructor intended the remark as good-natured humor or a wry riposte, his expression betrayed no hint. He simply resumed the lecture.[14]

The mere presence of women here at Dallas has provoked some controversy. As biblical literalists, students and faculty point to St. Paul's injunctions against allowing women as teachers in the Church in order to justify their exclusion from the ordained ministry, even though many Protestant groups over the past two decades have abolished their proscriptions against women's ordination, citing the broader, inclusive demands of the New Testament.[15] At Dallas, however, the seminary's constitution bars women from serving on the faculty. Although they have been allowed into selected degree programs and permitted to take courses as non-degree candidates for several years, women were admitted as candidates for the Master of Theology (the seminary's basic divinity degree) for the first time in the fall of 1986. Women now make up thirteen percent of the student body (as against the national average in Protestant seminaries of twenty-six percent, a figure that is much higher, approaching fifty percent, in liberal institutions).[16] But even though they are enrolled in the divinity program at Dallas, women are not allowed to take homiletics courses, the expectation being that they would never have occasion to preach, that their activities would be limited to some sort of parachurch work, teaching in a Christian school, or perhaps, in less rigid fundamentalist churches, administration or Christian education.

Apparently, however, such restrictions do not concern the female students. During my visit the current issue of *Kindred Spirit*, the seminary's glitzy, four-color public relations magazine, contained an article by Barbara A. Peil, a Master of Arts student in Christian education. Entitled "A Seasoned Approach," the article urged older Christian women to tutor younger women in their proper roles: "Young women need to be taught a biblical view of their roles and relationships with their husbands in order to truly liberate them to be all that God intended them to be and to experience the best that He has for them." God measures a woman's success in life, the author wrote, "by her relationship with her husband and children." Extolling the virtues of purity and self-control, Peil urged younger women to learn "the oft-maligned delights of homemaking."[17]

In such a climate, even modest attempts by women to enlarge the scope of their responsibilities meet with resistance. Holly Hankins completed her studies for the Master of Arts in biblical studies in December 1986, but in April 1987 she was working part-time as a clerk in the seminary bookstore. She hopes to find a job in a church somewhere but, she said, "I'm having a hard time finding a job because I'm a woman." Still, she has no designs on ordination because she believes that would be a violation of biblical teaching. Hankins would like a job as head of a women's ministries program in a church, a kind of nonordained pastor to women in the congregation. "Women should be counseled by women," she said, and that would take some of the counseling burden off the pastor.

Hankins, an attractive, articulate woman, has been something of a pioneer at Dallas Seminary—the first woman to serve on the student council and the first woman to pray publicly in the seminary chapel. She insists that neither the professors nor the students have looked down on her, but the placement office has provided little help. The head of placement, she said, "definitely believes" that a woman has no place on a church staff. "It's slow," she said of her job search. "Even after receiving my résumé, many churches tell me they have secretarial jobs available."

Defending traditional roles for women at Dallas Theological Seminary follows logically from both its epistemology and its cultural location. As biblical literalists, the faculty cannot maneuver around Paul's emphatic proscriptions against women in leadership positions.

Moreover, as the spiritual and intellectual descendants of fundamentalists who earlier in this century began dissenting from what they regarded as a secularizing society, their opposition to fuller roles for women coincides with their uneasiness with popular American culture. At a time when academic scholarship adopted the tenets of Darwinism and German higher criticism, and when the publicity surrounding the trial of John T. Scopes, a biology teacher from Tennessee, succeeded in portraying fundamentalists as rubes and anachronisms, fundamentalists began to perceive American culture as hostile. Whereas in the previous century evangelicals had shaped social and political agendas, in the twentieth century fundamentalists found themselves pushed to the periphery. Thus marginalized, they grew increasingly suspicious of the broader culture. Generations of children in fundamentalist households were instructed to eschew "worldliness" and to adhere to strict codes of morality that forbade card-playing, gambling, cosmetics, motion pictures, dancing, alcohol, and tobacco. Some of the proscriptions have eased somewhat in evangelical circles, but the suspicion of world-liness, of theological and cultural innovation, endures.

Norman Geisler, for instance, who describes himself as a "strong creationist," has testified in the courts in favor of permitting the Genesis account of creation to be taught along side of evolution in public schools. "I hold that God directly and immediately created every kind of thing, every form of life, and that there was no mac-roevolution between them," he insisted.[18]

Geisler along with other faculty and students at Dallas Seminary have also been active in the anti-abortion movement. A sign in the student center read:

> Join Drs Geisler and House
> and your Fellow Students to
> Protest the Destruction
> of Innocent Human Life
> at a Local Abortion Clinic
> Meet *each Wednesday right
> after chapel* in the parking
> lot by Academic 1

Several of the students I spoke with denied any necessary connection between conservative theology and conservative politics, although they acknowledged a correlation between the two. "I think there's something to be said for taking a conservative stance regarding abortion and subscribing to conservative Christianity," one man told me. "I think there's something to be said for taking a conservative stance against homosexuality and being a conservative Christian. I wouldn't vote for a politician who was for gay rights, because there you're dealing with morality."

I asked two students, Herb Bateman, who had come to Dallas Sem-inary from Philadelphia College of the Bible, and Jimmy Carter, a Southern Baptist from Tulsa, what was at stake in the doctrine of dispensational premillennialism. How does one's adherence to premillennialist ideas affect the way you live? "The imminent return of Christ affects the way I approach each day," Bateman said, "be-cause if I know that He can return at any moment I certainly want to make sure that my life on a daily basis is in accordance with what His will is, which is derived from the imperative statements of Scripture. Wherever I'm at, I'm to be living for Christ, and I know that with Him returning at any time I'll have to give an account for my life, and I'll be rewarded accordingly."[19]

Bateman added that a premillennialist interpretation of the Bible was "the best option available and the most consistent, but that's not to say that someone is any less a Christian because he believes that Christ will return *during* the tribulation rather than before. It's not an issue to die over."

Both Bateman and Carter felt more strongly about the inerrancy of the Scriptures. Bateman volunteered that he would "go to the wall" for the doctrine of inerrancy, and Carter said that he couldn't envision ever changing his views on that issue. I wondered if subscribing to the doctrine of inerrancy affected the way they read the Bible. "When you approach it as an inerrant text, it's not open to the subjectivity of man," Carter said. "By believing that the text is inerrant, we can go to it as the basis of our authority." Bateman concurred, adding that "if you throw that out, you lose some of your footing."

"We're taught a theological grid here, I won't deny that," Bateman acknowledged, a bit defensively, "but I don't think the Christian community is as closed-minded as the world would like to make us out to be. We're more than willing to open up and speak and dialogue. The closed-mindedness many times doesn't come from the Christian, it comes from the liberal." He paused. "If you've got the truth, what's there to fear in open dialogue?"

NOTES

1. Dallas Seminary's statement of purpose reads in part: "The Seminary is committed to the primacy of the authoritative, inerrant Scriptures. Its instruction, which includes teaching, defending, and applying the truths of the Christian faith, is given within the framework of evangelical, premillennial, dispensational theology."

2. Quoted in William G. McLoughlin, ed., *The American Evangelicals, 1800–1900: An Anthology* (New York: Harper & Row, 1968), p. 184.

3. Grace Union Presbytery, "Position Paper on Employment of Seminary Students" and "Policy Regarding Reception of Ministers." I am grateful to Carrie Washington, executive presbyter of the Presbytery of Newark and a former resident of Texas, for pointing this out to me.

4. John D. Hannah, "The Early Years of Lewis Sperry Chafer," *Bibliotheca Sacra* 144 (January–March 1987): 21, 22.

5. Records are incomplete, but Donald Kraus, Bibles editor at Oxford University Press, estimates that the press has sold anywhere from thirty to fifty million copies since 1909. According to Jonathan Weiss, sales manager at Oxford, the Scofield Bible has sold more than 4.2 million copies since 1967, eighty-five percent of them leatherbound editions, an indication of the Scofield Bible's continued popularity as a devotional tool.

6. Quoted in John A. Witmer, " 'What God Hath Wrought'—Fifty Years of Dallas Theological Seminary, Part I: God's Man and His Dream," *Bibliotheca Sacra* 130 (October 1973): 295.

7. Ibid., p. 292.

8. The divinity degree awarded at Dallas is the Master of Theology (Th.M.), the requirements for which include writing a thesis. Most seminaries offer the Master of Divinity (M.Div.) as their basic divinity degree and the Th.M. after another year of specialized study.

9. Henry Bettenson, ed., *Documents of the Christian Church* (New York: Oxford Univesity Press, 1947), p. 165.

10. James H. Thames, ed., *Dallas Theological Seminary: 1986–87 Catalog* (Dallas: Dallas Theological Seminary, 1986), p. 161.

11. Charles C. Ryrie, "What Is Dispensationalism?" rev. ed. (Dallas: Dallas Theological Seminary, 1986), [p. 5].

12. Norman Geisler, interview, 1 April 1987.

13. Several months after my visit, Dallas Theological Seminary dismissed three members of the faculty because of their apparent sympathies with charismatic theology; see Randy Frame, "Three Professors Part Paths with Dallas," *Christianity Today*, 5 February 1988, pp. 52–53.

14. Although he breezily dismissed the woman's query, Pentecost readily fielded questions from male students. Later in the lecture, seeking to illustrate the meaning of the term *leaven*, Pentecost asked: "Any of you girls bake bread?"

15. Typically, the biblical references cited against the ordination of women are 1 Tim. 2:11–12 and 1 Cor. 14:34. Those in favor of women's ordination point to Gal. 3:28, where Paul insists that in Christ there is "neither Jew nor Greek, there is neither slave nor free, there is neither male nor female; for you are all one in Christ Jesus" (RSV). Pentecost's reference to "ask their husbands at home" comes from 1 Cor. 14:35 (RSV).

16. Roy B. Zuck, academic dean at Dallas, interview, 2 April 1987; Ari L. Goldman, "As Call Comes, More Women Answer," *New York Times*, 19 October 1986.

17. Barbara A. Peil, "A Seasoned Approach," *Kindred Spirit* 11 (*Spring 1987*): 12, 13.

18. Geisler interview.

19. Herb Bateman and Jimmy Carter, interview, 3 April 1987.

3

On Location

A 1969 CHEVROLET MALIBU careened down a country road, its head-lights piercing the darkness. Soon the left front wheel veered across the yellow line. The car gathered speed and plunged off an embankment, landed on its nose in the ravine below, and then somersaulted onto its back in a creek.

A couple of beats after the rear tires stopped spinning, a voice yelled "Cut!" A company of onlookers burst into spontaneous applause. From the ravine the same voice inquired of his walkie-talkie, "Gloria, is Geoff okay?"

"Yes," another voice crackled, "we're okay, Don."

The operator of camera 1 invited the director to examine the final perspective. The automobile was framed squarely in the viewfinder. The director pronounced it perfect and exclaimed, "Jimmy, you're the best." He called across the creek to another cameraman: "John Leiendecker, how's it look?"

"Looks good, Don."

After acknowledging—and returning—the congratulations of his crew, the director allowed himself a little titter and muttered, almost under his breath, "God is good."

Indeed, the entire crew seemed to breathe a palpable sigh of relief. Unlike dialogue or interior shots, this scene could be shot only once; there would be no second take. It had to be perfect, and the consensus among the crew was that it was. All the hours, even days, of preparation had paid off. Gloria Fiorimonti, the stunt-woman, had drawn an imaginary X in the ravine, calculated speed and distances, and landed the nose of the car squarely on the X. The director of photography calibrated the camera angles according to Gloria's calculations. Pete Roseman, the gaffer, barked instructions to his lighting crew in order to carve the proper combination of light and shadow out of the September darkness. The sound man also captured the scene, the car roaring off the cliff and bouncing into the stream, then the eerie wash of water churning past the metal carcass.

"We'll dub a little more engine noise with that, Don, and it'll be real nice," he said.

"Good, Curt."

The euphoria and self-congratulation, however, passed quickly. The crew began preparing for the next scene, a shot of an empty beer can (which the driver of the car had tossed out the window during the previous night's shooting) meandering down the stream and colliding into the rear fender of the over-turned automobile.

It is a poignant scene, even to the spectators gathered on the bridge watching take after take of the beer can rolling down the bank and swirling toward the car. The red and white container won't tumble down the bank in any predictable way, so the scene has to be shot again and again—one crew member tossing it into the water and another retrieving it downstream—until it's just right.

The man responsible for getting it just right is Donald W. Thompson, the director. He checks camera angles, inquires about the lighting and sound, rehearses the actors' lines for the next scene. People constantly pepper him with questions: Where do you want the spectators? Will the noise of the still camera intrude onto the soundtrack during the crash scene? What about the catering truck? Almost an hour ago Thompson instructed his associate producer to radio for the helicopter as soon as the car landed in the ravine.

There's no time to lose; with a crew this size and a limited budget, delays are costly.

Yet Thompson finds time for a word of praise or encouragement. Late into the night he'll rub the shoulders of a weary colleague or offer coffee to an assistant. When Gloria Fiorimonti, the stunt-woman, announced she was returning to the West Coast, Thompson left the cameras and climbed out of the ravine to say farewell and offer his thanks. Amidst their goodbyes Gloria asked if he had a minute to share something she'd read in the Bible the other day.

Yes, there's time. There's always time. (Earlier in the evening Thompson had informed me that Gloria, the first and only woman inducted into the stuntmen's hall of fame, was a new, a recently converted, Christian.)

Gloria, wearing tight denims, a tee-shirt from Jackson Hole, Wy-oming, and a California tan, returned with a devotional booklet and began reading a meditation about God's strength, His ability to overcome adversity. She'd read that meditation the same day she first scouted this location. "I didn't tell you, Don," she confessed now, "but when I first saw this location I was terrified. I thought there was no way we could pull it off."

Apparently, sending an automobile off a cliff is not as easy as it looks. First, she needed a straight shot at the ramp, but the winding country road wouldn't allow it. She also had to thread the car into a narrow aperture between a tree on the left and the bridge abut-ment on the right, and all of this at a sufficient speed—thirty to thirty-five miles an hour—so that the automobile would sail off the cliff rather than just tumble into the ravine. God helped her over-come a difficult situation, she said, and in the process He taught her a valuable lesson about depending on Him.

Soon after Gloria headed home to California, the helicopter ar-rived. If this sleek, blue-and-white machine isn't exactly the star, it at least plays the title role in *Life Flight*, this movie about the genesis of helicopter ambulance service in central Iowa. Don Thompson's film dramatizes the early days of Life Flight, a program begun several years ago by Iowa Methodist Hospital in Des Moines and duplicated by hospitals elsewhere. Based on actual events, Thompson's screenplay depicts a series of accidents in remote areas whose victims survive because of the swift medical attention available by helicopter.

The screenplay also takes us into the lives of the people and families involved. The struggle of a veteran with memories of Vietnam and his fear of flying. An argument between a father and son just minutes before the angry, drunken son drives his car off the embankment. There are heroes aplenty in Thompson's screenplay: the helicopter, the veteran who overcomes his fears, the woman who pushes for Life Flight in the face of considerable bureaucratic resistance.

In the real world, however, life doesn't always imitate art. One scene in the movie, based on an actual incident, shows two people on a snowmobile disappearing into an icy lake. The helicopter manages to pull both victims out of the water and drag them to safety. In reality, however, the rescuers lost grip of one of the victims, who plunged to an icy death. While I was in Des Moines for the filming, Justin Charles Cupples, thirteen years old, was struck repeatedly in the chest by an older boy on a school playground in Newton, Iowa, thirty miles east of Des Moines. The blows were severe enough to dislodge a plastic heart valve that Justin had received weeks earlier to correct a birth defect. He collapsed onto the ground. Blood poured into his lungs. As Justin was being loaded aboard the Life Flight helicopter, he looked at his father and said, "Please don't let me die." During the helicopter ride to Des Moines, however, his heart stopped altogether.[1]

In *Life Flight*, the helicopter offers hope, a kind of redemption. But the real redemption Thompson wants to depict in his films is deeper and, to him, infinitely more important. All his movies during the past fifteen years have mixed action, suspense, and drama with a very unsubtle evangelical message. At a crisis point in the plot, the main characters kneel and give their lives to Christ. In *Blood on the Mountain*, an escaped convict learns God's forgiveness and asks to be saved from his sins. In *All the King's Horses* (whose stars Grant Goodeve and Dee Wallace went on to play, respectively, the eldest brother in the television serial *Eight is Enough* and the

mother in *E.T.*), the answer to a troubled marriage is conversion to
Christianity.

The evangelical message in *Life Flight*, Thompson insists, is a bit
more subtle—no longer the Scripture verses emblazoned on the
screen, but rather a tear signifying repentance in place of the full-
fledged conversion scene. It is a movie about God's will, a favorite
topic for Thompson, but one he hasn't tackled before because it is
so difficult to portray on screen. Discerning God's will, he believes,
is central to the Christian life. "I really want to be where God wants
me to be," he says. "It doesn't make your troubles go away, it's just
that God is in control of your life. He takes care of you."

Thompson's formula for happiness and success boils down to
"choosing God first, and the rest of it will fall into line." The choice
of this crash scene provides a good example. After a month of searching for the right location, he said, "I got lost one day going home,
and I came across this bridge and I thought, 'Holy smokes, it's
perfect!' I went home and told my wife, 'God designed that river
for this movie.' "

Don Thompson, a small, unprepossessing man who often wears
cowboy boots and western-style shirts, fairly brims with such illustrations of God's providence, and he enjoys nothing more than telling how God delivered him from difficult situations, how God made
the impossible possible. I have known Thompson since the early
seventies (he still delights in introducing me as one of his Sunday
school students), and I never cease to marvel at his indomitable
spirit, his boundless energy, and his boyish grin as he weaves together story after story about how God taught him this lesson or
another through difficult circumstances and insurmountable odds.
Each episode has its own moral, which Thompson invariably supplies in the form of a tidy aphorism, but there is nothing tiresome
or disingenuous about all this. Thompson is, quite simply, one of
the most remarkable people I have ever known, a man utterly without guile or pretension who sweeps you along with his irrepressible
optimism. He very nearly embodies, I think (though he would be
the first to deny it), the qualities most evangelical preachers have
in mind when they talk about a "godly Christian"—someone with

a conviction that seldom admits of doubt, who professes an intimacy with God, and who is always willing, even eager, to share his faith.

Thompson's vocation as a filmmaker supplies grist for his anecdotal mill; it also provides ample opportunity for Thompson's God to work His "magic." But Thompson recognizes that such serendipitous deliverances are no substitute for hard work, and he is eager to dispel the notion that he regards the Almighty as some sort of superhero who routinely rescues him from his own blunders or lack of preparation. Thompson approaches his craft, he says, with the attitude that "I have to work as if it all depends on Don, but pray as if it all depends on God. I don't want anybody to get the idea that God does this and God does that. I work my tail off," he said emphatically. Then his eyes brightened: "But God comes through when I need Him."

This attitude allows Thompson to face adversity with equanimity, with the confidence that "God has something better in store," perhaps a spiritual lesson of some kind. When I phoned him to make the final preparations for my visit, he recited a litany of difficulties that had plagued his shooting schedule: two weeks of steady rain (unusual for this time of year), the unavailability of the helicopter at critical junctures of the filming, even the decision of Iowa Methodist Hospital's board to press ahead with a long-delayed construction project. "But God has been good," he added after a sigh. "The Lord has really made His presence known to me these past weeks."

When I caught up with him on location, he repeated the same refrain. As we sat on the side of the highway late at night waiting for the crew to prepare for the next scene, he said, "It's been raining for three weeks, and we've been shooting for three weeks, but, praise God, we're still on schedule. I don't know how He does it. I'm to the point now where I don't even worry about the big problems," he continued, "I just leave them in the Lord's hands. I know He knows what He's doing. I've gone home nearly every night after filming and just cried because of all the problems, but the Lord keeps reminding me to leave it in His hands.

"When the people at Iowa Methodist Hospital told me that the board of directors had decided to go ahead with the demolition of one of the facades we were using for the movie, even though they'd been five days late getting me the helicopter they'd promised, I just shrugged my shoulders and said, 'Lord, you've got to get me through this.' Here it was pouring outside, and I had a day's worth of shooting to do in just a few hours before they began tearing the place down the next morning. But I walked outside and, suddenly, the weather cleared. We got everybody outside and shot all the scenes we needed." He smiled. "God is good."

Thompson's "divine connections" have apparently attracted notice in film circles. Occasionally, he said, people on the set will remark, " 'This is a Don Thompson picture; things always work out well.' " When I asked if he had that reputation in Hollywood, he lowered his voice, "Yeah, that's what I hear," obviously embarrassed, but also not a little pleased.

"One night we were in Gunnison, Colorado, filming a television special. I'd wanted snow and peaks and sunshine, and the locals told me, 'You won't get any sunshine up there in February. The snow will get about eighty inches deep up there. The cabin you want to use will be buried.' I told them to bring tractors in and keep it plowed out if they had to, but I wanted it to look virgin. And I was working with people from Hollywood who told me, 'You're crazy to come up here and shoot. This is the coldest place in the country. You've got scenes where this woman is supposed to be singing, but her lips will freeze.' I said, 'Well, I really believe this is where God wants me to do it.' And I don't know why, because usually when twenty or thirty people tell me I'm wrong I think, well, maybe I *am* wrong.

"It was a big company, a union shoot. We had twenty-two pieces of equipment, tractor-trailers, lining the road. And it was so cold that cables started to split. Peoples' leather script covers were splitting. It was so cold the generators wouldn't run. And I remember standing out there and these three guys, the union manager, the production manager, and the assistant director, walked towards me. All I could think of was Dodge City and *Gunsmoke*, and I thought, 'I'm dead.' One of them said, 'Do you know you just lost your client thirty thousand bucks because you picked this location?' I said,

'Well, the sun's out.' And then I said, 'I'm sorry, guys. I just feel we're supposed to be here.'

"Do you know what happened? The sun came out for four days in a row. The radio stations and newspapers said that had never happened in the history of that community. Never had there been sunshine all day long that time of year. One night we heard that a big blizzard would hit us the next day. I began to panic. But then one of the crew members—who wasn't a Christian, by the way, one of the most worldly women you'd ever want to meet—said, 'It won't come in. Not with this company. This is the company that moves clouds. I've seen it happen.' "

I may have seen it happen, too. During the early evening preparations for the crash scene Friday night, one of the sheriff's officers who had been assigned to block off the road and divert traffic announced over his loudspeaker that the Weather Service had just issued a thunderstorm watch until eleven o'clock that evening. Off in the distance to the west an ominous thunderhead, belching flashes of lightning, moved in our direction. Thompson and the rest of the crew seemed unperturbed, or at least preoccupied with other matters. When the car dropped into the ravine, the cloud had passed to the north, safely out of danger. It *really did*, I convinced myself at the time, appear to have changed course and veer north.

At the time, amidst the elation over the successful stunt, no one had deemed the weather worthy of comment. The next evening, however, when I arrived at the location, Thompson immediately pulled me aside. "I've got to tell you what happened," he said. "When we finished shooting last night at three-thirty (which was a miracle in itself), we got in our cars, everybody lined up and ready to go, and it started raining. Huge drops. It came down in torrents— well, not torrents, but it was raining hard. I was so grateful that we had finished. I just said, 'Praise God.' I was so excited I cried all the way home." He paused, then giggled, recognizing the irony. "Maybe it wasn't raining as hard as I thought. Maybe it was just me."

If God monitors the weather, God also receives credit for Thompson's success, both as a director and as a screenwriter. When he thought he had completed the script for *Life Flight*, he reread it and panicked. There was too much talk and not enough action, he concluded. Some of the transitions were still rough. "With two weeks until we started shooting, I knew I had six or seven weeks worth of work to do on the screenplay. I went home and got to work, and at one point I fell into bed and said, 'Lord, I got a problem I can't solve. There are major structural difficulties here.' God gave me the answer the next morning. I mean He just gave it to me on a silver platter."

Thompson described the scene. "Inside a house a mother and father are asleep, and all of a sudden you hear something crashing. The mother says, 'There's somebody in the house.' So the father gets up, goes to the closet and takes down a shoe box. Inside the shoe box there's a thirty-eight revolver and two cartridges. He takes the cartridges and puts two of them in the gun. He walks out into the hallway into the dark, and all of a sudden he sees this shadow— it looks like one of those guys out of the thirties, with a cape—and the shadow turns and a little girl says, 'Daddy, I have to go to the bathroom.'

"Then we leave the shot. When we come back the little girl is playing house. This is incredible! This is good cinema! She's got her high heels on, her dresses, her beads, and she goes into the closet to get Mommy's purse. She takes a stick and pulls the purse out and the shoe box with the gun falls onto the floor. She puts the hammer back and looks into the barrel and is playing with it. It's very scary. We show the shoe box empty. She's playing with it. She even points it directly into the camera, and you see her rotate the barrel and pull the trigger. The suspense builds because you know there are two loaded cartridges in there somewhere and you never know when it's going to go off. It could go off at any time.

"She says, 'Mom, come see what I found.' And just before her mom comes in she throws down the gun, picks up the doll, and says, 'Would you find my dolly's head?' So the mother thinks she's playing with the doll; the gun's buried in the toy box. Later on— it's nighttime now, the little girl is sleeping—she gets up, yawns, and starts playing with the doll. She sees the gun, puts down the doll, and starts doing the same thing again, pulling the trigger, rotating the barrel. The same routine. Finally she says, 'Mom, I want a drink of water.' "

At that point Thompson's cadence, though never deliberate, quickened to convey the drama along with the camera angles. "Then you see the mother coming down the hallway. Dutch tilt. Feet. Face. Dutch tilt. Feet. 'Click.' Feet. 'Click.' Feet. Face. 'Click.' All of a sudden the mother opens the door and blam! The gun goes off and hits her right in the chest.

"That sets up the rescue by the helicopter. And it leads into a critical transition in the story." He paused, nearly breathless with enthusiasm. "God gave me that. I didn't work that out. It just came. It's like I had to work everything else out really hard, but when it came down to where I was out of time, God said, 'I know you're out of time. Here.' "

When I suggested at one point in our conversations that making Christian films allowed Thompson to combine his two passions in life, his faith and motion pictures, he smiled. Then, after a pause, he wondered if faith wasn't more a gift than a passion.

Even so, he is clearly passionate about his convictions, and he finds it impossible to separate his faith from his filmmaking. "When I'm invited to universities to lecture about motion pictures, I tell them I'll come only if I can speak about my beliefs in addition to my films. You know what these film students ask me when I'm done? No one ever asks me about movies. One day I took a guy who worked on *Star Wars* because he was working with me on a film. But the students don't ask me about movies afterwards. They ask about the Lord."

Apart from his personality, Thompson also strikes me as exemplary in his literalistic approach to the Bible and, specifically, the seriousness with which he takes the various biblical prophecies concerning the end of time. He illustrates, moreover, the extent to which dispensational premillennialism, with its insistence on the imminent return of Christ, pervades the evangelical subculture in America and lends a sense of urgency to evangelical proselytization efforts. Thompson's most successful films—and perhaps the most controversial—depict the apocalyptic prophecies in the Bible, especially the books of Daniel and Revelation. "Those prophecy films were kind of hard," Thompson acknowledged at one point in our conversations, but he remains unapologetic.

A Thief in the Night, his first apocalyptic movie, filmed in 1972, takes the form of a dream. It opens with the sound of a clock ticking against a black background. As a shot of the clock on a nightstand comes slowly into focus, a message appears on the screen:

> Keep a sharp lookout! For you do not know when I will come, at evening, at midnight, early dawn or late daybreak. Don't let me find you sleeping!
>
> JESUS CHRIST

A voice over the radio interrupts with a special bulletin. "To say that the world is in a state of shock this morning would be to understate the situation." The camera pans slowly from the clock on the nightstand to a woman obviously just awakening from a nightmare. The voice continues: "Suddenly and without warning literally thousands, perhaps millions of people just disappeared. The few eyewitness accounts of these disappearances have not been clear, but one thing is certainly sure: Millions who were living on this earth last night are not here this morning."

The woman climbs out of bed and searches for her husband. "Jim? Jim?" Down the hallway and into the bathroom. There she sees an electric razor, still buzzing, in the sink. She screams, realizing that her husband has just disappeared.

In the next scene a young preacher exhorts a small group of listeners: "The world will be at ease, banquets and parties and weddings, just as it was in Noah's time before the sudden coming of the flood. People wouldn't believe what was going to happen until the flood actually arrived and took them all away. So shall my coming be. Two men will be working together in the fields. One will be taken, the other left. Two women will be going about their household tasks. One will be taken, and the other left. So be prepared, for you know not what day your Lord is coming.

"What does all this mean? It means exactly what it says. Any minute, any second, could be the last chance that anyone has to give himself to Jesus, because when He returns it will happen that fast—the Bible says in the twinkling of an eye. Millions of people will suddenly disappear, leave this earth to meet their Lord. And a shocked world will discover suddenly that what the Bible said is true. This is no joke. This is not a fairy tale. It will happen, just as surely as you and I are here right now.

"So, Christian, be alert. And, friend, if you haven't given your life to Christ, do it, and do it now, because the rapture will come and Christ will return. It says in the Bible that He will come as a thief in the night."

The preacher then joins several other sober-looking young people in a mournful, haunting melody:

> Life was filled with guns and war,
> and everyone got trampled on the floor.
> I wish we'd all been ready.
>
> Children died, the days grew cold,
> a piece of bread could buy a bag of gold.
> I wish we'd all been ready.
>
> There's no time to change your mind,
> the Son has come and you've been left behind.

The black background, the insistent chords of a synthesizer, and the deliberate beating of a drum render the words into a kind of requiem.

> A man and wife asleep in bed,
> she hears a noise and turns her head, he's gone.
> I wish we'd all been ready.
>
> Two men walking up a hill,
> one disappears and one's left standing still.
> I wish we'd all been ready.
>
> There's no time to change your mind,
> the Son has come and you've been left behind.[2]

The music dies and the scene fades to black.

The plot itself begins on the midway of a state fair, and it follows the lives of several young people in their early twenties who meet for the first time at the fair. One man, a rather devilish-looking sort who often lapses into Humphrey Bogart impersonations, immediately gravitates to a tall, blonde woman in a miniskirt. Another couple, Jim and Patty, the woman who awakens from the nightmare at the opening, eventually fall in love and marry midway through the movie. A third woman, the odd person out, wanders into an evangelistic tent and is born again, accepting Christ as her savior.

Although all the characters figure into the plot, Jim and Patty are the focal points. After a brush with death following a bite from an Indian cobra, Jim (a veterinary student) also is born again. But Patty resists. "I'm a Christian," she says early in the movie. "I go to church almost every week." Just any church, it turns out, isn't good enough. Her minister, the Reverend Turner, a theological liberal who refuses to interpret the Bible literally, debunks the Genesis creation account as a myth and, more important, refuses to believe the apocalyptic prophecies in the books of Daniel and Revelation.

If the Reverend Turner (played by Russell Doughten, the movie's executive producer and Thompson's partner) represents an evil, corrupting force, several characters point out the path of righteousness. There are repeated exhortations to "take Christ into your life" lest you be left behind when Jesus comes back to earth to remove the true Christians in the rapture, predicted in the fourth chapter of First Thessalonians. "We're living in the end times," a preacher warns.

The inevitable occurs. Suddenly on a summer afternoon, people find that their friends, the true Christians, have disappeared, including Jim. To deal with the crisis an organization called UNITE, the United Nations Imperium of Total Emergency, takes command. This sinister one-world government soon demands that all citizens take the "mark of the beast" described in Revelation. The wizened Reverend Turner, left behind at the rapture because of his unbelief, now recognizes the literal truth of the Bible. Disconsolate, he asks, "How many have I misled? How many are still here because of me?" On the basis of his new appreciation for Revelation, he counsels

Patty to resist the mark of the beast (a computerized rendition of the digits 666) because it is evil, and accepting it precludes any possibility of a "second chance" at salvation later in the apocalypse.

Patty, now a fugitive from UNITE, cannot purchase food without the computerized mark of the beast. Her friends betray her. She manages to elude a helicopter that searches for her in the woods; tired and frantic, she runs down a shimmering road. Then the music:

> Life was filled with guns and war,
> and everyone got trampled on the floor.
> I wish we'd all been ready.

A voice reverberates: "There will be no place to hide. There will be no place to get away anywhere." Surrounded by UNITE agents atop a large dam, Patty is forced onto a landing just above the cascading water. While trying to elude her captors, she slips . . . and then wakes up from her nightmare.

But the film's opening scene repeats itself. She looks for Jim, her husband, while the radio reports the strange disappearance of millions of people. When she finds the shaver buzzing in the bathroom sink, just as the music repeats "The Son has come and you've been left behind," Patty lets out a scream. A Bible verse appears on the screen: "But of that day and that hour knoweth no man, no not the angels which are in heaven, neither the Son, but the Father. Take heed, watch and pray for ye know not when the time is . . ."[3]

This is good, effective drama. Even chilling. You needn't sympathize with the message to be moved by the story, and many viewers identify readily with Patty, a "good person" whose goodness, nevertheless, according to the film's producers, will still leave her shy of heaven.

If the plot is a bit obvious in places, it's also quite compelling, especially when shown in an evangelical setting to people reared to take the apocalyptic passages of the Bible literally. Since its release in 1973, *A Thief in the Night* has been translated into three foreign languages, subtitled in countless others, and its international distribution continues strongly a decade and a half later. Six or seven hundred prints now circulate, in addition to videocassettes. In the

United States, where distribution is limited to church groups, camps, youth organizations, and the like, it is difficult to quantify the number of people who have seen the film. When I pressed Russell Doughten, Thompson's partner, for a figure, he reluctantly estimated that one hundred million people had seen *A Thief in the Night* in the United States, a figure, he hastened to add, that would include those who had seen it more than once. Even if you slash that number in half to account for hyperbole, fifty million is still a staggering figure, a viewership that would be the envy of many Hollywood producers.

For Doughten—and for Thompson—the more important statistic is the number of those who were converted as a result of viewing *A Thief in the Night*. Doughten estimated this figure in excess of four million, "a tremendous harvest of souls," especially for a movie that cost about $68,000 to produce (by the middle of 1984 the film had brought in $4.2 million in revenues). The film works best, they believe, when followed by an "altar call" or invitation to conversion. Typically, when the movie is over, a pastor, youth leader, or camp director will ask the audience to bow their heads in prayer. An organ might play softly in the background. The pastor will then ask people to examine their lives and ask themselves if they are ready for Christ's second coming. Have they invited Jesus into their hearts? "If Jesus should return tonight, or if you were killed on the way home this evening, would you be ready to meet God?" The movie's chilling ending, of course, sets this up nicely—Patty's abandonment, her growing horror as she realizes she's been left behind.

The success of any movie invites sequels, and Thompson has obliged. *A Distant Thunder*, *Image of the Beast*, and *Prodigal Planet* all depict life on earth after the rapture, after true Christians, the born-again believers, have ascended into heaven. The producers tout these films as a kind of pre-history—"a true story that is yet to happen"—portraying the brutality of existence during the tribulation prophesied in Revelation. Indeed, much of this is gruesome, replete with radiation sickness, blood-curdling screams, increased repression by UNITE, and stainless-steel guillotines. The events of the book of Revelation "could become a reality in your lifetime," the films warn. "Avoid these events by coming to Christ now."

Doesn't all this have the effect of frightening people into the kingdom of heaven? In the midst of her miseries in *A Distant Thunder*, Patty answers for the producers: "I would rather have been scared into heaven than have to go through this." I put the question to Doughten who, in contrast to Thompson, is soft-spoken and deliberate. His initial response was that "if they get into the kingdom through being scared, that's better than not making it at all." He continued: "Anybody who seriously reads the prophetic books or Revelation or Thessalonians or even Matthew 24 will be scared. There's some pretty heavy stuff in those prophecies. This is not for kindergarten. It's for those who are into the meat of the gospel. If you take seriously what's being said there, it's frightening. And it ought to be. All we've tried to do in the films is to put these things revealed in the Scripture into a dramatic setting. We're just trying to illustrate what's there. If it frightens you, then maybe it's your problem, because from our point of view that's what the Lord is telling you. If we can convince you that the tribulation period is going to be filled with strong confrontation between God and the forces of evil, and this is going to affect mankind to the point that one-third of the population will be destroyed as the various vials predicted in Revelation are poured out, well, that's pretty frightening."

So the apocalyptic writings in the Bible have no value apart from a literal, dispensationalist reading—as comfort to the distressed and persecuted early Christians, perhaps, an assurance that God will avenge their sufferings? "When I was a young Christian," Doughten said, "I was frightened of the prophecies in Scripture. They seemed so remote to me. I could only look on them as figurative. I didn't have the inner strength to consider that these things were absolutely true. But after I'd been a Christian three or four years, I began to get drawn into those things, and I began to look into the prophetic writings and decided that if the Lord is really sincere about these things, then what's coming is absolutely staggering. It goes beyond human comprehension. And in working on the scripts for the prophecy films, I had to study these prophecies deeply and let them seep into my soul and psyche, so when it came out, it would be true and honest. We had the sense that we were dealing seriously with the

Scriptures. People generally have one of two reactions to the prophecy films. Either people are scared to death and tell themselves it
isn't real, or they say, 'Forget it, nothing like that could ever be.'
But the Bible is true, and this is what the Bible says. We put a story
around it in order to reveal these things to modern audiences, but
the prophecy is true."

If Doughten, whose Hollywood credits include *The Blob*, provided the interpretive background for these apocalyptic films, it was
Thompson's restless, frenetic energy that translated the ideas or
messages into good, dramatic cinema, and herein lies his singular
contribution to Christian filmmaking. For decades, evangelicals
have shown movies at Bible camps or in Sunday evening services,
and many, like Thompson's, warned of the impending apocalypse
and implored viewers to repent. But almost invariably these were
poorly produced, low-budget films exhibiting acting skills that bor-
dered on the scandalous. One of them, *Missing Christians*, actually
depicted Christians levitating by way of harnesses up into something
that was supposed to be a cloud, or heaven, during the rapture.
When Thompson turned his cinematic skills to the subject, he produced a film that, despite its low budget and some infelicities in
acting, combined drama, action, and suspense into a convincing
portrayal of the "end times." It is only a slight exaggeration to say
that *A Thief in the Night* affected the evangelical film industry the
way that sound or color affected Hollywood.

Thompson's work also belies the persistent myth that evangelicals
are somehow anti-modern and suspicious of technology or innovation. The two issues must, I think, be separated. Yes, evangelicals
are anti-modern, but only in the sense that the term *modernity* is
invested with moral overtones. When modernity is defined as a
flight from "traditional" values—as politically conservative evangelicals want to define it—then there surely are anti-modernist elements within the evangelical subculture. But that does not mean
that evangelicals are chary about technology or innovation in general. Indeed, especially in the realm of communication, evangelicals
historically have been pioneers in the use of media. In the eighteenth century, George Whitefield triggered the Great Awakening
with his itinerant preaching, his oratorical skills, and his persuasive

rhetoric, techniques that patriots used to rally support for the American Revolution several decades later. During the Second Great Awakening early in the nineteenth century, Charles Grandison Finney employed "new measures," including the use of newspapers, to publicize his revivals. The benevolent societies of the nineteenth century and the highly organized Methodist circuit riders who evangelized the frontier prefigured the grass-roots organizations of political parties. In the twentieth century, Charles E. Fuller and other evangelists used the radio to communicate the gospel long before Franklin Roosevelt discovered its utility as a political device.

None of this suggests a fear of technology or innovation, although it is certainly true that evangelicals were slow in catching on to the evangelistic possibilities of motion pictures, due at least in part to lingering doubts about Hollywood morality and its "communist" sympathies. Thompson may not have eradicated those suspicions, but his films provide an illustration of evangelicals' willingness to use new media for evangelistic ends.

Thompson's work, in fact, has attracted praise from both the Christian and the secular film industry. Harry Bristow, a film distributor in Ambler, Pennsylvania, and president of the Christian Film Distributors Association, told me that Thompson, whom he called "the finest director in the industry," singlehandedly "revolutionized the Christian film business." Others have tried to emulate Thompson, Bristow said, but he still has no peer: "Nobody else in the Christian field can match up with him."[4] Jack Thompson, a movie producer in California who has worked with Don Thompson (no relation) on several films, considers him "a good filmmaker" who would "stack up very favorably" with the directors working out of Hollywood. "I think the world of him," Jack Thompson added, an assessment shared universally by those on the crew of *Life Flight*. "There's no better guy to work for," according to James Berry, director of photography and Hollywood veteran, "not in this business."[5]

Although not diffident about discussing his accomplishments, Thompson readily credits God with his professional success. Since *A Thief in the Night* came out in 1973, Thompson's films have won seventeen "Christian Oscars" from the Christian Film Distributors Association, which also named Thompson "Director of the Decade" for the 1970s. One of his more recent successes, a motivational film called *The Miracle Man*, released in 1986, won the International Silver Screen Award, Thompson's second. James Manilla of New York University's film department called it "just about the best scripted, best acted, best produced motivational program that I'd ever seen."[6] When Thompson learned that *Miracle Man* won the *New York Times* Film Critics' Award, he said he wasn't surprised in the least. "I knew God was in that project, and if God is in something, it's going to be successful."

With all this praise, why doesn't Thompson head to California and ply his skills there? "Ever since I was nine I've wanted to do a theatrical movie," he confessed, but when the offers came recently, he turned them down. In 1984, after a partnership of twelve years that had produced twelve pictures, Thompson and Russ Doughten agreed to go their separate ways. Doughten remained with Mark IV Pictures, while Thompson sought other work. He remembers those months between jobs as a time of personal crisis, a testing of his faith.

While unemployed, Thompson received an offer to make family films in Hollywood, an offer that included a six-figure income and a percentage of the company. "I'd have a home in Oregon and work in California," Thompson said. "Everything the flesh could want." Still, he hesitated. Why, his wife asked one day, wasn't he taking the job? "It seems like everything I would want," he replied, "and I don't know why we're not taking it, but I don't think the Holy Spirit is in it."

After signing on with American Media in Des Moines as a kind of freelance producer-director, Thompson received another offer to direct a theatrical film. As negotiations with the producer in California grew more serious, however, Thompson began to have reservations. "I looked at the script one day and said, 'I can't do this.' But negotiations were well under way—they were talking deals and money and contracts and shooting schedules—and I felt myself getting sucked into this movie that had sex in it, and it was a bad script. I finally went to my boss and said, 'Art, I'm sorry. If you have to fire me, you have to fire me, but I just can't do this movie.' I was scared, but I decided that I'm going to stand up for my principles and let God take care of me."

Arthur Bauer, president of American Media and Thompson's boss, understood and respected Thompson's position. "So I had to call the producer—a man whose credits include *Rocky, Cabaret, The Right Stuff*, and a lot of other successful films—and let him know. I said, 'In all honesty, your script is a piece of junk.' He said, 'Who the hell are you to tell me that? I've been in this business for thirty years, and I've made literally millions of dollars on motion pictures. And you're telling me my script is no good?' And I said, 'Yes, sir, with all due respect to your talent and creativity, your script is lousy.' Well, we fought over the phone for weeks, then I took the initiative with another writer in Dallas to rewrite the script. We spent two weeks on it. I sent it to the producer, and he got even madder. He said, 'That's not even the same story.' I said, 'No, sir, but in my opinion it's a darn sight better than what you had. It's hard enough for me to do a movie I'm in love with, let alone do it just for dollars.' He called me back about a month later. He was very nice. He said, 'Don, it hit me kind of hard when some kid from Des Moines, Iowa, was telling me what's good and what's bad, but that treatment you wrote is good, it's very good. Would you direct it if we did that one?' "

Thompson promised he would think about it, would pray about it. "I said, 'Lord, all I want to do is what You want me to do. If You want me to make church movies for the rest of my life, then praise God, hallelujah, I'll make church films. I just want to do what You want me to do. I don't want to make theatricals if You don't want me to.' The time came when I had to make a decision, so I got down on my knees. In the end, it wasn't difficult. All I had to do was choose God first, and the rest would fall into line. I told them, No, I wouldn't do it."

Thompson paused. "The funny thing is that I just love those Panavision cameras. They're the elite, the best in the world. But they're hard to get. You just can't get them for a film like *Life Flight*. So God said, 'You want a Panavision camera? I'll get you one.' We got a Panavision camera for this film. It was a miracle, but it was

God saying that I did the right thing in turning down that Hollywood movie."

How does God communicate? Only once in our conversations did Thompson catch himself using the phrase "God told me" or some variant. While recounting his decision to leave Mark IV Pictures, he said, "The Lord said to me—I hate it when people say that." He then continued with the phrase, "The Lord led me to believe. . . ." But Thompson clearly has a sense of divine guidance, a confidence that brooks no doubts or second thoughts.

Back in the mid-1970s, Thompson had visited a radio station in Des Moines for an interview. As he left, he became convinced that God was telling him to go back into radio. Thompson, who had spent many years as a disk jockey at KRNT in Des Moines, in what he called "big-time radio," resisted. "The Lord just kinda tapped me on the shoulder and said, 'I want you to do a Christian radio show.' And I remember saying out loud there in my car, 'Lord, no, I don't want to go back to radio.' But when the Holy Spirit talks to you, He never repeats Himself. He says it once, and you can choose to obey or not to obey, and I knew I'd be back on radio.

"I just kept driving. When I got back to my office that very morning I walked past the receptionist and told her, 'I'm going back into radio.' She said, 'Really? Where? When?' I said, 'I don't know.' I told the Lord, 'I'm not going to make one move to get back on radio. If You want me on, You'll have to do it.' Thirty minutes after I got back the manager from KWKY was in my office. As I had walked in the door, my assistant had been talking to him, and he told her he was looking for people who had been in radio to work for the station, a Christian station.

"As he sat in my office I told him I'd do it on one condition: 'I'm not going to take any orders from anybody. I know how to do this. At KRNT I had to take a lot of crap from a lot of people who didn't know what they were doing. If I go out to your station, I'm my own man, I do my own thing, and I'll pick the time.' He said, 'When do you want to go on?' I said, 'Ten to noon on Saturday.' He said, 'There are shows in that block that have been on for thirty years.

What am I going to do?' He came back the next day and said, 'I cancelled all those shows.'

"So I went out there and thought, 'This is dumb. Who's going to hear me in this stupid little station?'" But then I thought, 'This is where God wants you. Just do your best.' Pretty soon this little show became something of a classic; it's been on for eight years. I travel all around the state to speak and people come up and say, 'I listen to your show every Saturday.' "

Thompson's weekly radio show features music of the 1950s. He sees this program, like his films, as evangelistic. "People will listen to that radio show who aren't Christians, who couldn't care less about Christianity." Thompson intersperses the music with anecdotes, lighthearted shenanigans, and sound effects, and he concludes the program with a story or two about God's goodness, His provision in difficult situations, a feature of the program that listeners have come to call "Don's Storybook."

The program has become so popular that even when Thompson is off on location or traveling somewhere, the station runs tapes of previous broadcasts. One morning during the filming of *The Shepherd*, a movie about a military aviator, Thompson had reached the end of his rope with all the difficulties he had encountered with the weather and various technical problems. "I was driving to the set, and I started crying and said, 'God, I can't do this anymore. I just can't. I just don't know where to go.' It was eleven forty-five, and I thought I'd switch on the car radio and listen to some music and feel better. My show was on, and my 'Storybook' was on. And what I said was just what I needed to hear. I started laughing, because God really has a great sense of humor. I said, 'God, only You would use *me* to tell *me* it's going to be all right!' "

What's ahead for Thompson? "I don't know if God wants me to make theatrical features. There are people right now raising money for pictures they want me to direct. Big things are starting to happen for me, and they frighten me, they terrify me, because I can't live in the world of those people." He paused. Thompson, pensive now, sat cross-legged in the grass along the side of the road as the crew prepared for the next scene. "Someone asked me not long ago what my ultimate goal was. I hadn't thought about it before, but I knew immediately." He plucked a blade of grass and held it in his teeth. "My goal is when I get to heaven to have God walk up to me and say, 'You did a good job.' I want to be able to face Him and say, 'I did my best.' "

NOTES

1. Nick Lamberto, "Frail Heart Torn by Blow, Boy Needs Transplant," *Des Moines Register*, 26 September 1986, p. A1; idem, "Boy's Final Plea: 'Please Don't Let Me Die,' " ibid., 27 September 1986, p. A1.

2. "I Wish We'd All Been Ready," words and music by Larry Norman, © 1969, 1971 Beechwood Music Corp. and J. C. Love Publishing Co. All rights administered by Beechwood Music Corp. Used by permission.

3. Mark 13:32 (KJV). The final message on the screen reads: "The End . . . is near!"

4. Harry Bristow, 24 June 1983, in International Cinema Artists Corporation booklet; idem, telephone conversation.

5. Jack Thompson, telephone conversation, 12 January 1987; James L. Berry, interview, 12 September 1986.

6. James Manilla, "Making Miracles in the Heartland," *Industrial Photography* (April 1986): 20, 53.

4

Phoenix Prophet

IT IS CURTIS FRISBY'S JOB to "warm up" the audience for his father, much the same way that Ed McMahon does for Johnny Carson or Ira Sankey did for evangelist Dwight L. Moody in the nineteenth century. Curt, a dark-haired man in his mid-twenties, struts onto the stage in shiny black trousers and a sportcoat with sleeves hiked up to his elbows. He grabs the microphone with a kind of practiced insouciance and exhorts the audience to "give God a clap offering." The congregation obeys. He then asks, "How many love the Lord with all your heart?" More applause. With the backup of an electric guitar, drums, several singers, and an electronic organ played in a way that suggests a skating rink rather than a cathedral, he croons several songs, all the while imploring the congregation to join in by singing and clapping in rhythm. Several in the audience have brought tambourines. "Let's give God a clap offering," he says again. Then: "Gimme a J-E-S-U-S!" The audience responds at the appropriate junctures. "Ya' know," he says, "the more you praise God, the more happier you get." Another chant: "I'm saved." A lusty echo from the crowd, then: "By the blood of Jesus Christ."[1]

A large, amiable man in his late thirties, identified simply as

Brother Max, steps to the microphone to announce the offering. There is no prolonged appeal, just a comment that a building like theirs isn't inexpensive. Indeed not. The Capstone Cathedral in Phoenix, Arizona, was built in 1971 at a cost well in excess of $1 million. Rising from the desert floor, the four walls of this square, concrete building slope upward at a gentle angle, and at the apex sits a steel-ribbed pyramid, forty feet square at its base and rising to a point thirty-one feet higher. The eighteen-ton pyramid is sheathed in a pattern of blue-green and red glass, and, from a distance, the effect is that of a large, gaudy jewel sitting atop some otherworldly launching pad.[2] To enter this Capstone Cathedral, you approach the building across a small berm that surrounds the structure and then step down into one of several entrances, small gashes in the foundation of the pyramid. Once inside, a huge space opens before you, unimpeded by structural supports. The floor slopes down toward the southwest corner where it meets the semicircular fronting of the stage, snuggled like a slice of pie into the corner. The sense of scale here is overwhelming. Row upon row of theater seats—enough for two thousand people—fan out from the stage and up to the far reaches of the building.

Except for the podium, which sits beneath a bank of television lights, the platform itself is ordinary enough, cluttered in the back with amplifiers, drums, a piano, and the electronic organ. As the wooden pulpit, fixed at center stage, rises from the floor it becomes slightly broader at the top. A large, deep chevron is etched in the facing, beginning at the top two corners and extending almost to the floor. Toward the bottom of the chevron sits a white star within a circle. Inside of the two triangles formed by the upper parts of the chevron are red and blue stripes, overlaid by two bolts of lightning that begin near the top two corners and angle toward the star. Knowing that people at the Capstone Cathedral place a great deal of stock in symbolism, I asked one woman what this meant. "Wings of power," she replied matter-of-factly, in a tone that suggested any fool would know that. "It means the Lord's wings of power."

Back on stage, with the congregation now suitably prepared, arms flailing and clapping, Brother Max says, "And now, the watchman on our walls . . . Evangelist Neal Frisby!" From behind a curtain at the back of the platform a small, stocky man, wearing a spearmint-green sportcoat and a loosely knotted tie, rushes to the pulpit, waving a Bible to acknowledge his welcome.

"The Lord bless your hearts tonight," he begins. He then speaks about "the great things God is doing" in the crusade, this series of nightly revival meetings during the winter of 1987. Frisby launches into his sermon, which he delivers in clipped sentences and an uneven cadence. Much of it sounds like a stream of consciousness. He frequently concludes sentences—or fragments—with the phrase, "and so forth like that," as he hurries on to his next thought. In order to elicit a response from the congregation, he'll ask, "Amen?" or "How many of ya' believe that?" A sprinkling of applause or shouted affirmations follow each question. When Frisby wants to emphasize a thought, he tacks the inflection "ah" onto the end of his phrases: "There is coming a time-ah, when the glory of the Lord-ah, will appear to the faithful-ah." There is very little sustained argumentation here, just a random jumping from one thought to the next.

But the congregation of about one hundred people doesn't seem to mind. Tonight, Thursday evening, is Miracle Deliverance Night at the crusade, so Frisby's meditation centers around the spiritual power of healing, a phenomenon that accounts for much of his renown. At the conclusion of the sermon he instructs those who seek healing or those who can attest to such healing to gather in two lines, one at either end of the stage. On his left are those who want some kind of healing—tumors, back troubles, stomach troubles, eye problems, respiratory problems, drug or alcohol dependency. "We'll get the drugs out and make the alcohol run," he promises. "There is nothing too big or too large for the Lord." On his right, are those who will come and testify about such healing, physical or spiritual, in the past. Queues of about twenty-five people gather at the steps on either side of the platform.

Frisby begins with the testimony line. A young black woman (perhaps one-third of Frisby's congregation, many of whom travel weekly from Los Angeles, is black), breathless and nearly incoherent with enthusiasm, says that she "became real" through Brother Frisby's ministry, "and that's where it's at," she continues. "God wants you to be real for Him." While she was pregnant several years ago, she said, "a force tripped me," and her son, now seven years old, was born mentally retarded. But now, praise God, through Brother Frisby's ministry, the boy is healed. "He's a genius. He's only seven years old, but he can read on a twelve-year-old level." This woman flies in from California every week, she says, "because this church is real."

Frisby then turns to the healing line. A young boy, perhaps eight years old, walks to the evangelist. (During this part of the service Frisby turned around in the pulpit, with his back to the audience, and the people who came up to face him were hidden behind Frisby and the large lectern.) "I can't breathe too good," the boy says. Frisby places his hand on the boy's forehead and asks Jesus to heal him. At the conclusion of the brief prayer, Frisby says, "Now take a deep breath. You couldn't do that before, could ya'?" The boy mumbles something, which apparently falls short of the wholesale affirmation Frisby was looking for, so he hedges: "As you obey, Jesus will keep on healing you." The boy heads off the stage and back to his seat. Frisby adds, "Sometimes the little fellas don't know how to say it, but it turns out okay."

He takes a few more from the healing line and then alternates between the two. A man who asked healing for arthritis testifies that God had healed his car. A young woman claims deliverance from "female problems." An elderly woman using a cane walks on stage. She says that Frisby has removed her bunions through prayer in the past, and she comes now for healing in her hips; one leg, she says, is longer than the other. Frisby touches her forehead and prays for healing. "Lord, heal this woman. By the power of your Spirit, adjust her hips. Take away the pain-ah!" The prayer completed, he asks, "What happened there? I really felt the Spirit adjust hips. Did one leg get longer? Walk around there. What do you feel?"

"It feels like it's getting even," the woman says, rather tentatively. "You don't need that cane anymore," Frisby announces. "Jesus has healed you!" Then to the audience: "Give the Lord a hand clap." The woman walks down the steps, across in front of the stage, and to her seat—using her cane. (The same woman returned to the healing line Sunday evening, the last day of the revival, this time without the cane. "I'd like a little more healing in my knees," she said.)

A teenager in denims and a dark tee-shirt approaches Frisby and asks for prayer. "I'm not doing too good in school," he says. Frisby grabs his forehead and unleashes a thunderous prayer calling on God to "give this boy some of Your special power-ah!" At the end of the prayer, the evangelist asks, "What happened there?" The young man looks a bit shaken, like he'd gotten more than he bargained for. He backs away, shakes his head, and answers, "I really felt the Spirit." Frisby sends him off and says, "Give the Lord a hand clap."

Another woman, one of Frisby's longtime followers in Phoenix, insists that "for eighteen years I haven't used a doctor. When I get sick I just call up and ask for Brother Frisby." Indeed, the evangelist dispenses healing as effortlessly as physicians write prescriptions. He treats coughs, colds ("I command the cold to go in the name of the Lord"), even toothaches ("Put the tooth back where it belongs, Jesus-ah"). Sometimes at the conclusion of the prayer, before Frisby invites a response, he'll say, "Oooh-wee. It really came out of me that time!" Or: "Did you feel that? The power really surges."

Frisby prays for everyone who comes onto the platform. Sometimes the prayer elicits no visible response. With others, however, it unleashes all manner of ecstatic behavior—tears, wailing, shaking arms and limbs, fibrillating voices (speaking in tongues), jumping up and down. People sometimes stagger away as though reeling from a jolt of electricity. "I feel good. I love ya', Lord. I feel great," one woman exclaims, waving her arms. Frisby clearly relishes such gyrations or outpourings of the Spirit. "Let's give the Lord a hand clap."

Frisby is not diffident about his healing powers. In the past he has claimed a ninety-nine percent success rate, and he frequently boasts that he has created ear drums and other body parts. These "creative miracles," as he calls them, date to the very beginning of his ministry in the 1960s. "Eardrums, one right after another, were created; legs were lengthened, one right after another," he wrote in his autobiography. "Backbones, nerves, and spinal parts were created. Hip sockets have been created, even when there was no

ball." The list continues. "I have seen enamel put back on teeth. I
have even prayed for corns and they have fallen off in people's socks,
or just disappeared!"[3]

Unlike other pentecostal revival services that might continue long
into the night, Frisby concludes his about an hour or an hour and
a half after it begins. When the healings are over, he turns to the
congregation, reminds them of the next meeting, and then invites
them to "come to Jesus." "I'm going to pray a mass prayer here,"
he says. At that signal everyone leaves his or her seat and files to
the platform. The music, now deafening, begins again, laced with
a heavy beat. Frisby cups his hands around the microphone and
emits a series of unintelligible, gutteral sounds. As the congregation,
gathered in front of him, claps in rhythm to the music, the evangelist
gesticulates with his arms, sweeping them first to the left, then to
the right, all the while barking strange noises into the microphone.
The only word I could understand amidst the banter was an emphatic, drawn-out "Jee-sus-ah." He leaves the pulpit briefly to dance
to one side of the stage and then the other, sweeping his arms in a
kind of ritualized motion. Coming back to the podium, he turns his
back to the audience, now whipped into a frenzy, thrusts his arms
into the air, throws back his head, and trots offstage behind the
same curtain whence he emerged.

Frisby's antics, especially in the surreal setting of his Capstone
Cathedral, lend a kind of carnival atmosphere to his meetings. But
the claims about his healing prowess are not terribly exceptional.
Since the turn of the century, faith healers have abounded in America, and even in the nineteenth century various evangelicals propagated divine remedies for physical ailments. In the early 1830s,
Sylvester Graham, a Presbyterian evangelist and temperance
preacher, developed a cracker as a health and dietary aid; the Graham cracker is still popular today. Ellen Gould White, afflicted from
childhood with various physical disorders, had several visions that
revealed the secrets of good health. White, leader of the Seventh-
day Adventists, founded the Western Health Reform Institute in
Battle Creek, Michigan, under the auspices of which John Harvey
Kellogg invented corn flakes and other health foods. Mary Baker

Eddy believed that deliverance from physical affliction lay in the spiritual realm. Even the science of chiropractic, developed by D. D. Palmer in Davenport, Iowa, in the 1890s, grew to some extent out of religious impulses and convictions.

When the pentecostal or sanctified movement—grounded in the belief that the Holy Spirit anoints true Christians with special spiritual gifts—began to gather force in American evangelicalism early in the twentieth century, healing became one of the spiritual gifts that pentecostals claimed as evidence of sanctification. Later in the century, the media propelled some of the faith healers to prominence. Through radio, Kathryn Kuhlman of Pittsburgh built a national reputation out of her gifts of healing. Oral Roberts, whom Frisby admires, parlayed his into a huge empire centered in Tulsa, Oklahoma. Neal Frisby belongs in that tradition, though he is clearly on the fringes, but there is another dimension that sets him even farther apart from the pentecostal mainstream: He believes he is a prophet sent from God, the final prophet before the end of time.[4]

The Capstone Cathedral (also known as the Temple of Destiny, the Headstone, or the Great Pyramid), it turns out, is fraught with apocalyptic significance. Its construction in the early 1970s prefigures the rebuilding of the temple in Jerusalem.[5] Frisby claims that God designed it, and that the dimensions were revealed to Frisby (who then apparently relayed them to Ray Parrish, an architect in Scottsdale).[6] "He even told me where to build it," Frisby claims. The seven concrete layers that recede upward toward the cap represent the seven ages of the church or the seven thunders of Revelation 10.[7] The tiers also symbolize the seven great prophets or messengers of Christianity, beginning with Paul the apostle and concluding with the "Star Prophet," William Branham, a pentecostal preacher who claimed a visitation from an angel on May 7, 1946, and whom Frisby considers his mentor and predecessor.[8]

For an understanding of the top pyramid of green and red glass, the capstone, Frisby asks his followers to look at a one-dollar bill. "On the back side of a dollar and at the left corner is the sign of the PYRAMID and at the top we see the 'Capstone' separated forming a 'Capstone Eye' with glory around it, revealing the 'all seeing eye' of God was rejected!" The base of the pyramid, moreover, "depicts the large groups that started in the 7 Church Ages through history and as it gets closer to the top it shows how the Lord narrows down a small group separated in the eye to take away!" Thus, the capstone depicts the true followers of God (the followers of Frisby) who will be taken in the rapture. The capstone also represents Frisby himself, who believes he is the final prophet, the culmination of history and revelation, God's mouthpiece in these last days.[9]

The symbolism continues inside. Every few rows the color of the seats extending from the platform changes. This spectrum of color symbolizes both Frisby, the "Rainbow Prophet" predicted in Revelation 10, and his followers, "the Rainbow Elect of God." The star on the pulpit represents Jesus, "the bright and morning star"; the blue stripes signify the bruises Jesus sustained before His crucifixion and the red stripes the blood He shed for the sins of humanity. The lightning bolts represent the power of God's revelation given to Frisby, who writes: "In Bible symbology when lightning cuts through the air this portrays a spirit message going forth."[10] A sign above an accordion door to the left of the platform, along the south edge of the building, reads THE VEIL in block letters. This is Frisby's inner sanctum, the last of a series of three chambers reserved for his use. In coming years, as the eschaton approaches, Frisby believes that the United States will pass laws against spiritual healing. The area behind the veil, then, will serve as a place of healing. Frisby, I was told, does much of his meditation and prayer here in the "chamber of revelation," but it is also used now, albeit infrequently, as a place for "special healings" or "special ministrations of the Spirit." Frisby says that just before construction workers covered the floor in the room behind the veil, "the Lord Jesus gave me some secrets and I put them underneath and I will not reveal them until later." This sanctum is the rough equivalent of the holy of holies in the Old Testament, a place reserved to the high priest and cordoned off from the people by the veil of the temple.[11]

How did Frisby come to his calling as a prophet? Born July 23, 1933, in Strong, Arkansas, Neal Vincent Frisby, a scrappy kid, had a troubled early life. "I always had a desire to be a conqueror, a champion," he confessed in his autobiography, without elaboration.

After moving to California, he completed the ninth grade and then went to barber college. Following the birth of her second child, Frisby's wife, still in her teens, committed suicide, an action Frisby now attributes to possession by a demon, "a melancholy spirit from the devil." Shortly thereafter, he went to an Assemblies of God church and was converted. "When I was saved my heart was healed instantly," he wrote. "It was miraculous!" Later, he spoke in tongues and became convinced that "the Spirit of God bade me go preach and pray for the sick."[12]

Frisby, however, resisted that call. He began to drink heavily, neglecting his family and his barber shop. "After a year of hard drinking, and begging the Lord to just save me, but not call me to preach, I began to have convulsions, the last stage of alcoholism. I began to use dope. In my convulsions I chewed my tongue. My bones would come out of joint and have to be put back in." Frisby went to hospital psychiatric wards several times and entered the state mental asylum for treatment, where he witnessed all manner of demon possession. But his problem, he knew, was spiritual: "Sin brings on insanity and sickness." Frisby found deliverance only when he resolved "to have it out with the devil." "I told the Lord I would do what He wanted me to do," he wrote. "Instantly by the power of God, and I lie not, a light feeling hit me. The demons had departed. I had no craving to drink, no seizures or convulsions."[13]

Frisby embarked on a forty-day fast, consuming nothing but water, in the course of which God came to him on the seventh, twenty-first, and thirty-seventh days, and said, according to Frisby, " 'There shall not anything stand before thee all the days of thy ministry. As I was with Moses I will be with thee! Be thou strong and full of courage!' "[14] God also endowed Frisby with the extraordinary power of "creative miracles" that at times, he insists, is so overwhelming that people find it frightening. "Even now," Frisby wrote in his autobiography, "I can't stay around anyone on the platform for very long because the anointing will wear them down. There is something strange about it." During this fast, he also became convinced of his prophetic calling: "The anointing is upon me. God spoke to me and said, 'The words I speak unto thee, write them and put them into a book.' " Frisby also declared, "I am a man given to prophetic visions [of] the glory of the Lord in a vision of white shekinah."[15]

How does this prophet interpret his calling? Frisby views himself as a messenger who "speaks by Divine Revelation and a Prophetic Spirit that goes beyond all gifts and utters the exact words of God to the Elect of his age and thunders the judgement of God on a nation!"[16] At irregular intervals since 1967, Frisby has issued prophetic scrolls to his followers. These scrolls, printed in two colors on a kind of parchment, contain his revelations from God. The introduction to a collection of the scrolls sets forth their importance: "Throughout the entire history of the world no work has been placed before the public which is as comprehensive revealing the fundamental truths of the Bible as this timely book on prophecy and its fulfillment!" As the end of time approaches, Frisby declared, "the Lord will release true wisdom unto His children through the dynamic scrolls"; furthermore: "One should carefully read this Literature in prayer because it is a written revelation by the supernatural wisdom of God! The writer does not claim infallibility, but we definitely believe the events, dates and symbols were placed in correct position close as humanly possible under divine inspiration!"[17]

Like many evangelicals, Frisby insists upon a literal reading of the Bible, from Genesis to Revelation. This hermeneutic, together with the conviction that he is a latter-day prophet, leads to a kind of fixation with apocalyptic prophecies in the Scriptures. Unlike other evangelical clergy who are content to study apocalyptic writings, discern the signs, and preach the importance of repentance, however, Frisby is eager to locate himself within God's prophetic scheme for the end of the world. He finds his niche, he believes, in Revelation 8. The apostle John, in the midst of his apocalyptic visions, sees a Lamb upon a throne (generally interpreted as Jesus Christ, "the Lamb of God who takes away the sins of the world"). In the sixth chapter, the Lamb opens the first six seals, one by one, and out come, in succession, four different colored horses, the martyrs, and, finally, various signs in the heavens—earthquakes, falling stars, a solar eclipse. After the sixth seal, chapter 7 records an interlude. "When the Lamb opened the seventh seal," Revelation

8:1 reads, "there was silence in heaven for about half an hour." In chapter 10, after the sounding of six trumpets, John records another interlude and the arrival of an angel, "coming down from heaven, wrapped in a cloud, with a rainbow over his head." "He had a little scroll open in his hand," John continued. "And when the seven thunders had sounded, I was about to write, but I heard a voice from heaven saying, 'Seal up what the seven thunders have said, and do not write it down.' "[18]

This silence, Neal Frisby believes, prevailed until recently, when God designated Frisby as this Rainbow Prophet or "the mighty rainbow cap angel" in the last days who would reveal the hidden messages of God and inaugurate a "great rainbow revival," replete with all manner of divine signs: "The dramatic flashing appearance of lightning and thunder miracles will occur! Tremendous anointing is coming to create parts of the body, at times all will be healed!"[19] This, Frisby believes, is his place in prophetic history: a source of divine healing and revelation who communicates the workings of God—and the contents of the unopened seventh seal—on parchment scrolls. "In the scrolls Jesus isn't adding to the Bible or taking away," Frisby writes, "but a continuing work of the spirit revealing a highly inspired written key message to reveal the 7th seal that was opened." His scrolls, Frisby believes, contain the "Key to interpret the secrets to the book of Revelations!" Even the U.S. dollar bill confirms this. Beneath the pyramid on the reverse side is the inscription THE GREAT SEAL, which, Frisby believes, refers to the seventh seal, described in the book of Revelation.[20]

Frisby's prophecies, revealed on these scrolls, range from the predictable to the bizarre. He inveighs against such commonplace evangelical targets as rock music, drugs, alcohol, homosexuality, communism, and Roman Catholicism.[21] In the 1960s he predicted the emergence of a U.S. president who "does much for the poor and religion" and who would "move toward uniting church and state." "How quick this president rises I'm not certain," Frisby wrote, "but I will tell you who he is if I get permission from the Lord." He predicts the unification of the three Cs—communism, Catholicism, and capitalism—to form one kingdom that seeks to replace the "great C" (Christ).[22]

He also thinks that the ancient Hebrew prophet Nahum "saw the (last car) not the first one made! It was rocket turbin, electric or radar controlled."[23] Late in the 1960s he advised his readers that America's highways "will undergo vast changes in the 70's and radar controlling will come into view about the time Christ appears." Frisby worries about such issues as transportation during the millennium, in light of Zechariah's prophecy that people would go to Jerusalem to worship once a year. "This would be utterly impossible with out some kind of huge swift space craft, (possibly some new gravity free super sonic or atomic craft!)," Frisby wrote, but then he offered consolation: "Never the less the Lord may supply the transportation, 'He has supernatural craft.'" Some prophecies build on popular fears, such as the prediction in the 1960s that an earthquake would plunge much of California into the ocean. Back then he also predicted the rise of Ronald Reagan, "a man preordained and predestined," to national prominence. In Reagan's strategic defense initiative ("Star Wars") of the 1980s, Frisby doubtless found vindication for another vision of the late 1960s: "I am shown paralyzing rays of light far ahead of the atomic bomb are being invented. Cosmicide radiation which rends people helpless will be discovered and used from outer space and land!"[24]

All of Frisby's prophecies point to the imminent end of human history and the beginning of the apocalyptic events foretold in the Bible. Frisby welcomes the end. He already feels caught up in the inexorable sequence of events: "The cycles and dates converging and innerlocking together in astounding fashion prove we are in the hands of Divine Providence!"[25] Like other preachers who seek to interpret the signs of the times in order to predict the impending eschaton, Frisby has his own ideas about the sequence of events. First comes the rapture, when the *true* Christians—those who subscribe to his "Capstone Ministry"—are taken from earth and united with Christ in heaven. The tribulation, a time of trial and testing for those left behind, begins immediately, followed in three-and-one-half years by the Battle of Armageddon predicted in Revelation 16. The millennium directly precedes the great white throne judgment of Revelation 20, when those with names recorded in the book of life go to heaven and those not found there are cast into the lake of fire. Finally, according to the penultimate chapter of Revelation, "a new heaven and a new earth" appear.[26]

All of this, Frisby believes, is imminent. One of his scenarios reads like this: "If God should allow by Divine intervention that the Rapture should go past 1977, my feeling then in Revelation time cycles is the Tribulation will start in 1983, Armageddon in 1986. The Church would leave between 1977-83 or sooner. But this I know by divine wisdom Armageddon will not take place until after January 1976."[27]

Interwoven with all these calculations are the familiar evangelical intimations that the unsaved must be saved and the elect must live holy lives and eschew evil, for the apocalyptic moment is close at hand. "We can safely say it looks like He is pointing to the ending of things. Early or late 70's," Frisby says at one point in his transcription of God's messages. "However, if it goes past the 80's it will all totally end by 1986. AMEN! But I really feel the 70's will tell the complete story of the end." Elsewhere, commenting on the apocalyptic end of time predicted in Revelation, he wrote, "I definitely feel it will all be finished before 1986."[28] When I heard Frisby in February 1987, the dates had changed. He spoke obliquely about three five-year periods and said that the end would come before the conclusion of the third five years.

While he insists that "I am not writing an extra Bible only fulfilling it," Frisby is certainly convinced that the scrolls contain divine revelation. "I speak by the mouth of the Lord!" he declares in one scroll. Sentences often begin with phrases like, "The Lord told me . . . " or "God showed me that . . . "; elsewhere he writes, "I am sent with 'the angel of the Lord to warn you' " and "that great angel is standing by my side." At one point Frisby claimed to relive the visions of Daniel, the Hebrew prophet in the Old Testament. "I feel a strong anointing," he wrote at the beginning of Scroll 8, "taking me back to the days of Daniel, and entering a new depth of Revelation."[29]

He admonishes his readers: "Soon these Scrolls will be the most valuable possession you own. Remember the Bible will be changed by man soon or taken, but not these Scrolls. The wise will see what God is doing through me." The scrolls, according to Frisby, also contain supernatural powers. "Reading these scrolls," he wrote, "will relieve and protect against mental disorders."[30] Indeed, Frisby's followers take these scrolls quite seriously. I spoke with one man, a follower since the early 1970s, who told me that he studied the scrolls regularly and had marked his copy at home with glosses and cross-references.

To undergird his prophecies, Frisby turns to solar eclipses and astrology, numerology (most often relating to his birthdate), and photographs of his Capstone Cathedral, all interleaved into the volume of prophetic scrolls.[31] The captions under each photograph—and often the text of the scrolls themselves—explain some supernatural wonder revealed in the photograph, very often a cloud formation that shows the face of God perched above the capstone. "Now I am going to reveal something here that is going to dumbfound the world," he announced in Scroll 61. "The stone the builders rejected (Christ—Mark 12:10) was photographed on top of the building, and has become the head of the corner." Once he publishes this photograph, Frisby wrote, "there isn't anything anybody can do but just stand and fall back in awe!"[32]

Many of the photographs suffer from some sort of aberration caused by double exposures, lens flares from shooting into the sun, or poor developing. But rather than tossing these pictures into the wastebasket or firing off an angry letter to Eastman Kodak, Frisby believes they reveal some divine mystery. "The Lord has given us the most sacred and rarest photographs ever seen before," Frisby boasts. In these photographs, he sees angel wings, golden halos, pillars of fire, and, most often, shekinah glory.[33] The Capstone Cathedral itself, the central subject in all these photographs, plays a central role in the coming apocalypse, and Frisby enjoins his followers to visit the building before Christ's return.[34]

Neal Frisby, this stocky man with dark hair and a receding hairline who wears sportcoats of canary yellow and powder blue and spearmint green, looks like a truck driver or maybe a small-town insurance salesman, the kind of man you might expect to find at the local diner kibbitzing with the guys. In truth, however, in recent years (for reasons I never learned) Frisby has grown increasingly reclusive and misanthropic. He and his family live on the church property in a two-story house surrounded by an eight-foot cinder-block wall. Brother Max, Frisby's assistant, told me that he had never had an extended conversation with Frisby; they had exchanged words only casually and in passing. When I made discreet inquiries about speaking with Frisby, I was told in no uncertain terms that he would not be available and that he rarely gave a personal audience. How do members of his congregation communicate with him? Apparently they don't, except for whatever contact they have in the healing or the praise lines during the services, although I was assured that Frisby would respond to a written note or question from a member of the congregation.

Frisby's day begins at four or five in the morning, when he goes into his private chambers and begins a regimen of prayer and writing that continues virtually all day. Frisby closets himself away in this "chamber of revelation" and writes his prophecies. From time to time, the text itself offers a few clues about this process. A parenthetical sentence in Scroll 40 reads: "while writing this late at night in my room I am also receiving something to do with the World Market and USA business exchange! It is important I am shown the years 1976–77."[35] Elsewhere, he writes: "I am lifted up above the world catastrophe (Armageddon) and All ages will be used in the last war. I saw children, young men and women and old men armed prepared to fight the last great war, as Russia and the Orientals came down on Israel."[36] Beyond that, there are remarkably few clues about this enigmatic prophet.

There are, however, some tantalizing glimpses. In searching through clipping files at a local library, I discovered several newspaper articles about Frisby and his nephews. In August 1984, his nephews exploded half a stick of dynamite in the back yard of the assistant police chief, claiming that the policeman's son owed them $600 for guns they had sold him. The nephews subsequently led an undercover agent from the Bureau of Alcohol, Tobacco and Firearms, posing as a gun buyer, to their cache of weapons. The agent purchased four hand grenades, eleven bombs, and several sticks of dynamite from Frisby's nephews; he passed on the submachine guns equipped with silencers, but stayed long enough to hear one nephew boast that he could blow up cars without a trace. "My dynamite is the strongest on the market," he said. "You put this under some-body's car, and you're going to lift it off the ground."[37] The case never came to trial. Frisby's nephews were granted probation after Frisby wrote a letter on Capstone stationery attesting to their regular church attendance. (After learning about this incident, and knowing about Frisby's passion for secrecy, I winced whenever I turned the ignition on my car.)

Apparently, Frisby's congregation remains unperturbed about such matters, although there has been a dramatic ebbing of his popularity in recent years. In his salad days of the early 1970s, several people told me, the crowds would begin arriving at four-thirty for an eight o'clock meeting. The line for healing sometimes extended from the platform, down through the auditorium, and out the front door, a distance of several hundred feet. I saw film clips of the building, seating two thousand, filled to capacity.[38] Along the walls of two sides of the pyramid sit banks of metal files containing Frisby's mailing list, which includes, I was told, the names of twelve million followers around the country and the world.[39]

The remnant of the faithful, down now to 100 or perhaps 150, is a mixed lot. During the first night of the crusade I sat near a woman, a member of the local Assembly of God, who was visiting the Cap-stone Cathedral out of curiosity. She expressed wonderment at both the service and the congregation. "This is really—I don't know how to say it—a lower-class crowd," she said, "which surprises me, be-cause this is a well-to-do neighborhood." Indeed, most of the people hardly looked affluent. A sizable percentage of the congregation is black. I saw a good number of elderly people—some of whom arrived in wheelchairs, others with canes or walkers—hoping no doubt for some miraculous deliverance from physical suffering. I noticed pre-scription bottles in the side pockets of several purses. I asked one older woman, a kindly person who stood behind one of the tables selling literature, about the old days and why attendance at Capstone had slackened so badly. "People just don't want to do God's will," she said. "They come for healing, but they don't want to follow the teachings of the Lord." I suspected that the real answer was a bit less spiritual. Frisby is a good example of an evangelical figure who gathers a following because of his charisma and his claims of healing power. At the same time, Frisby, who elevated himself to the status of prophet, was accountable to no one; because of the increasingly freakish twists in his theology, moreover, erstwhile followers became disenchanted and fell away.

But those who remain faithful—the elect—will be rewarded, Frisby promises. "Now the 'Capstone' people (the Sons of God) is called in the Thunders! Like Enoch they walked with God and will be translated! This is the 'Rod iron elect', little is heard of them at first, but they are the most powerful group who ever came on the face of the earth!"[40]

The promise of power in the afterlife to compensate for suffering and powerlessness in this life? I wondered.

As the crusade drew to a close, it became clear that I'd be unable to penetrate this veil of secrecy around Frisby. On Sunday morning, the final day of the revival, however, I conceived a plan. Several times Frisby had announced that on Sunday he would have a special prayer line for those who had come from out of town, giving them a chance to request healing either for themselves or for others. I figured that I qualified. The week before, moreover, a student had visited my office, and when the conversation came around to this impending trip, she volunteered that she had recently lost the hearing in one ear. This provided the perfect pretext, I reasoned, and as the line snaked forward, I rehearsed my appeal. Three women in front of me, all dressed alike and all from Los Angeles, went away crying, dancing, and shouting. Then came my turn.

"Brother Frisby," I began, feeling every bit the impostor, "I have a friend named Alexandra who recently lost the hearing in one ear. Could you heal her in the power of Jesus's name?" Frisby rose to the challenge, ears being something of a specialty. "Well, we'll pray for her right here," he announced. "Can she come to the meetings, or is she too far away?"

"She's too far away."

The Rainbow Prophet grabbed the back of my neck with his left hand and placed his right hand on my forehead. Having watched the prayer line several times now, I knew that the correct posture at this moment was to cast aside my inhibitions, throw my arms up in the air, and close my eyes. I don't recall all of Frisby's prayer, although I remember a few words and phrases: "don't know what has affected this girl's hearing," "let her feel the anointing of Your Spirit all through her body," "heal her," "name of Jesus." As the prayer continued, the evangelist began to shake me, while bearing down with increasing pressure on my forehead. When he finished, he let out a little "whooo-ee," released me from his grasp, and stepped away as though thrown backwards by the recoil of a rifle. He was looking for some sort of response, I realized later. Surely I disappointed him when I muttered "thank you," shook his hand, and walked away.

What did I feel? Nothing. Just a sweaty palm on my forehead, shaking and pushing.

As the plane lifted out of Phoenix on Monday morning after the revival, I searched the flat, barren landscape below for the Capstone Cathedral, the jewel atop the pyramid. Neal Frisby was, perhaps even now, I thought, scratching away at his latest prophetic scroll, or maybe flailing away at some private demon that retreats before him like a desert mirage. Like the city here in this desolate Valley of the Sun, I thought, Frisby was a kind of phoenix himself, rising out of the ashes of despair to become, of all things, the Rainbow Prophet.

The day after I arrived home, I phoned Alexandra. "How's the ear?" I asked. I tried to sound mischievous and conspiratorial, but I was genuinely curious.

"No change," she said.

NOTES

1. This account derives from impressions gathered over the course of several meetings during the February 1987 crusade.

2. On the design of the Capstone Cathedral, see "Glass-Dome Capstone Believed Largest Phoenix Church," *Arizona Republic*, 21 February 1971; Henry Fuller, "Capstone Cathedral Rises from the Desert," ibid., 11 July 1971.

3. W. V. Grant, *Creative Miracles* (Dallas: Faith Clinic, n.d.), pp. 17, 18. This booklet, purportedly written by W. V. Grant, a fellow evangelist, actually consists of three chapters: the first is a kind of introduction by Grant; chapters 2 and 3 are first-person, autobiographical narratives by Frisby.

4. Frisby's unusual theology has prompted David Edwin Harrell, Jr., to dub him the "most bizarre prophet of the 1970s" (*All Things Are Possible: The Healing and Charismatic Revivals in Modern America* [Bloomington: Indiana University Press, 1975], p. 221).

5. Neal Frisby, *The Revelation of the Written Scrolls and the Word of God as Given to Neal Vincent Frisby* (Phoenix: n.p., n.d.), pp. 183–84. Frisby also refers to the building as the Lord's "holy Temple" (p. 210).

6. See Fuller, "Capstone Cathedral Rises from the Desert."

7. Frisby clearly believes we are living in the seventh age, but although this idea of church ages is a tenet of dispensational theology, I ran across no reference to the term *dispensation* in his writings.

8. Frisby claims to have seen visions of Branham's death in advance; see Frisby, *Revelation of the Written Scrolls*, p. 54. Regarding Paul as the first messenger, see ibid., p. 111. On William Branham, see Harrell, *All Things Are Possible*, pp. 159–65; C. Douglas Weaver, *The Healer-Prophet, William Marrion Branham: A Study of the Prophetic in American Pentecostalism* (Macon, Ga.: Mercer University Press, 1987).

9. Frisby, *Revelation of the Written Scrolls.*, p. 149; cf. p. 191. Frisby often stops just short of making this claim explicitly, but it is surely implied in his writings. See, for example, ibid., p. 127. He also uses his birthdate (in logic I cannot decipher) to confirm this; see ibid., p. 134. At the conclusion of Scroll 57, Frisby responds to queries about the identity of various prophets mentioned in previous scrolls. He says, "The last one mentioned is the writer of scrolls" (p. 189).

10. Ibid., pp. 111, 173. For further significance of the rainbow motif, see ibid., p. 169.

11. Ibid., p. 183; see also p. 194.

12. Grant, *Creative Miracles*, pp. 10, 21, 11, 23.

13. Ibid., pp. 12, 26.

14. Frisby, *Revelation of the Written Scrolls*, p. 133. It has always intrigued me that God speaks seventeenth-century English.

15. Grant, *Creative Miracles*, pp. 18, 19. *Shekinah* means divine presence.

16. Frisby, *Revelation of the Written Scrolls*, p. 83.

17. Ibid., pp. 5, 89. Even the compilation of the scrolls has significance: "The Lord shows Bro. Frisby the hour has arrived to put the Scrolls in Book Form to reveal to his special partners and Crusade friends some remarkable prophecy visions God gave him personally of the future of the world!" (p. 7). Later, he writes: "The significance of what I have been writing is a final message to the Bride [Church]—and pronouncing judgment on the nation" (p. 158).

18. Rev. 8:1; 10:1–11 (RSV).

19. Frisby, *Revelation of the Written Scrolls*, p. 152; Frisby uses the designations "Rainbow Prophet" and "Rainbow Angel" interchangeably and says that the Rainbow Angel "will be transformed into a prophet" (p. 168). The designation "mighty rainbow cap angel" occurs on p. 227.

20. Ibid., pp. 110, 111, 149. Frisby, a diffident man, is careful to shrug off any divine infallibility, even as he professes to speak the mind of God: "I want to make this plain, I am no special person because I am used in writing the scrolls. But Jesus is the special one" (p. 112). Regarding the dollar bill, Frisby holds that God "put all this on a dollar instead of a 20 or 100 dollar bill, being (one) would be seen or handled more as a greater witness! Also the USA currency is in almost every nation witnessing this very thing" (pp. 149–50). I am quoting Frisby verbatim throughout, including his erratic spellings and syntax.

21. He writes: "The U.S.A., Israel and England will go through great tribulation for being involved with Babylon (Catholics) at the end" (ibid., p. 59). During one meeting he charged that music videos provided "a well-rounded Satanic education."

22. Ibid., pp. 55, 56.

23. Ibid., p. 69.

24. Ibid., pp. 73, 75, 92, 95, 106, 148. Of Reagan, Frisby wrote that "Ronald Reagan could cause an upset for the presidency" (p. 87). The scrolls in the printed collection are undated, but this one also included prophecies for the late 1960s and early 1970s. Frisby later altered his prediction for atomic destruction and spoke of the neutron bomb (p. 155).

25. Ibid., p. 146.

26. Rev. 21:1 (RSV). On the exclusiveness of the elect, Frisby says, "The world will have to except the 'Capstone Ministry' of the last message or they will have to except the brimstone message of the lake of fire!" But later in the same paragraph he hedges: "I am not saying this will be the only work of God, but it is an Elect major work of His!" (Frisby, *Revelation of the Written Scrolls*, p. 161).

27. Frisby, *Revelation of the Written Scrolls*, p. 137. At times Frisby seems to equate Armageddon with some sort of atomic destruction; see ibid., p. 141.

28. Ibid., pp. 78, 108, 131. Elsewhere, he writes: "According to Gods

true time it would almost seem impossible for the world to continue after 1986" (p. 137).

29. Ibid., pp. 162, 113, 66, 67. Frisby concluded this section: "And I, Neal, understood and wrote these things and worshipped Him who is the beginning and the end, standing beside me. Amen" (p. 68).

30. Ibid., p. 63.

31. Ibid., pp. 105, 159, 215, 217–18. Frisby devotes an entire scroll (no. 68) to the importance of numbers; ibid., pp. 226–28.

32. Ibid., p. 203.

33. Ibid., pp. 221, 234–35.

34. Ibid., p. 205. He writes: "The Temple here is just full of the power of God, a thick presence is in it! There is only one life to live, and everyone should see Capstone before His return. We want all to come and be healed, no disease can stand here. When a person lines up with the Headstone, diseases and devils fall like the lightning!"

35. Ibid., p. 145.

36. Ibid., p. 155.

37. From transcript of court records, quoted in Tom Fitzpatrick, "Bombing Case Intriguing, But Suspects' Ties Blew It Out of Water," *Arizona Republic*, 29 August 1985; see also idem, "Gun Case Involving Officer's Son, Preacher's Nephews Inspires Questions," ibid., 5 September 1984; Susan Leonard, "2 Brothers Held In Blast at Home of Police Official," ibid., 30 August 1984; "Phoenix Man Pleads Guilty in Threat Case," ibid., 20 December 1984; "Defendant Admits Bombing at Phoenix Lawman's Home," ibid., 5 March 1985.

38. A newspaper article written in 1973 put the congregation at eight hundred; Max Jennings, "Hallelujah! Ailments Vanish at Revival," *Arizona Republic*, 23 February 1973.

39. The figure of twelve million was quoted to me several times, although one person indicated that the active list was eight million. Given the attendance at the crusade, these figures seemed exaggerated.

40. Frisby, *Revelation of the Written Scrolls*, p. 162.

5

Adirondack Fundamentalism

IN THE EARLY MORNING HOURS, Schroon Lake is gray and placid. Wispy clouds tumble over the pine-covered hillsides that surround the lake. Steam rises from the water. A lone canoe paddles by. For a brief moment, the sun pushes past the clouds but then settles back into exile.

When the receding glaciers carved Schroon Lake into the Adirondack mountains of upstate New York, they left a ninety-acre island at the north end of the lake. There, pine trees sprouted among the glacial rocks, and thus surrounded by frigid mountain water, the island became an ideal location for a youth camp.

Jack Wyrtzen, a fundamentalist Bible teacher from New York City, took possession in 1946, at about the same time that motor travel began to diminish the attractiveness of the resorts dotting the Adirondacks. He has since added an inn, a family campground, a ranch, and a Bible institute—hundreds of acres, all told—to his empire, the Word of Life Fellowship, in and around Schroon Lake. Word of Life also includes radio broadcasts on more than one hundred stations around the world, mission enterprises in places as diverse as Peru, Hungary, Israel, and New Zealand, various traveling evangelists, musicians, and drama troupes, and over a thousand Bible clubs held in churches throughout the country. All of this consumes an annual budget of about $12 million, but the youth camp, "for young people and college-career young adults aged 13 to 30," remains the centerpiece of Word of Life.[1]

I'm not sure there is any way I could document this, but I suspect that the greatest fear that haunts evangelical parents is that their children will not follow in their footsteps, that they will not sustain the same level of piety as their parents—stated baldly, that they are headed for hell rather than heaven. Such themes as waywardness and redemption provide the grist for countless evangelical sermons; the parable of the prodigal son, I am convinced, is one of the most popular texts in the evangelical subculture. Prayer meetings fairly reverberate with petitions for this or that son or daughter who has wandered from the faith. In recent decades, many churches, reflecting the concerns of parents in the congregation, have hired youth pastors, whose job it is to keep children safely within the evangelical fold, to shield them from the perils of worldliness.

Indeed, there is ample cause for concern. What can be harder than passing on religious verve and vitality from one generation to the next, especially within a tradition that defines itself by the conversion process, that transition from darkness to light, from sinfulness to redemption? The Puritans of the seventeenth century faced this problem and never fully resolved it. New England's founding generation had forsaken fortune and family in England in order to carve a godly commonwealth out of the wilderness of Massachusetts. By the time the second generation approached adulthood, the spirituality of the founding generation had taken on heroic proportions, and when this next generation was asked as a requirement for church membership to stand before their elders in the meetinghouse and give an account of their conversions, most of them refused, knowing full well that their piety paled before that of their elders. Before long, the Puritans discerned in their midst a spiritual malaise that they called declension, and by the latter half of the seventeenth century the pulpits of New England resounded with calls to repentance.

In his novel *The Chosen*, Chaim Potok illustrates how this generational problem plays itself out within a different context. Reb Saunders, a pious, learned man venerated by his Hasidic followers, wants desperately to pass along the mantle of religious leadership to his eldest son, Danny, a precocious child who has studied the Talmud exhaustively all of his life and who regularly astounds his father's congregation with his grasp of even the most recondite Jewish sacred writings. Danny Saunders, the elders all agree, would be a worthy spiritual successor to his father.

But Danny Saunders's restless mind leads him in other directions, to intellectual pursuits outside the narrow confines of his father's calling and to friendships outside of his Hasidic community. When it finally becomes clear that Danny will not follow in his father's footsteps, Reb Saunders bids his son an anguished farewell, whereupon Danny Saunders, shorn of his earlocks and no longer dressed in black Hasidic hat and coat, walks down the street and toward a new life very different from the sheltered existence he has known.[2]

It doesn't take much imagination to appreciate the quandary of parents who want to pass along to their children the faith that has shaped their lives and solved for them the riddle of eternity. You want to shelter your children from the temptations that assail them at every turn. You want to school them in the Scriptures and in the theology that you know to be correct. And you also want them to be models of godliness, a credit not only to the faith but also to you as wise, godly parents.

Yet at the same time, such sheltering diminishes the drama of their own spiritual conversions when—and if—those conversions do occur. Whereas your embracing of the gospel had delivered you from a life of, say, alcohol or drugs or promiscuity, theirs serves merely as a ratification of the beliefs and lifestyle that you, their parents, have drilled into them since infancy. (The prodigal son's older brother who stayed at home, after all, never knew the contrast between the perils of the world and the security of home, and he envied the lavish party his father threw for his brother's homecoming.) On the other hand, neglecting your children's spiritual nurture will not suffice either, for that entails the considerable risk of trusting them (through God's leading, of course) to come to Christ of their own volition.

Ever since the 1925 Scopes Trial convinced fundamentalists that the broader American culture had turned hostile to their interests, fundamentalists have busied themselves devising various institutions to insulate themselves and their children from the depredations of the world. (In fact, the terms *worldly* and *worldliness* are probably the closest most evangelicals come to epithets; these words are often spoken sneeringly, in a tone at the same time condescending and cautionary.) First, the fundamentalists separated out of mainline denominations so that they could maintain a theology untainted by liberalism or, in the argot of the day, "modernism." Evangelicals then established their own mission boards, Christian schools, Bible institutes, colleges, and, eventually, seminaries. For children, Sunday school provided socialization and instruction in the rudiments of evangelical theology. Once the children had grown, you could ship them off to a Bible institute where they might prepare for the pastorate, missionary work, or some other kind of "Christian service."

But by the 1940s many fundamentalist parents recognized a gap in this system. How do you shelter your children from the onslaughts of the world during those critical teenage years when, with hormones swirling furiously, temptations reach their zenith?

About this time Jack Wyrtzen devised a summer Bible camp for teenagers, a sanctuary for fundamentalist parents to send their children, a place where strict parietal rules would be enforced and, more important, where some sort of religious commitment would be exacted.

A small pontoon provides ferry service between the western shores of Schroon Lake and Word of Life Island. As you approach, a boathouse with the legend A VERY SPECIAL ISLAND comes into view. Once on the landing, a sign welcomes you to Word of Life Island and, beyond that, a second notice warns: ALL VISITORS MUST REPORT TO THE OFFICE AND SIGN IN! A winding pathway leads to a large frame building called the Pine Pavilion.

The Pine Pavilion is a squarish building constructed on a hillside, with terraces of long, wooden benches sloping down toward the stage. Flags and red-white-and-blue bunting festoon the interior. In the northeast corner, a large wooden sign reads:

> CHRIST WALKS ON THIS ISLAND
> WILL YOU MEET HIM HERE?

Green porcelain warehouse-style lamps hang from the rafters.

The evening service begins at seven, and several announcements over a public-address system warn campers to be on time. Soon, a torrent of energetic campers tumbles into the building. Most of them are white and dressed in standard teenage fashions—tee-shirts, denims, sneakers, large, oversized sweatshirts.

Ten minutes into the meeting, as the sun sets across Schroon Lake, the Pine Pavilion is rocking. It's military week on the island, and the campers have been divided into Army and Navy teams. A series of games, challenges, and good-natured rivalry has been devised by the camp directors to generate spirit, teamwork, and enthusiasm. Apparently they've succeeded. Some of the counselors wear camouflage fatigues, and not infrequently amidst the singing of various evangelical songs and choruses, the pavilion erupts in rival chants of "Army! Army!" and "Navy! Navy!" Each team sings its fight song—"Anchors Aweigh" and "The Caissons Keep Rolling Along"—accompanied by spirited stomping, and soon, amidst all this excitement, the building begins to smell faintly of adolescent sweat. [3]

The crowd reverts to rhythmic clapping and stomping when a middle-aged man in a plaid, open-necked shirt plays "When the Roll Is Called Up Yonder" on his trumpet, triple-tonguing the second verse. When he finishes, more applause, shouting, hooting, and stomping. The pavilion quiets somewhat as a pretty blonde woman in her late teens, wearing a khaki skirt and a navy blazer, mounts the stage. She sings several songs to the accompaniment of taped music played over the sound system. After one of the songs, she exhorts the audience in a kind of breathless whisper: "It's so important to keep your standards high. You know, it's a nasty world out there." The next song, "Build on Higher Ground," reiterates that theme:

> Build your house above the ocean.
> Build your house on higher ground.
> Build above the world's commotion
> And its mesmerizing sound.

The music finishes with a flourish, and after an announcement encouraging campers to purchase a Ryrie Study Bible and books by Chuck Swindoll at the bookstore, the young soprano joins the trumpet player for a duet, "I've Just Seen Jesus," a fitting complement, I thought, to the sign in the northeast corner of the pavilion.

Jack Wyrtzen, a snowy-haired man in white pants and a floral-print tropical shirt, comes to the podium. He reminds the campers about some of the rules that govern life on the island. Everyone must wear a robe or sweat clothes to the beach. Shorts must be at least fingertip length. Word of Life promotional literature has already spelled out these regulations in some detail. "Please keep modesty in mind regarding all clothing," the literature counsels, adding that campers should bring a Bible and "sportswear for daytime activities, dress-up clothes (dress shirt and slacks for guys, dress for girls) for Sunday and some evening meals, modest one-piece bathing suit (I Tim. 2:9) and beach robe."[4]

Wyrtzen is an old fashioned, unvarnished fundamentalist. An affable, bespeckled man, his photographs in Word of Life promotional materials invariably show him with a large, open-mouthed grin, wearing an expression that suggests he has just told you the funniest joke in the world and is awaiting your reaction. He opens with a prayer asking God that everyone in the building will be "born again by the Word of God." Immediately thereafter, he asks how many in the audience have Bibles. Virtually everyone thrusts a Bible high into the air. As he announces this evening's text, he tells the audience that he hopes "before the night is done you will come to the Lamb of God." For the first nineteen years of his life, he says, "nobody told me about Jesus Christ" in the liberal churches he attended. The United

States Army, in fact, is "the greatest denomination in the U.S.," because that's where Wyrtzen became a Christian.

Fundamentalists are fond of belittling the pretensions of mainline, liberal churches, and Wyrtzen is no exception. He uses certain code words or phrases to indicate his derision of theological liberals. The one he employs most often is "First Church." He will tell of some member of "First Church" who came to one of Wyrtzen's rallies, heard the gospel for the first time, and went away born again. Or some worldly woman, also a member of "First Church," who "got saved" at Word of Life and now is "on fire for the Lord." The audience, many of whom have apparently heard this nomenclature before, picks up on this right away, snorting disapprovingly at the reference to theological liberals and the putative name of their churches.

But tonight Wyrtzen is not interested in preaching to the converted; he wants to bring more of the unsaved into the fold. After telling of various sinners—including a woman he refers to as the "blonde bomber"—whose lives have been transformed by Jesus, and after warning of the torments of hell, he asks, "Have you been to Calvary?" He implores the campers to come to Jesus and leads them in a slow, mournful chorus that evokes Jesus's death at Calvary:

> Dying there for me,
> Dying there for me.
> Jesus died, was crucified.
> Dying there for me.

"You need to confess you are a sinner and believe Jesus died for you," Wyrtzen says. "Invite Him into your heart right now." Wyrtzen makes it easy, providing a formula prayer for the wavering: "Dear Jesus, I confess that I am a sinner. Thank you for dying on the cross for me. Come into my heart and save me now. Amen."

All heads are bowed. All eyes closed. The meeting's raucous beginning is long forgotten. Wyrtzen asks for a show of hands from those who prayed the prayer. A few timid arms reach upward. Wyrtzen acknowledges each one. "Yes, I see that hand. Is there another?" He pleads a bit longer and then closes the meeting with this stark admonition: "If you leave this building without Jesus, you're guilty of His crucifixion."

The harvest tonight is disappointing, but it's still early in the week. Wyrtzen has a whole stable of speakers, Bible teachers, and counselors who will hammer the message home in the next few days. The entire schedule, in fact, is calculated to produce a maximum yield of converts and rededications, those who publicly reaffirm their conversions and resolve to live holier lives.

The day begins with breakfast at eight, followed by a morning of Bible study. After lunch, the campers have an afternoon of play—swimming, water skiing, basketball, volleyball—before supper and the evening meeting, either a rally in the pavilion or around a campfire. After the meeting, the counselors organize more competitive games between the Army and Navy teams. Even with lights-out at ten-thirty, fatigue sets in, what with all the fresh air, sunshine, and just plain fun. But that's part of the scheme as well, for there is a certain rhythm the organizers are trying to impose. The religious appeals begin early in the week at the rallies and in the morning sessions. By Wednesday evening's campfire, a sense of camaraderie, of shared experience, has set in. Campers are beginning to see their friends profess conversions or rededications, and nothing motivates an adolescent better than the example of his or her peers.

Figuring unpredictably into this mix is that confounding, exhilarating phenomenon: the summer romance. The people at Word of Life Island tolerate such courtships and even encourage them with a special dinner on Wednesday night to which boys are encouraged to bring dates. Parents back home, who are praying fervently for their child's spiritual renewal, also tolerate the courting that takes place at teen camp. They figure that their child's chances of meeting a nice Christian girl or boy at Bible camp are certainly greater than back home in a public high school. They trust Jack Wyrtzen and his staff, moreover, to police such romances carefully, lest passions run awry.

I kissed a girl for the first time at Bible camp—and, come to think of it, the second, third, and fourth times—all of it quite innocent, of course. Somewhere along the shores of Rainbow Lake a tree still bears the initials "R.B. + C.S.," chiseled into the bark with a jackknife. Word of Life Island bears the markings of similar romances and infatuations, flames that burn brightly, last through several exchanges of letters, but then generally flicker and die before the leaves fall:

Erika & Howard
I love Dave
Dawn & John
Kyle + Deanna
Leon and Joan

Some have thoughtfully included the date in their memorials, as if establishing a statute of limitations:

85 Denise -n- John
I ♥ Joel Hoffman '86

Adolescent love is a sweet and wonderful thing, and if your beloved is a good Christian girl—"wholesome" is the adjective my parents always favored—then your resistance to the gospel weakens further.

By the time the Friday night campfire comes around, you are tired to the bone. You've never played so hard, swum so far, or slept so little. You are sunburned and mosquito-bitten; you have several proud bruises to show your sister. A sense of melancholy sets in because you know that tomorrow you must say goodbye to all the friends you've made at camp that week: the cabinmates who put corn flakes and shaving cream in the bottom of your sleeping bag and who helped you ambush one of the girls' cabins, the counselor who listened and became a friend, and most of all the lovely girl with the cornflower-blue eyes seated next to you. You have been peppered all week with invitations to receive Christ into your life and warnings about the fate of those who refuse. You may not have another chance, you are told; Jesus may come at any time—before the week is out, before morning, even before the campfire ends. Don't let Him find you unsaved. It's easy. Come to Jesus. Just ask Him into your heart and live for Him.

The counselors at Word of Life Island refer to the Friday campfire as the "say so" meeting, taken from Psalm 107:2: "Let the redeemed of the Lord say so." Other Bible camps have different names. "Testimony service" or "afterglow" are rather common. Some camps used to refer to the final campfire, quite seriously, as a "faggot fire," a reference to the practice of grabbing the unburned end of one of the embers and tossing it into the fire as you begin your testimony about what Jesus has done in your life that past week. There is an illusion of spontaneity in these services, but for anyone who has witnessed more than a couple of them at Bible camps across the country, there is a remarkable uniformity to these gatherings. Having stared into a few fundamentalist campfires myself, I well remember the rhythms, the emotions, the ritualized adolescent behavior that takes place around the fire.

The service at Word of Life Island opens with singing; one of the counselors has supplied a guitar. The purpose of the say so meeting, another counselor informs the gathering, is to provide a chance for campers to tell what the Lord has done in their lives. He continues: "I'd just like to begin by saying that I've grown a lot this week. Pastor Jim's Bible studies have taught me a lot about what it means to be a Christian and to live for the Lord. I don't know about the rest of you, but I just praise the Lord for Pastor Jim and for the insight God has given him into the Scriptures."[5]

A few appreciative murmurs follow and then a short silence as half a dozen people sitting there in the encroaching darkness summon the courage to stand and address the other campers. The fire is still struggling to take hold. The sun has just disappeared beyond the ridge at the west end of the lake, and all eyes are adjusting to the twilight.

There are no takers yet, the Spirit hasn't yet moved, so the guitarist begins strumming the chords for "Cum by Yah," and after the first few bars everyone joins in:

> Cum by yah, my Lord, cum by yah.
> Cum by yah, my Lord, cum by yah.
> Cum by yah, my Lord, cum by yah.
> O, Lord, cum by yah.

The plaintive, doleful melody functions as a kind of invocation: Come here, Jesus, and grace this gathering with Your presence.

Once the music dies, Joyce Johnson is ready. She rises confidently to her feet. All eyes move briefly from the fire to see who is talking and then, after a moment, settle back on the flames. There will be no dramatic confession here; Joyce Johnson, everyone at camp knows by now, is too good for that. Instead, this is a kind of homily disguised as self-disclosure. "I've been coming to camp ever since I was eight years old," she begins, "and once again the Lord has really worked in my life. He's shown me some new things out of His Word this week, and I know I'll be a better witness for the Lord during this next year." The tone then shifts from self-congratulatory to admonitory. "If anybody here isn't a Christian, my prayer is that you'll accept Jesus as your savior before tonight is over, before you leave this island tomorrow. You may never have another chance to receive Jesus into your heart."

After a decent interval, Candy Schroeder stands. "I'm not sure what I'm gonna say," she confesses with an uneasy chuckle, "but I wanted to tell you what the Lord has been doing in my life. For a while now I've been seeking the Lord's will for my life, and I've been praying for His guidance—especially to know what to do after I graduate from high school next year." She pauses, then wipes the corners of her eyes with the back of her hand. The length of the silence is uncomfortable for those seated around the fire, and only a few steal a glance at Candy, standing there in denims and a loose, gray sweatshirt. "I'm just so grateful to my parents," she continues between sobs, "and to everyone who has prayed for me. On Tuesday during the missionary hour, the Lord just spoke to my heart. When Reverend Hunt told about the millions of unsaved people down in Argentina, I just knew that the Lord was calling me to be a missionary to all those people who have never heard the gospel, to all those people—" she pauses again, biting her lower lip, "to all those people who are lost without Jesus." A dozen "amens" greet this happy news, and they are repeated sporadically as Candy Schroeder reveals her plans to attend a Bible institute after high school and then go to South America as a missionary.

Paul Snyder, a big, strapping kid of fourteen, is next. "I didn't grow up in a Christian home," he says. "In fact, my parents are members of the Lutheran church back in Easton, Pennsylvania, and they didn't want me to come. When my friend Mike here invited me to Word of Life, I wasn't sure, either, but then he told me how much fun it was, so I convinced my mom and dad to let me come." The fire is thriving now, shooting flames and sparks upward into the darkness like a kind of offering. The mosquitos have arrived, searching for patches of flesh. A small motorboat trolls by, its green and red lights slicing through the darkness. "I sure am glad I came, though, because on Thursday night after the rally I gave my life to Christ. I had always thought I was a Christian because I went to church with my parents. But when I asked Don, my counselor, if I was going to heaven, he told me that unless I asked Jesus into my heart I would go to hell when I died. Well," Paul continues, halting slightly, "I gave my life to Christ. I'm a new, baby Christian. I'm going to read my Bible every day and tell all my friends at school about the Lord."

The guitarist thinks it's time for another song:

> Seek ye first the kingdom of God
> and His righteousness
> and all these things shall be added unto you.
> Hallelu-hallelujah.

The sweet, soft words echo across the lake. Paul Snyder's testimony has stirred something inside of Amy Durkin, because last year at this time she, too, gave her life to Jesus for the first time. She remembers now the feeling, the euphoria, and also her resolve to live a Christian life.

"I became a Christian here at camp last summer," Amy says, almost apologetically. "But once school started I fell in with the wrong crowd. Many of my friends are worldly, and I thought I was a strong enough Christian to stand up to them—" she begins to cry, "but I wasn't. Pretty soon I was just as worldly as the rest of them—going to movies and dances and stuff like that." Amy stops to regain her composure. The mournful cry of a loon reverberates across the lake. "But this year is going to be different. I've rededicated my

life to the Lord this week, and I'm going to live for Him and bring
my Bible with me to school every day and witness to my friends."

There are countless subtle variations to this rededication soliloquy, but most of them recount a previous commitment to Christ
and a resolve to maintain high standards of godliness in the midst
of a sinful and decadent world. But somehow, something went
wrong—perhaps the lack of parental support or the absence of a
good church youth program. Most often, however, even the most
resolute convert from Bible camp caves in to peer pressure. "It's
not easy being a Christian in my high school," is a familiar refrain.

Indeed not. If being a Christian as the people here define it means
abstaining from drinking, smoking, dancing, movies, and perhaps
even bowling and roller-skating (because of their "worldly" connotations), it doesn't take long for an evangelical high school student
to become a pariah among his or her peers—or, more frequently,
a kind of cipher on the social scene. The options then become either
finding a new support network—a church youth group, perhaps—
or compromising your fundamentalist scruples in order to fit in with
your peers. If your parents are evangelical Christians, they want
you to do the former, of course, but doing so exacts a price. It's not
easy turning your back on your peers, rejecting the companionship
and approval of friends at school for the comparatively unfulfilling
friendships of people your own age at church.

No, it's not easy being an evangelical in high school. Carl Watkins,
I think, understands that. For some time now I had been watching
him shift uneasily on the stony ground; he seemed to be summoning
the courage to get up and speak. Now, finally, Carl unfolds his tall,
gangly frame, shuffles his feet uneasily, and clears his throat.

"My father is a preacher," Carl begins, "so I was raised in a
Christian home. But I haven't always lived a good Christian witness.
I'm not even sure that the kids at school know I'm a Christian."
Carl stares at his shoetops. "I mean, sometimes I go out drinking
with my friends. I know that's not right. I know that's not what the
Lord wants me to do, but, I don't know, I just do it."

As he continues his halting confession, I begin to see myself in
Carl Watkins. I see a Little Leaguer who had to miss all his Wednesday games, even the all-star game, because Wednesday was prayer-

meeting night. I see in Carl Watkins an eighth-grader forced to sit on the sidelines during square dances in gym class and a teenager who couldn't wear bluejeans to school because his parents thought they would damage his Christian testimony. I see a high school graduate who never overcame his sense of alienation from his peers.

"I don't mean to hurt my parents," Carl continues, his voice cracking now, "but I guess, I don't know, that I always feel like I'm supposed to be perfect, to be this super-Christian at church and at school. But I'm not." Carl thrusts his hands deep into his pockets and shrugs his shoulders. "I really love my mom and dad. And I'm so grateful to the Lord for allowing me to grow up in a Christian home."

I also see in Carl Watkins a teenager contemplating the consequences of his rebellion, recounting sermon illustrations about eternity—time utterly without end, going on and on and on. If a tiny sparrow flew around the world and took a sip from the ocean at each pass, so the sermon illustration goes, by the time the ocean was dry, eternity would only have begun. Eternity was an awfully long time to be burning in hell, that lake of fire and brimstone.

"I ask you to pray for me this year," Carl concludes, "as I try to live a good Christian life." His gaze rests on the flames for a brief moment, and then he sits down. The fire crackles and spits sparks into the air. Carl Watkins reaches back and turns up the collar of his jacket against the sudden autumn chill that whips across the lake. Off to the east, a new moon hangs in the late-August darkness. Carl shifts once more and squeezes the hand of the girl with the cornflower-blue eyes seated next to him.

In another era, in another camp, I sat next to a fire and shifted uneasily on the stony ground. My repeated attempts to appropriate the faith of my parents were desultory and imperfect, as I realized even then. Summer camp was where I tried annually to get it right, to conjure the same piety that my elders showed, to claim the elusive "victory in Christ" that they professed. More often than not, what I felt instead was defeat and inadequacy, a gnawing sense that the persistent doubts I harbored about God and Christianity or my

occasional transgressions of the fundamentalist behavioral codes
would consign me to damnation.

Therein lay the conundrum. What I did not see then—indeed,
could not have seen—was that the "gospel" presented to me was
really an adumbration of the New Testament "good news." Much
of the news I heard was bad—that I deserved damnation for my
sinfulness and that if I didn't do something about it quickly I would
certainly receive my just deserts. The solution to the predicament,
as I understood it, was not to rely utterly on the grace of God, as
Martin Luther recognized in the sixteenth century; rather, the way
of salvation seemed to lay in subscribing to a set of doctrines and
then hewing to strict standards of morality, usually expressed in
negative terms: Don't dance, drink, smoke, swear, or attend movies.

That differed, I suspect, from the message that brought my parents into the evangelical fold. They heard about their sinfulness,
yes, but the complementary element of the law is God's grace, which
saves us in spite of ourselves. Therein, as Luther realized, lies true
freedom and liberation—not in the observance of tiresome moralistic
schemes, but in the celebration of deliverance from sin in Christ.
In time, first-generation evangelical converts learn the canon of
evangelical taboos, but only *after* their experience of grace. For
their children, however, the sequence often is reversed. As an evangelical parent, if you are concerned (understandably) about the spiritual welfare of your children, you will establish guidelines for them
so they will grow up in the faith, or, more accurately, grow up with
all the trappings of godliness. Their "conversions" then become
adolescent (or pre-adolescent) rites of passage, often accompanied
by fabricated emotions in order to convince their peers, their parents, and, most important, themselves of their sincerity.

The difficulty, however, is that Christianity has already been defined for them in behaviorial terms—do this, don't do that—rather
than in terms that Luther would have approved: We all are sinners
by dint of *who we are*, not *what we do*, and therefore we rely abjectly
on God's mercy. For a child in a fundamentalist household, a second-
generation evangelical who already adheres to most of the standards
of "godly" behavior, it is difficult to grasp the significance of any

such conversion, since it demands no alteration of behavior. Instead of assurance, very often they feel anger and resentment because their conversions failed to deliver the religious euphoria and freedom from doubt implied in their parents' promises.

What brings Carl Watkins and Amy Durkin back to Word of Life Island year after year, I suspect, is the same mixture of motivations that took me back to Rainbow Lake summer after summer during my teenage years. Our parents want us there, in the first place, not only because Bible camp offers a sheltered, protective environment, but also because of their abiding hope that we will someday, somehow claim their faith as our own. That's easier to do, of course, in the company of those who have professed their own conversions—certainly much easier than in the alien, godless environment of the public schools back home.

Aside from the perennial, elusive quest for summer romance, we are at camp, many of us, for the same reason that our parents want us there. We too want to claim the faith, not merely to win our parents' approval, but also because of a deep yearning for a religious experience that will meet our expectations and dispel our anxieties. We seek above all an experience that will yield the spiritual fulfillment we see (or think we see) in our parents. That experience comes to some. Others grasp it for a time and then lose it, year after year. Still others find the standards too high and abandon the quest in frustration or despair.

For people of faith, of course, and for people who want to pass their faith to the next generation, there is no easy solution to this predicament. Abandoning children to their own devices violates everything evangelicals believe about nurture, and yet mapping their children's spiritual pilgrimages may, in the end, deprive them of the kind of forceful, dramatic conversion that shaped the parents' lives.

Will evangelicalism, then, inevitably suffer from a gradual enervation of religious ardor as the faith passes from one generation to the next? Sociologists like Max Weber, who talks about the routinization of religion, insist that the answer is yes. Fervent evangelical parents pray that the answer is no.

NOTES

1. *Word of Life 1987 Annual* (Schroon Lake, N.Y.: Word of Life Fellowship, 1986).

2. Chaim Potok, *The Chosen* (New York: Simon & Schuster, 1967).

3. This is a composite description taken from the observation of several evening rallies at the Pine Pavilion during the summers of 1984 and 1987.

4. *Word of Life 1987 Annual.* 1 Tim. 2:9 reads: "women should adorn themselves modestly and sensibly in seemly apparel, not with braided hair or gold or pearls or costly attire" (RSV). These rules apply to all campers in all the Word of Life camps, including the adults at Word of Life Inn.

5. This account of the campfire is entirely fictionalized—the only such passage in this book. It is based, nevertheless, on conversations with campers and counselors at Word of Life Island as well as on observations of meetings there. It is also based on personal experience and reminiscences from many summers at several different Bible camps.

6

Campaign Journal

SATURDAY, FEBRUARY 6, 1988   In the Masonic Lodge in downtown Des Moines, Iowa, I approached a young man who appeared to be in charge of the gathering. "Can you tell me where I might find Sarah Leslie?" I asked. "Oh, you're one of Sarah's people, too," he said, pointing to an attractive woman in her mid-thirties. "So am I."

Sarah Leslie and about one hundred other Republican Party activists had gathered for a G.O.P. precinct caucus training session in order to prepare for the Iowa caucuses coming up in two days. For Leslie, however, an evangelical who understands the political process better than many politicians, the session was just a refresher course; in fact, she had many other things on the agenda today, so she slipped out early.

Next stop: a live radio interview in Norwalk, Iowa, on KWKY, a thousand-watt station that features evangelical Christian programming. With the caucuses only two days away, most of the real organizing is completed; it's a matter now of seeing that "her people," most of them evangelicals who are newly active in the political process, go to the caucuses and make their voices heard. "We've actually been working on the 1988 caucuses for about five years now," she told me. "Now we want to make sure that our people get out on Monday night and express their views."

The radio provides an effective vehicle for doing just that. Sarah Leslie is president of the Iowa Right to Life Committee, an anti-abortion organization, and Donald Thompson, host of the radio program, played one of Leslie's radio commercials encouraging voters to attend the caucuses. "Remember," the spot concluded, "if you don't attend, if you don't participate, you're giving up more than a vote. You're giving up an opportunity to change the pro-abortion, anti-family agenda at work in our country today. Don't miss this chance to represent life on February eighth."

A battery of other commercials followed, all of them urging listeners to attend the caucuses, then another of Leslie's radio spots. "First, we had abortion, and they said that was all they wanted." The voice was Sarah Leslie's. "Twenty million babies ago. Then we had infanticide, killing handicapped newborn babies. Now we have euthanasia, killing the elderly and sick. Will you be their next victim?" The commercial concluded: "Vote for life at your precinct caucus on February eighth. If you care, you'll be there." Yet another commercial implored listeners to "vote for Jack Kemp, the pro-family candidate who can win the presidency."

Two days before the Iowa precinct caucuses, it was clear that a real fight had developed for the evangelical vote. All the Republican candidates have courted this constituency, but the two who claimed the most support were Kemp, a Republican congressman from upstate New York, and Pat Robertson, the former head of the Christian Broadcasting Network who resigned his Southern Baptist ordination just prior to announcing his candidacy. Both had campaigned feverishly in Iowa, although the consensus was that Robertson had the superior organization. Indeed, Robertson promised to surprise the pundits with his showing on Monday night, and he claimed that he would bring in thousands of conservative evangelicals, many of whom had never participated in caucuses before. Kemp, on the other hand, who bills himself as the true ideological heir of Ronald Reagan, had sought to shore up his base among conservatives of all stripes, including evangelicals, by emphasizing his opposition to abortion.

Although Sarah Leslie, as president of a federal political action committee, feels she can take no public stand in support of one candidate or another, she privately favors Kemp in large part because she feels he has a better shot at the nomination. On the radio program, however, she said only that there are five pro-life candidates running for president; no Democrat in the race passes muster, but all the Republicans, except for Alexander Haig, whom Leslie regarded as "soft" on the issue, are considered acceptable to the pro-life activists. Part of the reason why the Iowa Right to Life Committee has endorsed no candidate, Leslie explained, is that "we want to stay united on our issue."

Thompson, the host of the radio program, announced that Leslie would take questions from listeners. One query regarding the term "reproductive freedom" came in during a commercial break. When Thompson asked Leslie if she wanted to tackle that one, she replied, "Oh yeah, I've got some good ammo on that." Back on the air, Leslie explained that "reproductive freedom" simply means abortion-on-demand, that it was just a code term that the pro-abortion lobby uses to camouflage its agenda.

Another question came from a woman who said she was a registered Democrat but had Republican views. Did she have to attend a Democratic caucus? "No," Leslie said. "The Republican caucus may want her to somehow identify herself as a Republican. She may go to a Republican caucus, but she may have to re-register if the caucus asks her to do so." Leslie has heard that question a thousand times by now, coming from Democrats who are disgruntled with the failure of the Democratic Party to oppose abortion.

Thompson asked Leslie why Christians, evangelicals, should attend the caucuses Monday night. Leslie explained that the eyes of the nation will be on Iowa Monday, and this presents an opportunity for the evangelical voice to be heard around the country. "Look at it this way," she explained. "You're standing on a stage, and the spotlight's on you. And we're Christians. If we as Christians don't speak out, nobody else is going to do it."

Thompson, who would be attending a caucus for the first time on Monday, chimed in. "If you believe that these children should not be aborted, then get out and do something about it. It may make the difference."

"That's right," Leslie added. "You might be that one vote at the precinct caucus that might turn it into a pro-life caucus."

After the radio program and on the way to lunch, Leslie explained her background and how she became involved in the fight against abortion. Sarah Leslie grew up in Plainfield, Illinois, a small town southwest of Chicago. Her parents were quite active in the civil rights movement, she said, so it was not much of a jump for her to become involved in the pro-life movement, which she regards as a logical extension of civil rights.

"I had a good friend when I was in high school. She had a boyfriend, and they started messing around sexually. Pretty soon she thought she was pregnant, but she was too scared to tell anyone or talk about it, and by the time she was four or five months along and she was starting to show, she figured she had no choice but to tell her folks. So she did, and they took her to some small-town doctor, and he told them about an abortion clinic in New York. So they flew her out to this abortion clinic. She had no idea at that time what an abortion was; all she knew was that it would take away her pregnancy. When she came back, she had a horror story to tell me. And she told it and told it and told it. She would call me every day for six months and cry and cry. The story was that she had to go through induced labor—horrible pain—and she was all alone. When she had finished giving birth to a dead baby, she saw dead babies in buckets all over the clinic. And this was legal in New York. The whole place was filthy and dirty. There were bugs crawling, there were mice. It was awful. But the most horrible aspect to her was that she killed her baby and that she'd had no choice in the matter. She just couldn't get over the whole experience.

"When I think about that ordeal," Leslie said, "I realize that my friend's experience had an impact on me, too. It affected my life a lot more than I realized at the time."

There were several more stops along the way to the presidency of the Iowa Right to Life Committee. An interest in Eastern mysticism led Leslie into the drug culture around 1970. She recalls hallucinations, experimentation with heroin, speed, alcohol. She remembers the death of a friend from an overdose. "Four months after I had gotten involved in the drug scene, I had lost my boyfriend. I made a conscious decision one day—it was September of 1970—that I did not care anymore about anything." Leslie seriously contemplated suicide and credits "the power of the Lord" with sparing her life.

Leslie left high school early on a junior-admission program at Drake University in Des Moines. "I had some friends in high school who were involved in the Jesus freak movement, and I had sat down with one girl and asked her to tell me what she believed. When I got to Drake I was still searching, so I went to some Inter-Varsity meetings and became friends with some of the people there. I did some speed one night that really knocked me out, and the next evening as I was waiting for my friends I encountered a girl with red hair who was holding a Bible in her arms. She looked at me and said, 'Do you know Jesus?' Right then and there, I accepted the Lord. It was November 12, 1971. I didn't do anything. The Lord came to me. That's when I became a Christian.

"This girl talked to me for awhile and then said that she would bring some friends by because I needed to be discipled. The people she brought to the door the next day were from Berkeley, California. They'd been through that whole scene, and they'd become Christians. They were Jesus freaks. They discipled me for the next six months, and I couldn't have done it without them. I never have seen or heard from them since then. All I can say is that they knew exactly how to disciple someone who'd been through what I'd been through. They just knew all the right Bible verses and how Satan was going to tempt me."

Leslie had organized a luncheon at the Crystal Tree, a posh restaurant near the airport in Des Moines. As the guests assembled, Senator Paul Simon of Illinois, a candidate for the Democratic nomination, walked over to the table and shook hands all around. Except for a visitor from New York, however, Simon's effort was wasted; everyone else at the table considered him an unacceptable candidate because of his pro-choice position, despite the fact that he is a devout

Lutheran and the son and brother of Lutheran ministers. It was an awkward moment. When Simon asked who or what the group represented, there was some dissembling. Leslie finally answered, "Oh, this is just sort of an ad hoc group." The senator seemed satisfied, if a bit confused, and walked away.

The purpose of the luncheon was to rally the faithful. Those in attendance included Leslie; her husband, Lynn, an assistant director of personnel for the City of Des Moines; Donald Thompson, the radio host and a filmmaker;* the Reverend Craig Nelson, a recent graduate of Grace Theological Seminary in Indiana and now pastor of the Easton Baptist Church in Des Moines; and Mary Ann Gilbert from Indianola, Iowa, who handed me a business card identifying her as field representative for a Webster City-based organization called Iowans for Israel. Two members of the party arrived late: Congressman Chris Smith from New Jersey, who was in Iowa for the weekend to campaign for Jack Kemp, and Gaius Ives, the man from the Kemp campaign responsible for chauffeuring Smith to various engagements. Although he had known the congressman only a few hours, it appeared Ives was already a dedicated sycophant.

Smith, formerly the executive director of the New Jersey Right to Life organization, won election to Congress in 1980. At lunch, he emphasized his anti-abortion credentials and repeated other conservative nostrums such as support for the contras in Central America and the necessity to remain vigilant against the Soviets. But he was also eager to push Kemp. Many of his sentences began, "Jack and I served together on a committee that . . . " or, "Jack and I both feel that. . . . "

Most of the people there already were in the Kemp camp, so Smith was preaching to the choir. The conversation around the table soon turned to expectations for Monday night. "Totally new groups of people are coming out to the caucuses for the first time," Sarah Leslie announced. Someone else reported that various evangelical churches were calling their congregations and telling them to go to the caucuses. The excitement already was building, and the consensus around the table was that there would be a large body of

*This is the same Donald Thompson whose profile appears in Chapter 3.

evangelicals at the caucuses this year who had never attended before.

The Iowa Right to Life Committee occupies a small suite of base-ment-level offices in northwest Des Moines. On the wall opposite the front door is a painting of Jesus kneeling in pain with an aborted fetus in His right hand. On another wall a poster reads: THE BABY WAS GONE . . . TAMMY HAD AN ABORTION AT 16. Elsewhere, a pho-tograph of a fetus carries the inscription, "Speak out for the silenced minority," and a copy of a proclamation by the governor of Iowa declares January 22, 1986, as "Respect Life Day" across the state.

Two days before the caucuses, there was an air of dishevelment in the empty offices, the desks and tables filled with dog-eared telephone directories and empty soda bottles. The state maps taped to the walls showing congressional and legistative districts and the county maps showing precincts were marked and worn. On the floor in front of Leslie's desk lay a crib mattress and a child's pillow, and a large box of toys sat in one of the back offices.

Leslie volunteers her time for the Iowa Right to Life Committee, and so her children, Colin, Kate, and Meggie, often spend their afternoons in the office. Leslie has a woman come into her home three days a week to care for the children, but the fifty dollars every week is taking a toll on the family budget, and as soon as the caucuses are past, she said, she and Lynn will have to sit down and make some tough decisions. She spoke about the possibility of selling one of their cars or even their home, a modest, two-story frame house in West Des Moines, in order to make ends meet. Still, she harbors no regrets. "Most of us have such a conscience about our issue that if we've got available funds we'll sink them all into the cause, and we'll sacrifice if we have to. Sometimes you feel like a martyr, but most of the time you just figure that's the cost of doing something you believe in." She paused. "I think there's also a sense of urgency to the movement. Among those of us who are actively working, something is broken in our hearts. Every day I am painfully aware that four thousand babies are being murdered—every single day."

The Leslie children are robust and active. They romped freely amidst the congenial chaos of the family household in the Valley Junction area of West Des Moines. "We've got three kids in a two-bedroom house," Leslie had told me as we approached the front door. Meggie, the youngest, was born in August 1986, but shortly thereafter, Leslie, a nursing mother, carted young Meggie along the campaign trail, working for the re-elections of Governor Terry Branstad and Senator Roger Jepsen (Branstad was successful; Jepsen lost to Tom Harkin, a Democrat). Meggie and her siblings competed with a flurry of phone calls for the attention of their mother, but about four o'clock in the afternoon, Leslie disappeared upstairs and, in what seemed like record time, made three beds, administered three baths, and folded a pile of laundry.

Leslie alternates between housewife and political activist with practiced ease. The night before, as she was preparing two dishes for a church potluck dinner, she received word that the Iowa Senate was considering legislation to establish a mandatory curriculum on contraception and family planning for the public schools. She excused herself early from the dinner, went to the office and ran off several hundred copies of a "legislative alert" that she then took back to the potluck dinner. There, the pastor and other members of the First Assembly of God helped her stuff envelopes so that her network of activists around the state would be poised to lobby against the legislation when it came up again the following week. "In this business," she said, "you see the power of being a Christian. The enemy would just come in like a flood if we didn't stand there."

SUNDAY, FEBRUARY 7, 1988   St. John's Lutheran Church, at the corner of Sixth Avenue and Keosauqua, is one of the venerable congregations in downtown Des Moines. On the Sunday before the Iowa caucuses, the Reverend Dr. Jerry Schmalenberger wanted to encourage his congregation to attend the caucuses. "Christ instructs us to take part in the government in which we live," he said. "I believe if we mainline, reasonable Christians don't take part in current politics, there will be those highly organized and much more fervent who will. They will represent Christianity in a way that is almost foreign to us and certainly will be an embarrassment to many. It will be a bitter pill for our brand of Christianity in the future."[1]

Schmalenberger clearly had his eyes on the evangelicals when he warned that "single-issue voters are the most dangerous." "Fundamentalists frighten me," he confessed, although he acknowledged them as "our brothers and sisters in Christ." The pastor assured his congregation that he would attend his neighborhood caucus. "If I go to a Democratic caucus, I'll do my best to insist that the caucus be honest about promising all sorts of give-aways with no tax increase and still reduce the national debt," he said. "If I go to a Republican caucus, I'll try my best to let others at the caucus know you can be a Christian and a 'Bible believer' without being a far–right-wing believe-as-I-do-or-you're-going-to-hell-for-sure person."

"We are also Bible-believing Christians," Schmalenberger in-sisted. "But the Holy Spirit speaks a different message to us from the same inspired word of God. It says we are to be peacemakers and learn to love our enemies and turn the other cheek and go the second mile." Schmalenberger stopped short of endorsing any po-litical candidate or party, but he said he wanted a president who "will stand up for my human rights to dissent," for the rights of women, including "complete reproductive rights over their own bodies."

Such liberal notions do not sit well with most evangelicals, es-pecially amidst the highly charged political atmosphere in Iowa this weekend. When Schmalenberger's sermon came up in my conver-sations with Sarah Leslie, she laughed derisively and dismissed it with a wave of her hand. Across town on this Sunday morning, a much larger congregation heard a different message.

The First Federated Church in northwest Des Moines is anything but old and venerable. It is one of the new breed of evangelical churches that looks more like a concert auditorium or a sporting arena than a church. First Federated features television floodlights, roving cameramen, canned music, applause, blow-dried preachers, and a sound system that will knock your necktie askew. Politics was there, too. The pastor, the Reverend Tom Allen, introduced Pat Robertson's daughter and son-in-law, Senator Robert and Elizabeth Dole, and Senator Charles Grassley, one of Dole's principal sup-porters in Iowa. "We need to be in prayer for the caucuses tomorrow night," Allen said, and his own pastoral prayer echoed the same themes that many of the Republican candidates had been sounding out on the stump. We need in this country to choose "righteousness over unrighteousness" and "that which is moral over that which is immoral," he said.[2]

Sunday evening services the day before the caucuses gave the candidates another chance to ply the religious vote. At six o'clock, the Reverend Paul Bawden of the Westchester Evangelical Free Church introduced Congressman Jack Kemp to his congregation and asked Kemp for a "brief word of encouragement." Kemp, who has a well-earned reputation for being anything but brief, stepped to the pulpit, introduced his wife, Joanne, and asked, "How can you be a Christian and *not* be involved in the political process?" He said there were three "great issues" in this political campaign: "the defense of Western Judeo-Christian values," the defense of "family and family values," and "the defense of the free-enterprise system." Kemp spoke of James Madison's "dear, dear Christian mother" and asserted that the U.S. Constitution was "inspired by the inspired word of the Bible." After about twenty minutes, Kemp urged the congregation to participate in the caucuses the next night and then walked down the aisle, pumping hands the whole way, just like any other candidate might work a union hall. At the narthex, the press entourage rejoined him, and they all drove off into the night toward another evangelical Sunday evening service.[3]

MONDAY, FEBRUARY 8, 1988   Caucus day. An inch or two of snow blanketed the state during the night, a reminder that Iowa lives according to the rhythms of nature, not the vagaries of the political process.

Maxine Sielman and I agreed to trade interviews this morning in Norwalk. Sielman, a gray-haired mother of five and now a grand-mother, hosts the "Breakfast at KWKY" program each weekday morning, a show heard by nearly one hundred thousand people around the state. After the program, it was my turn to ask questions.

Sielman, a member of First Federated Church in Des Moines, said that she had been involved in party politics for only a couple of years, but in that brief time she had been elected to the county and then the state central committee of the Republican Party. Yet 1988 would be her first presidential precinct caucus.

Abortion, she said, was the main issue that brought her into the

political process. "I was concerned as both a parent and a grand-
parent with what was happening in our country. I was ashamed that
I had not been a voice when the Supreme Court legalized abortion
fifteen years earlier." Sielman's range of political interests has since
broadened. "I have a real concern for defense spending," she said.
"It bothers me to think that we can trust the Soviets now. I heard
it said that a number of years ago Daniel Ortega of Nicaragua came
to this country with his military uniform, his slicked-back hair, and
his professional glasses, and he was a communist. He comes now
to our country with his designer clothes, his long hairstyle, and his
designer glasses, but do we realize he's still a communist? I think
there are some values being lost because we're not willing to back
a country in trouble, whereas but for the grace of God that country
could be us.

"When the last shot is fired, I want to be there, knowing that I
did everything that I could do to make a difference. I really do
believe that our freedoms are being taken from us one by one. I do
not have the right to pray in school, and yet my children are being
taught witchcraft in school. I don't have the freedom to express my
views as a Bible-believing Christian in the schools, yet at the same
time humanists can instruct my children. Here in Iowa, in fact, one
parent was insulted because there was a prayer given at a baccalaureate service. There are no more baccalaureate services in Iowa
because of this one parent. Now I as a parent wish to have my
freedoms respected and maintained, and yet this individual, I feel,
has infringed upon my rights as a citizen. Where is the balance in
all this? There are times when I would love to find another Plymouth
Rock and get in my boat and look for that free country where everyone would be free again and be respected as a human being and
given the dignity that each human being is entitled to."

Sielman insisted that it is not so much because she is an evangelical
that she became interested in politics. "I'm a grandmother and I'm
a mother and I'm a woman, and I've had enough. It's time now to
pick up my skillet and my rolling pin and charge. It's time to say,
'I'm a homemaker, and I'm proud of it, and I carry that title with
dignity.' "

Who's the enemy? "Satan. We're living in Satan's territory. This is spiritual warfare that takes many forms. It invades television. The media, the way the media has taken control of this country. Abortion. When the history of our age will be written, the books will ask, 'Where were the real Americans when they were slaughtering millions of babies—innocent babies?' The most dangerous place to be these days is inside a mother's womb. Where were the Americans when they allowed the minds of their children, the next generation of leaders, to be polluted by the filth that was coming through the television set? We are a blind, selfish generation."

In addition to her other activities, Sielman serves as head of the Iowa chapter of Concerned Women for America, a conservative, evangelical, Washington-based lobby organization that claims over five hundred thousand members across the country. "I think women are the key to turning this nation around. I firmly believe that this is why Satan went to Eve, not Adam. I think the influence that women have on society Satan knew back in the Garden of Eden. He knew that if he could convince Eve, she could convince Adam. And so, therefore, if Satan can deceive women about the role God created them for, then the women will be able to confuse and influence men. I firmly believe the role of a woman today is to nurture our next generation. She has the power within her hands to either make or break a nation. A good woman can make a bad man good, but a bad woman can make a good man bad. A woman has tremendous influence upon her husband and her children. That frightens me, in a way, because I think women today have been confused about their roles as women. The secret to a woman's role, I believe, is authority and being submissive. And I feel that just as God asked the woman to bear children because He knew that she wouldn't want to put up with a pregnant man for nine months or He knew that a man could not tolerate the pain of having a child, God also asked her to be submissive, which is one of the hardest things that a woman is asked to do. But therein comes real peace. As we submit to God and become all we can be under God's authority, we find fulfillment. There's no limit to what women can do today."

Can they change the country? "Women *will* change the country. Women are the real key for turning this country around. When women can find their value in their relationship with Jesus Christ and see themselves as God made them, this frees them to go about doing whatever it is that God puts in their lives. I firmly believe that God has always worked through women. I think He's looking for women today to work through."

This idealization of femininity and domesticity is a relatively new phenomenon in Christian history, dating only to the nineteenth century. Historically, Christian theology has viewed women as temptresses, the descendants of Eve. In the nineteenth century, however, as men began to seek their livelihoods outside of the home and the farm, women, with the increased leisure time available to them because of the growing commercial economy that freed them from making soap and clothes and butchering meat, began to view the home as their particular domain. A passel of Victorian magazines advertised consumer goods through the mail and offered advice about decorating. Whereas the seventeenth-century Puritan father had assumed responsibility for the spiritual well-being of his family, Protestant women in the nineteenth century came to take responsibility both for the home and for the religious nurture of their families. The clergy lionized the piety of women and held them up as models of true godliness. Even Alexis de Tocqueville observed that in America, "women are the protectors of morals."[4]

The ideal of feminine spirituality and domesticity still has a powerful hold on the evangelical subculture, as I had discovered at Dallas Seminary. "Much like a thermostat, a woman determines the emotional climate in her home," a female student at Dallas had written in the seminary's magazine. "No other part of the world will be more affected by her influence than the place she lives, loves, and nurtures every day."[5] Men, who traffic daily with the world, are seen as vulnerable to worldly enticements, whereas a godly wife and mother will resist such blandishments. The feminist movement of the past quarter-century has bypassed most evangelical women precisely because it threatens these Victorian myths. Phyllis Schlafly, who led the successful fight against ratification of the proposed equal rights amendment to the Constitution, remains enormously popular in evangelical circles, despite the fact that she is Roman Catholic.

There is another dimension to the mythology that has energized evangelical political involvement over the past decade. In addition to the domestic ideal and the myth of feminine spiritual superiority, many evangelicals also subscribe to the political myth about America's "Christian" origins that Kemp alluded to on Sunday evening when he referred to James Madison's "dear, dear Christian mother" and to the belief that the Constitution was inspired by the inspired Word of God. Evangelicals have been eager in recent years to recast American history according to the shibboleths of the political right. These new histories have asserted (in the face of contrary evidence) that America was settled almost exclusively for religious reasons, and this revisionism has also given rise to rather comic attempts to transform people like Thomas Jefferson, Thomas Paine, James Madison, and Abraham Lincoln into something like fundamentalists.[6]

But these mythologies, both domestic and political, serve a useful purpose for activist evangelicals because they conjure images of a halcyon past when evangelical Protestant values prevailed in American culture, when a woman tended her domain in the household and thereby ensured the spiritual welfare of her family. The mythologies, no matter how far removed from reality, energize political involvement by serving as constant reminders of how decent and righteous America *used* to be and how far we have yet to go in order to reclaim those ideals.

Beyond the mythology, however, there is a symbolism that represents the displacement evangelicals feel in a pluralistic world that they believe has turned against them and their values. What symbolizes their alienation and vulnerability better than anything else is a fetus.[7] "The most dangerous place to be these days," Maxine Sielman had said, "is inside a mother's womb." There is nothing more pure and innocent than a fetus. Indeed, the fetus serves as a marvelous symbol, not only for its Freudian or psychoanalytical connotations of crawling back into the womb to escape the buffetings of the world, but also because it represents evangelicals' own sense of beleaguerment and helplessness. Despite their political successes in the past decade, contemporary fundamentalists, like their predecessors in the 1920s, still see American culture as alien and their own survival as precarious. They must exercise extraordinary vigilance lest the forces of evil and darkness, usually identified as "secular humanism," overtake them.

I don't mean to trivialize the issue. Many evangelicals (and others) have put forward persuasive and even eloquent arguments against abortion; I find some of those arguments compelling, and most of them sincere. But it strikes me, at first glance, as an odd issue to serve as a rallying point for evangelical political activism. There is nothing in the Bible that *explicitly* condemns abortion, and the pro-life position does not appear to arise out of any abstract devotion to the sanctity of human life. Many pro-life evangelicals, for instance, also favor capital punishment, and the majority of evangelicals have seldom shied away from the exercise of military force.* I wonder, then, if evangelicals have reacted so vociferously to the abortion issue because they identify with the vulnerability of the fetus, its susceptibility to larger, alien forces outside the womb. Abortion, moreover, blatantly violates their two-pronged mythology. First, it contradicts the political myth of America as a Christian nation because it provides them with irrefutable evidence of the political process run amok; the Supreme Court, after all, sanctioned abortion in the first place, and venal, ungodly politicians have refused to override that travesty. Second, abortion violates the domestic Victorian myth of feminine spirituality: If women guarded their purity and contented themselves with their God-given roles as mothers and housewives they would not seek abortions in the first place.

For people like Sarah Leslie, Maxine Sielman, and countless other evangelicals, then, there may be a sense of urgency to their political activism that transcends mere advocacy. They, like the fetus, are engaged in a struggle for survival in what they view as an alien and threatening culture, and God is surely on their side in fending off the slaughter of the innocents.

Maxine Sielman believes that one of the foot-soldiers in this crusade against evil in central Iowa is DeAnne Sikes, from nearby Indianola. When I talked with her on the phone several weeks earlier to arrange an interview, Sikes, a full-time homemaker and

---

*In this respect, the "pro-life" moniker, which the activists prefer to "anti-abortion," is something of a misnomer.

mother of three, spoke about the importance of "lobbying from the kitchen table" in those few quiet moments during the day when the dishes are done, beds made, and the children are either napping or in school. Until recently, she told me in her living room in Indianola, she had never written a letter to a senator or a congressman, never lobbied for anything. Now, she said, "they know me by name. I now realize I have a right to walk into that office and let them know how I feel. A couple of years ago I would *never* have done that. I would have been so intimidated."

No more. Through her involvement in Concerned Women for America, Sikes has learned to channel her indignation into the political process, arguing for continued aid to the contras of Central America, for a strong defense, against sex education in public schools, and against abortion. "I'm furious about abortion," she said, her voice rising. "Nothing makes me angrier than to think about people murdering human beings, especially these late-term fetuses. I know now that my vote is going to make a difference. Senators and legislators *do* listen. They have to listen when there's hundreds of thousands of us saying 'This has to stop.' "

The Iowa chapter of Concerned Women for America is still fairly new, but both Maxine Sielman and DeAnne Sikes pointed to one victory that they considered significant. "When we got back from the national convention in Washington," Sikes said, "we were all fired up and full of patriotism. We met in a public library in Des Moines, and we wanted to open the meeting with the Pledge of Allegiance, but there were no American flags anywhere in the library. We made some phone calls and got the American Legion to take it on as a project and supply all the public libraries with American flags. We've gotten so lackadaisical in America that children in many schools don't even say the Pledge of Allegiance. In Nevada, Iowa, they leave out 'under God' and just say 'one nation, indivisible, with liberty and justice for all.' We just can't let that happen."

I asked Sikes, a Robertson supporter, what was at stake in the Iowa caucuses that evening. "I think tonight, for the first time ever, America is going to see grass-roots, evangelical, fundamentalist people crawl out from where we've been hiding in our pews and saying, 'This is how I feel; I'm supporting a candidate who stands for traditional values.' I am tired of the trend in this country of a few very liberal Americans controlling what happens." Sikes singled out the American Civil Liberties Union and People for the American Way as examples of pernicious liberal influences that she hopes to counteract by her involvement. "This is all totally new to me," she acknowledged. "I think most of the evangelicals, the church folks who will attend the caucuses this evening, have never been to a caucus before."

Back in Des Moines at the offices of the Iowa Right to Life Committee, Sarah Leslie was surprisingly calm and unruffled (even she seemed a bit surprised at this) at mid-afternoon on caucus day. She had fielded more calls asking for candidates' positions on abortion, and she had again coached others on what to expect at their precinct caucuses. "I guess we've done all we can do," she said, locking the office door. "We've got prayer chains going right now all across the state." She still expected a big turnout from her people.

At the first precinct in West Des Moines, both the Republicans and the Democrats met at the West Des Moines Community Center, albeit on opposite sides of a partition. Sarah Leslie was responsible for convening the Republican caucus at seven o'clock, and by the time I arrived at six forty-five, it was clear that the Robertson people were present in large numbers. "There's already a Robertson move to oust me as chairman," Leslie informed me as soon as I walked into the room. That movement never developed, but the Robertson people dominated the caucus at will. After checking the credentials of everyone in the room, Leslie called the caucus to order and then distributed tiny sheets of paper listing the names of the Republican candidates. When the straw poll was tallied, Pat Robertson received thirty-eight votes, nearly fifty percent of the eighty-one Republicans in attendance. Robert Dole was next with seventeen, George Bush had twelve, Kemp eight, Pierre du Pont four, and one expressed no preference.

If Leslie, a Kemp supporter, was a bit stunned by the results, she betrayed no hint of it but rather continued with the business of the caucus. She opened the floor for nominations to the county convention, and each nominee then came to the front of the room and declared which candidate he or she favored and why. The Robertson people predominated. "He best represents what is good for the family," one Robertson candidate for delegate said. "I support Pat Robertson based on his Christian beliefs," said another. An eighteen-year-old girl affirmed her support for Robertson and added, "I think it's really neat that teenagers can get involved in the political process."

Virtually all of the Robertson candidates for delegate conceded that this was the first precinct caucus they had ever attended. That clearly engendered resentment from the party regulars, some of whom allowed their frustration to boil over with angry warnings that Robertson was unelectable and that the presence of his supporters represented an unwelcome intrusion. "I'm a sixth-generation Republican," one man shouted, "and what I've seen here tonight is disgusting. This man will never be elected president, and if you insist on pushing him on the Republican Party, that's the quickest way to make sure that the people next door elect *their* man as president," he said, pointing to the partition.

Such appeals were largely unavailing. Of the four delegates elected from the precinct to the county convention, two were for Robertson, one for Kemp, and one (Sarah Leslie, a Kemp partisan) nominally uncommitted.

The crowd had dwindled considerably by the time the caucus got around to passing resolutions for the party platform. What followed was a kind of free-for-all, a conservative wish list. Proposals in favor of a balanced-budget amendment to the Constitution, a line-item veto for the president, mandatory retirement for Supreme Court justices, and the abolition of the Electoral College all passed by acclamation. "Hold the line on taxes," one man shouted; the caucus agreed. The issue of education aroused the most interest and the most passion. The caucus resolved to abolish the Department of Education, to allow a moment of silence for prayer in public schools, to mandate the daily recitation of the Pledge of Allegiance, and to support the voucher system, which would effectively provide public support for private, parochial, and religious schools by giving each child a voucher for use at any school of the parents' choice. When the discussion turned to school-based clinics, Leslie finally had her moment. The sentiment of the caucus was to oppose school clinics which, conservatives contend, exist primarily to provide contraceptives and abortion referrals. Leslie, as chairman of the caucus, gently directed the group's attention to a sheet of resolutions that the Iowa Right to Life Committee had prepared for this purpose. The caucus unanimously concurred with the printed resolution opposing school-based clinics and thereby declared itself, by Sarah Leslie's definition, a "pro-life caucus."

For the national media, whose trucks and equipment blanketed downtown Des Moines, the real story of the evening was Pat Robertson. Robertson's "secret army," as it had become known in recent weeks, turned out in impressive numbers, giving the former television evangelist twenty-five percent of the Republican vote, a second-place showing behind Robert Dole's thirty-seven percent but well ahead of George Bush's nineteen percent. Jack Kemp won the allegiance of only eleven percent of Iowa's Republican voters.

At Robertson's headquarters at the International Trade Center in Des Moines, the crowd was abuzz with excitement. The candidate himself appeared several times, smiled benignly at the cheering supporters above him in the mezzanine, and then rode off in his limousine. "It's almost, like we say, you've got to give God the credit," Robertson declared in an interview.[8]

A young woman standing next to me in the crowd had driven all the way from East Lansing, Michigan, to be part of the victory celebration. When I asked if she was surprised by Robertson's strong second-place showing, she hesitated, smiled, and said, "I was hoping he'd come in first." On the other side of me, two local campaign workers festooned with Robertson buttons clearly were relishing their candidate's success as they watched the networks' coverage on a bank of television sets. "This is big news. This is big news," one of them said, almost breathless with excitement. "Satan has controlled politics for too long." His friend agreed. "I guess everybody knows now that Christians are serious."

SATURDAY, FEBRUARY 13, 1988 Cherry Marsh of West Lebanon, New Hampshire, has never met Sarah Leslie, DeAnne Sikes, or Maxine Sielman, but she was grateful indeed for their efforts to propel the issues that are important to her to the forefront of the political debate in Iowa. As a leader of Concerned Women for America in New Hampshire, Marsh is also disturbed about legalized abortion and what she considers the lack of moral leadership in America.

Her candidate is Pat Robertson. Indeed, hers is a Pat Robertson family, with a bumper sticker that reads "Women for Robertson '88" on their yellow Chevrolet sedan. Cherry's husband, Keith, is one of the pastors of the Dartmouth Area Christian Fellowship, a pentecostal congregation in Hanover, New Hampshire. Even Hannah, their five-year-old daughter, has caught the campaign spirit. She refers affectionately to "Pat" in the same way that other children might express their attachment to a teddy bear or a pet turtle. "When Pat becomes president, he won't say that, will he, Mommy?" Hannah said after her mother repeated one of the slogans of the pro-choice movement.

During the car ride between Hanover and Concord, about an hour away, I had the opportunity to ask Keith and Cherry Marsh, both political novices, about their involvement in Robertson's campaign. They remembered well their first encounter with Robertson at a pastors' luncheon in Concord, the state capital. "We really were impressed," Cherry said. At that time, Keith added, Robertson hadn't yet announced his candidacy but was traveling around the country soliciting advice about whether or not he should run for president. "The consensus of the meeting," Keith said, "was, 'God bless you, Pat; we don't think you can win, but you can raise some issues in the course of the campaign.' "

Both Keith and Cherry Marsh have since changed their minds about Robertson's chances. After his strong showing in Iowa, the Marshes became convinced that Robertson will eventually become the Republican nominee for president in 1988. Keith predicted a second-place finish in New Hampshire's primary on Tuesday, but added, "I think he could win." Indeed, both Keith and Cherry exuded an air of expectation, even giddiness, about their candidate's chances. Robertson, they pointed out, is well-organized in the South, where the so-called Super Tuesday primaries would take place in less than a month. "That's what's so fun working on this campaign," Keith said. "You know you're not alone." Cherry agreed.

"We women volunteer in the evening, bring coffee to the campaign office, pray together, and get on the phones," she said. "We feel that we're making an impact. We're raising the standard of right-eousness in this state. It takes time, it takes work to leave our cozy, warm homes. But it's been fun. We're all rookies, really."

Rookies. Yes, that was the word. At the Robertson celebration in downtown Des Moines the previous Monday, I had been struck by the demeanor of the crowd. They seemed uncomfortable, a bit out of place with all the flummery that accompanies a political campaign. Many seemed to wear their campaign buttons and the styrofoam "straw" hats uneasily, as though they weren't quite sure about the protocol of politics, like a high school junior at the prom uncertain about which lapel to pin his boutonnière on, his eyes darting fur-tively to search for clues from others in the room. The celebration at Robertson headquarters, though loud and jubilant, lacked the raucous abandon and the unabashed silliness of most political rallies. Many of those in attendance looked uncomfortable, as though they would rather be home in front of the television or in church at Wednesday night prayer meeting.

Indeed, according to polls, about three-fifths of Pat Robertson's supporters in Iowa had participated in the caucuses for the first time. The same pattern seemed to obtain in New Hampshire, where evangelicals like Keith and Cherry Marsh, with no previous en-gagement in politics, were becoming involved in the political pro-cess. "History will remember Pat Robertson because he's showing us Christians that we're a lot bigger than we thought we were," Keith said. "This campaign is knitting a lot of people together."

A few minutes after we arrived at the New Hampshire Highway Hotel in Concord, a huge Robertson motorcade, stretching two miles in length and numbering about two hundred vehicles, pulled into the parking lot. Cars, pickup trucks, even some motor homes all wore large, royal-blue Robertson signs. Robertson supporters emerged shivering from the cold into the lobby of the sprawling, two-story, white frame hotel. Campaign organizers had arranged for a buffet dinner upstairs at the hotel. The Marshes opted for Burger King down the street; I decided to mingle with the Robertson peo-ple. On the way to dinner, Madeline Flagg, who described herself as a born-again Christian from Nashua, New Hampshire, said that this was her first political campaign and that she had joined up with Robertson because "he understands the issues that affect us as a family. He believes in a strong defense. We don't feel we can trust the Soviets." Robertson's showing in Iowa, she said, indicated that he represents "the true conservative voters, not just born-again Christians."

I heard similar sentiments at the dinner table, many of them mixed with the kind of starchy conservativism for which New Hampshire is famous. When I asked Frank Anderson why he had settled on Robertson in 1988, he said the decision hadn't been that difficult. He quickly ruled out Bush, Dole, and Haig because of their ties to the Trilateral Commission and the Council on Foreign Relations. Jack Kemp, he said, was "too much of a statist." Beverlie Tuttle of Danbury, a born-again Christian for ten years and a member of Concerned Women for America, is a veteran of political battles. She and her husband publish a newspaper called *The Truth*, the cover of which carried a picture of a wooden horse with a sign that read: "The I.N.F. Treaty is a TROJAN HORSE." Tuttle believes that Ronald Reagan sold out to the communists by signing the treaty limiting nuclear warheads in Europe, and she cloaked her opposition to the treaty in biblical terms. "The Bible tells us not to be unequally yoked with unbelievers," she said. "Signing a treaty with atheists is being unequally yoked."[9]

For the past two weekends I'd been lunching and dining with conservatives, be they Jack Kemp's people or Pat Robertson's, and I'd grown a bit weary of the steady diet of paranoia and conspiracy theories. I heard endless accounts of Russian perfidy, the conspiracy of liberals in Washington, the abject failure of public schools to educate children (this argument is especially curious in Iowa, which for years has enjoyed the highest literacy rate in the nation). Pat Robertson and, to some extent, Jack Kemp apparently have tapped into this discontent. Some of the printed banners Robertson's campaign distributed read: NO AID TO COMMUNISTS, RESTORE FAMILY VALUES, AMERICA FIRST IN DEFENSE, and IMPROVE OUR SCHOOLS.

Back downstairs in the New Hampshire Highway Hotel, a large

crowd gathered in the ballroom for an evening rally featuring the candidate himself. Reporters and photographers milled about the room talking to Robertson loyalists and snapping pictures of entire families dressed in Robertson tee-shirts. At about seven o'clock, an energetic young woman dressed in white sweatpants and a white Robertson sweatshirt grabbed the microphone and shouted, "Let's get our blood flowing. Pat Robertson's going to be the next president of the United States!"

After the first of three renditions of "This Land is Your Land," the woman shouted, "Amen! Hallelujah! Righteousness exalts this nation!" She then taught the audience a campaign song, the words of which were distributed on "Americans for Robertson" letterheads. Sung (loosely) to the tune of "Row, Row, Row Your Boat," the words read:

> We're Pat's grass roots!
> Watch us grow!
> Taller, Taller, Taller, Taller!
> Smotherin' out the foe!

Everyone in the ballroom then rose spontaneously to the strains of "God Bless America," followed immediately by "America the Beautiful" and "My Country 'Tis of Thee." When it came time for "The Battle Hymn of the Republic," the crowd was getting warmed up. They clapped and stomped on the wooden floor, all the while singing "Mine eyes have seen the glory of the coming of the Lord."

When I sat down next to Keith and Cherry Marsh, near the stage, the crowd was in the midst of a chant: "We want Pat! We want Pat!" Cherry looked a bit sheepish. "This is the place where we cut loose," she said almost apologetically. "This is where we have fun." By seven forty-five the ballroom was filled, and a uniformed Army sergeant came to the microphone to lead the audience in the Pledge of Allegiance. When the recitation came around to "one nation under God," several people around me shouted "under God" in a defiant tone. During the singing of "The Star-Spangled Banner," the audience waved their styrofoam hats from side to side in unison.

The enthusiasm of the audience rarely waned, even during a

succession of musical selections and speeches from lesser-light politicians eager to bask in Pat Robertson's spotlight. The master of ceremonies introduced one of the singers as "a young lady, the mother of five, and a perfect example of what this country stands for." Kelly Griswold walked onstage and sang "Ready for the Times to Get Better," which, she said, "is what's going to happen when Pat becomes president." Next to me, Juanita Cashulines, a Robertson volunteer from Hudson, New Hampshire, nodded in agreement. "The Lord's on our side," she said.

Meldrim Thompson, governor of New Hampshire from 1973 to 1979, is chairman of Pat Robertson's campaign in New Hampshire. When it came time to introduce Thompson, one of the junior politicians waxed rhapsodic, describing the former governor, who once proposed equipping the New Hampshire National Guard with nuclear weapons, as the "patriarch of conservatives in New Hampshire" and "one of the most wisest, most respected men in American politics." Thompson, a short, ruddy-faced man, acknowledged the cheers from the audience and then introduced Robertson. At that moment, the rally's enthusiasm reached a crescendo. "We want Pat! We want Pat!" The crowd's awkwardness and tentativeness, so evident earlier in the evening, gave way to boundless enthusiasm and adulation. Cameras flashed. Placards swayed. Keith and Cherry Marsh cheered and waved their hats high in the air. "Look at all them press people," one woman said, pointing to the phalanx of photographers and cameramen. "A month ago there were only three or four of them."

"When I look at all your faces and see your enthusiasm," Robertson began, "I believe we're going to see victory on Tuesday." The audience agreed. "I am *not* a politician," he continued, sounding a theme that plays well in New Hampshire. "As president of the United States, I am free to serve God as I see fit and to serve all the people of the United States." Several people shouted "Amen!" during Robertson's speech, especially as he proclaimed his support for individual initiative, freedom from communism, strong families, and "the preservation of life for the unborn." One voice said, "God bless you, Pat."

Robertson plunged into the audience to shake hands, to "press the flesh," as Lyndon Johnson used to say. Keith and Cherry Marsh passed up the chance to pump the candidate's hand, preferring to avoid the crush of people around Robertson. "I've shaken his hand before," Keith explained. Outside in the parking lot, however, a friend of the Marshes, a woman in her fifties and a member of Keith's congregation, ran up to the car. "He knows us. He knows us," she exclaimed breathlessly. "He said, 'God's going to work a wonder. I just know it.'"

SUNDAY, FEBRUARY 14, 1988   The Dartmouth Area Christian Fellowship meets in the Nugget Theater in downtown Hanover. The worship is pentecostal, an informal mix of guitars, singing, flailing arms, and spontaneous shouting from the congregation: "Thank you, Jesus!" "You're the king of all the earth!" Toward the front of the theater, one member of the congregation seems to be coaching a newcomer on the various techniques for waving his arms in the air. He then places his hand on the newcomer's head and unleashes a lengthy prayer that lasts through several songs. Some of the exhortations from the audience take the first-person voice of God: "I have given you spiritual gifts. You are a gifted people. . . . You don't know when, but my Son is returning."

After an hour or so, the meeting adjourned for a brief intermission. Cherry Marsh introduced me to Rob and Margaret Drye from Plainfield, members of the congregation and Robertson supporters who are also active in the pro-life movement. The Dryes quickly volunteered that they were schooling their children at home and that their defiance of state regulations had involved them in all sorts of legal tangles. "We're not going to send our kids into the snake pit of the public schools," Rob said disdainfully. "The whole curriculum is designed to turn children against their parents." I asked if they weren't worried about their children's socialization in that they were separated from their peers. "Yes, we worry about socialization," Margaret said. "That's why our children are *not* in public schools."

At the front of the theater, Keith Marsh stepped behind a lectern and said, "Okay, saints, let's sit down now." He then invited members of the congregation to offer testimonies about what God had done in their lives. Two days away from the primary, politics was on the mind of some. "I just want to tell everyone who's concerned about the political scene in this country that Jesus Christ is the answer," one young man said. "We really need to pray for God's will to be done." Another man exhorted the congregation to "go out and vote on Tuesday. Ask God to bring forth who He wants to bring forth in this country."

An air of triumphalism tinged some of the declarations. "We know who the winning side is," someone said. "It's us." When one man casually let it drop that "I'll be voting for Pat Robertson on Tuesday," Keith Marsh hurried to the podium. "We don't endorse political candidates as a church," he pointed out. "Amen?"

For many evangelicals in America, the realm of politics is still alien terrain, and the propriety of various political activities is disputed. In the fifties, sixties, and seventies, many evangelical seminaries explicitly instructed their students not to express themselves politically in any way lest they compromise the effectiveness of their ministries. Evangelicals on the whole viewed politics with suspicion as a "worldly" domain unworthy of their participation beyond mere voting. It was not always so. In the nineteenth century, evangelicals shaped the nation's social and political agenda with their concern for such issues as abolitionism, prison reform, temperance, and sabbatarianism. Lyman Beecher mounted a moral crusade to outlaw duelling, and various missionary and benevolent societies worked for the amelioration of society.[10] Such activity coincided with their postmillennialist theological views.

By the turn of the twentieth century, however, teeming, squalid cities and rapacious industrialists hardly looked liked fixtures of a millennial kingdom. Premillennialism, with its expectation of a sudden, cataclysmic judgment of sinful society, better suited the temper of evangelicals at the turn of the century. By the time of the Scopes Trial in 1925, they were convinced that American culture was hopelessly damned, so they turned inward, awaiting their rapture into heaven.

Such attitudes did not lend themselves to political activism, and for half a century—from the Scopes Trial in 1925 until Jimmy Carter's campaign for the presidency, beginning in 1975—evangelicals largely steered clear of politics. By the late 1970s, ironically, many evangelicals, led by Jerry Falwell, Baptist minister and founder of Moral Majority, turned against Carter and saw in Ronald Reagan the kind of crusader who could arrest the moral decline in America by reinstituting prayer in schools, outlawing abortion, and stemming the tide of communism. Reagan's lack of success on those fronts only increased the determination of evangelicals to advance their agenda, and in 1988 they began looking for a new champion.

Still, there are anomalies in this moral crusade being waged in the precincts of Iowa and the purlieus of New Hampshire. The mood of triumphalism that surrounds Pat Robertson's campaign is curious in that most of Robertson's evangelical followers still claim to be premillennialists—that is, they expect the imminent return of Christ and the judgment of a sinful world—but they are acting increasingly like postmillennialists who have taken it upon themselves to usher in Christ's millennial kingdom. Indeed, there are many evangelicals whose premillennial scruples still will not allow them to participate in politics. In the course of our conversations, Keith Marsh recounted an argument that Robertson faced at the pastors' luncheon in Concord as he was deciding whether to run for president. "Wait a minute," one of the ministers said. "The next event on the eschatological clock is the return of Christ. Things in society should get *worse* rather than better. If Christians worked to turn our nation around, that would be a humanistic effort and delay Christ's return." In the euphoria of the 1988 presidential campaign, however, many evangelicals have brushed aside such naysayers, even though they may not admit to a shift in theology or even be aware of any contradiction between their premillennial convictions and their postmillennial activities.

Keith and Cherry Marsh are not bothered by such contradictions. At their home in West Lebanon, over a Sunday dinner of Yankee pot roast, carrots, homemade rolls, and mashed potatoes, I asked the Marshes and their friends, Dan and Barbara Gornell, to assess their first foray into politics. Barbara Gornell, a schoolteacher for many years, linked the evangelical surge into politics with the emergence of the Christian-school movement. "The curriculum in those schools emphasizes government through God, and this whole generation is coming up with biblical principles for government," she said. These principles are then picked up by the parents. "As you educate the children," she said, "you educate the parents."

Dan Gornell, who recently retired after a career in the Air Force, said he thoroughly enjoyed his volunteer work for Robertson's campaign. His daily duties include driving around in his pickup truck every morning and replacing all the Robertson lawn signs that had been torn down or vandalized the night before. In the past, he said, "there was a mindset that Christians shouldn't get involved in politics. But look at the Bible." He pointed to the examples of Moses and Gideon as political figures, and he placed Robertson in the same tradition as the leaders of ancient Israel.

"Pat Robertson has come along to champion our cause," Barbara Gornell said. "We're as amazed about it as everyone else, but we've got to make a stand here. The conviction of knowing you're doing something right keeps you going. Our ranks are thickening, and people are getting excited. This campaign has relieved a frustration in my life. I really *can* do something to change the system."

What would happen, I asked, if Robertson's campaign fizzled or if he were denied a place on the Republican ticket by a political deal of one kind or another. All agreed that they would be disappointed but that they would still work for the Republican nominee in November. Cherry Marsh conceded, however, that "I don't think we would work as hard for anyone else."

"It's a victory that Pat is even running," Keith Marsh said. "He has emboldened us not to be ashamed of our faith and beliefs. We're in it for the long haul," he added. "We'll be back in four years."

Cherry agreed. "We're not going to give up," she said.

NOTES

1. From the 9:00 a.m. service, 7 February 1988; see also William Simbro, "Robertson to be Target of Sermon," *Des Moines Register*, 6 February 1988, p. 8A.

2. From the 10:15 a.m. service, 7 February 1988.

3. From the 6:00 p.m. service, 7 February 1988.

4. Alexis de Tocqueville, *Democracy in America*, ed. Henry Steele

Commager, trans. Henry Reeve (New York: Oxford University Press, 1947), p. 199. On nineteenth-century femininity and domesticity, see Colleen McDannell, *The Christian Home in Victorian America, 1840–1900* (Bloomington: Indiana University Press, 1986); Ann Douglas, *The Feminization of American Culture* (New York: Knopf, 1977).

5. Barbara A. Peil, "A Seasoned Approach," *Kindred Spirit* 11 (Spring 1987): 13.

6. A good example of this genre is Peter Marshall and David Manuel, *The Light and the Glory* (Old Tappan, N.J.: Revell, 1977). For an evangelical response to this revisionism, see Mark A. Noll, Nathan O. Hatch, and George M. Marsden, *The Search for Christian America* (Westchester, Ill.: Crossway Books, 1983).

7. Douglas Frank started me thinking about the fetus as symbol. I am grateful to him for allowing me to develop this idea here.

8. Quoted in Michael Oreskes, "Almost 'Got to Give God Credit,' Robertson Says in Thanking Staff," *New York Times*, 9 February 1988, pp. A1, B7.

9. Tuttle was referring to a passage found in 2 Cor. 6:14.

10. On the social concerns of evangelicals in the nineteenth century, see Timothy L. Smith, *Revivalism and Social Reform in Mid-Nineteenth-Century America* (Nashville: Abindgon Press, 1957); Charles C. Cole, Jr., *The Social Ideas of the Northern Evangelists, 1826–1860* (New York: Columbia University Press, 1954).

7

Mississippi Missions

ON JANUARY 15, 1987, the day I arrived in Jackson, the Mississippi legislature voted to set aside the third Monday in January as a state holiday in honor of Martin Luther King, Jr. The holiday, the legislature decided, would also commemorate the Confederate general Robert E. Lee. In Mississippi, apparently, when one hand giveth, the other taketh away.

Much of Mississippi still enjoys (yes, enjoys) a reputation as one of the last bastions of the Old South, a holdout against desegregation, civil rights, and change. Mississippi waited until 1986 to set up kindergartens in public schools, the same year it made schooling mandatory for the first time; children in Mississippi now have to remain in school until age ten. Not until 1975 did the state require that justices of the peace have at least a high school education.

Over the past century, however, Mississippi's most stubborn resistance to change has centered in race relations. Here in the state that provided the Confederacy with its only president, many whites still refer to the Civil War as the War Between the States, a moniker that insists that the South was an independent, sovereign nation. Ross Barnett, segregationist governor of Mississippi from 1960 to

1964, used to tell his white constituents, "The Negro is different because God made him different to punish him."[1]

If God ever flagged in His "punishment" of blacks, there were always plenty of whites in Mississippi ready to assume the responsibility. In 1964 three civil rights workers were slain and buried secretly in an earthen dam near Philadelphia, in Neshoba County. The year before, Medgar Evers, head of the National Association for the Advancement of Colored People in Mississippi, was murdered at his home in Jackson. In September 1962, President Kennedy called in Army troops to quell the rioting in Oxford occasioned by the registration of James Meredith at the University of Mississippi. When a reporter asked if he didn't find it a lonely life as the only black on an all-white campus, Meredith replied evenly, "I've been living a lonely life a long time."[2]

In 1947, another young black man, also very much alone, stood at the train station in Jackson, Mississippi, with a lunch, a second-grade education, one change of clothes, three dollars, and a ticket to California. Even at sixteen, John Perkins would write later, "a guy has a lot to remember. And a lot to forget."[3]

As Perkins headed west, he recalled his childhood. Born to boot-legging sharecroppers outside New Hebron, in the Piney Woods section of central Mississippi, his mother had died of pellagra, a painful disease caused by protein deficiency, when Perkins was only seven months old. His father, seeking work, left about the same time. But what most seared his memory was a Saturday afternoon in New Hebron during the long, hot summer of 1946. His older brother Clyde, recently returned from Germany with combat ribbons, a Purple Heart, and an honorable discharge, stood in the alleyway queue for the "colored" entrance to Carolyn's Theater. A deputy marshal walked by, barked, "You niggers quiet down," and then, for reasons never clear, brandished his club. After sustaining one blow, Clyde Perkins grabbed the weapon and scuffled with the lawman, who then stepped back, pulled his gun, and pumped two shots into the black man's stomach.

Clyde Perkins died several hours later.

In California, half a world away from New Hebron, John Perkins traded his twenty-dollar-a-month Mississippi wages for ninety-eight cents an hour at the Union Pacific Foundry in South Gate. Far away from the blatant, overt racism of Mississippi, Perkins encountered a world of possibilities and opportunities. He worked as a union organizer, served a tour of duty in Korea, got married, and held a succession of jobs that placed him on the road to middle-class respectability. He also undertook a spiritual quest that began with the Jehovah's Witnesses, continued with Christian Science and the Father Divine Peace Mission, and settled finally at evangelical Christianity.

Soon after Perkins "said yes to Jesus Christ," he became convinced that God wanted him back in Mississippi, the very place he had left "for good" in 1947.[4] When John and Vera Mae Perkins and five children clambered out of their '56 Chevy on June 9, 1960, they found a state that had changed little since that young man had left thirteen years earlier. The racial hatred he had encountered as a boy still festered. Blacks remained trapped in a cycle of poverty, despair, and oppression.

Yet Perkins's faith, he maintains, allowed him to face these conditions with energy and determination rather than resignation and despair. He insists that he did not return to Mississippi with any strong ideological convictions or strategies, that he was influenced only tangentially by Gandhi, Martin Luther King, or the economic philosophies of the Nation of Islam.[5] Instead, while working at a job picking cotton, he began simply to foster a sense of community and eventually to organize various religious and social programs in Mendenhall that soon became known as Voice of Calvary Ministries.[6] He started vacation Bible schools in the summertime, taught classes in Bible at public schools, and purchased a large tent for religious meetings that featured Bible study as well as preaching. Perkins settled in and quickly expanded his activities, despite harassment from local whites.[7]

There are still two sides of the railroad tracks in Mendenhall, Mississippi. To the east, on a gentle rise overlooking the rest of the town, sits the white section, an area of well-manicured lawns and freshly painted houses on a grid of carefully calibrated streets. Turning east at Mendenhall's only stoplight on Old Highway 49, you enter a wide Main Street flanked by meticulously clean stores. The street leads up the hill to the Simpson County courthouse, an imposing nineteenth-century structure crowned by a golden dome.

The "quarters" (the old slave quarters) lie in a flood plain on the other side of the tracks. Here the streets (some of them paved) meander randomly. Soft-drink vending machines sit on cluttered porches, delapidated automobiles rust in patches of weeds in otherwise barren front yards. There is plenty of squalor and neglect and bleakness here in the quarters. Yet amidst evidence of decay and indifference, other signs, however tentative, indicate hope.

One of first problems that Perkins addressed after he settled in Mendenhall was housing. Most of the buildings in the quarters were owned by white landlords on the other side of the tracks who extorted a good deal of rent each week, but who provided little or nothing in the way of basic maintenance. When black tenants attempted to improve their living environment by making repairs or painting walls, landlords often succeeded in evicting them for "tampering" with the building. After the evictions and with no further investment of time or capital, the landlord would simply let the building again, this time at an increased rent that reflected the improvements made by the evicted tenant. Such a system understandably bred cynicism among residents of the quarters and quashed any incentive to improve their living conditions. Perkins believed that the answer lay in a fundamental recasting of landlord-tenant relations. With help from outside contributions and a loan from the Farmers Home Administration (FHA), a co-op housing group built five low-cost duplex apartments that still provide safe, sturdy housing in the quarters.

For Perkins, this sort of social activism was perfectly compatible with his understanding of evangelical Christianity, which he saw as addressing the *physical* needs of the poor as well as their spiritual needs. He had returned from California convinced that the emphasis on emotion and ecstasy so characteristic of black religion had served to inhibit real progress—intellectual and social—among rural blacks. "I saw very quickly after I returned to Mississippi that my gospel and their gospel were not relevant to the needs of the people," he recalled. "I had to combat the emotional, simplistic gospel that black folks had already accepted. It provided an emotional outlet for them, but little else."[8]

Perkins, of course, was not the first to draw such conclusions. The famous essay, "Faith of Our Fathers" by W. E. B. DuBois, identified three elements of slave religion, "the Preacher, the Music, and the Frenzy," and added that the latter "was the one more devoutly believed in than all the rest."[9] Daniel Alexander Payne, nineteenth-century bishop in the African Methodist Episcopal Church, believed that the real difference between master and slave lay in knowledge. Payne spent most of his ecclesiastical career urging the formation of colleges, seminaries, and curricula for the development of black leaders. During a tour of the Reconstruction South, William Wells Brown, sometimes called America's first black man of letters, visited "one of the most refined congregations in Nashville," where he encountered all manner of religious frenzy. Believing that such demonstrations were a scourge to black social, religious, and political advancement, Brown advocated an educated ministry but allowed that, "It will be difficult to erase from the mind of the negro of the South, the prevailing idea that outward demonstrations, such as, shouting, the loud 'amen,' and the most boisterous noise in prayer, are not necessary adjuncts to piety."[10]

As a result of Perkins's efforts, black religious piety in Mendenhall now encompasses worldly concerns as well as otherworldly. Under the auspices of Mendenhall Ministries (originally, Voice of Calvary Ministries), black evangelicals in the quarters operate a thrift store, which offers low-cost food, clothing, furniture, appliances, gardening supplies, and other necessities for poor residents. The Summer Enrichment Program employs high school and college students to tutor grammar school children in study skills. A savings plan requires young people to put half their earnings into savings, both as a way to learn discipline and to provide funds for college. Outside of town a farm, purchased in 1980, provides food, a modest income for the organization, and training in agricultural techniques for local farmers.

In 1976 two Northern blacks, Dennis Adams, a physician, and his wife, Judi, an educator, came to Mendenhall. Although the government reneged on its promise to forgive eighty percent of his medical school debts if he practiced in a low-income clinic, Dr. Adams decided to stay, even though he earned as director of the Mendenhall Cooperative Health Center only a fraction of what he might make in another setting or in private practice.

Judi Adams, a striking, well-spoken woman who now assists in the administration of these various programs, initially invested her energies in the Genesis One School, a two-story cinder-block building that houses cheery, well-appointed classrooms. The school, organized by the community to provide a quality education for blacks and other poor people in the region who found such opportunities denied them in Mendenhall schools, now boasts that its graduates outshine their public school counterparts. This education, moreover, complete with remedial tutoring, school supplies, and two meals a day, commands only $650 a year in tuition—a sum, nevertheless, beyond the means of many parents in the area, who exchange volunteer work for a reduction in tuition.

Down the street from the school, the R. A. Buckley Christian Youth Center provides vocational training and recreation in the form of a gymnasium and, according to Judi Adams, "the best-equipped weightroom in the county." The Community Law Office, situated nearby in a small steel building, provides free or low-cost legal services to the poor of Simpson County. An assortment of pamphlets in the lobby offers general advice on the legal tangles routinely faced by the poor: threats of eviction, what to do if arrested, how to file for bankruptcy, how to avoid foreclosure. The staff includes a full-time attorney, several paralegal assistants, and interns from such institutions as Stanford, Duke, and Harvard law schools. In addition to its advocacy for individuals, the Community Law Office has filed class-action desegregation suits and has recently developed a three-session People's Law School to apprise the poor of their basic legal rights.

There is a sense of hard-won permanence in all this bustle in the quarters, a tribute to determination in the face of discouraging odds. From its inception, the work in Mendenhall has met with suspicion, if not outright hostility. Any organization that enlists the cooperation of blacks and whites is viewed askance in Mississippi—it is a "civil

rights outfit" that threatens traditional notions of order. Life is seldom easy in the quarters, on the wrong side of the tracks, down
the hill from the courthouse that sits atop the slope of Main Street
in Mendenhall.

John Perkins knows what it means to live in the shadow of the
Simpson County courthouse, knows about the unsubtlety of Mississippi justice. While spending a night in the county jail after pro-
testing the beating of a young black by the police, Perkins conceived
the idea of an economic boycott of Mendenhall businesses. Because
the economic and political interests in Mendenhall were so en-
twined, he reasoned, such a boycott by blacks would be the best
means to call attention to their systematic repression, the persistent
denial of economic opportunity, harassment by law-enforcement
officials, and the continued segregation of schools.

In the ensuing months, beginning the week before Christmas
1969, the blacks of Simpson County stayed away from the stores on
Main Street and organized their own cooperative. Each Saturday,
armed with a parade permit, they gathered at Voice of Calvary, the
ministry's headquarters, and snaked their way through the quarters,
across the tracks and Highway 49, up Main Street to the courthouse,
chanting "Do right, white man, do right."

Under constant surveillance by the Mississippi Highway Patrol,
Perkins and other participants recognized that such an assault on
Southern norms would not go unavenged. Law-enforcement officials
finally pounced on Saturday, February 7, 1970. After tailing two
vans of students who were returning to Tougaloo College after participating in the weekly march, a Mississippi patrolman signaled one
of the vans to pull over just beyond the Simpson County line in
Rankin County. Soon one of the students telephoned Perkins to say
that they were in the Rankin County jail in Brandon. When Perkins
and two others arrived to set bail, they were met outside the courthouse by a dozen highway patrolmen who searched them, arrested
them, and began beating them even before they reached the building. Sheriff Jonathan Edwards came over to Perkins and announced,
"This is the smart nigger, and this is a new ballgame. You're not in
Simpson County now; you are in Brandon."[11]

Then the beatings began in earnest. One of the students later testified that the sheriff assailed Perkins so vigorously that his "shirt tail came out." After a time, five deputies and twice that number of highway patrolmen took over. Thrown to the floor, Perkins tried to shield himself by rolling up into a ball, but "they just kept on beating and stomping me, kicking me in the head, in the ribs, in the groin." One officer jammed a fork up Perkins's nose and then crammed it down his throat before beating him to the ground again. [12]

Others, including some of the students, sustained injuries in jail that night, but Perkins remembers that while lapsing in and out of consciousness he resolved to face the issue of racism in Mississippi with a new strategy. Looking into the eyes of his attackers, into eyes contorted by hatred, he recalled later, "I saw what hate had done to those people." The white man "was a victim of his own racism," and the only way he could acquire a sense of worth was to subjugate the black man. "When I saw that, I just couldn't hate back."[13]

Although at the time some of the students feared otherwise, Perkins survived that night in the Rankin County jail, but he received no satisfaction at the hands of Mississippi justice: The criminal charges against him (for "contributing to the delinquency of a minor" by allegedly encouraging one of the students to remain in jail rather than leave, as the sheriff wanted) and his civil suit against the state of Mississippi ended in compromise settlements. Perkins insists that his ordeal in Brandon and in Mississippi courtrooms did not embitter him; instead he resolved "to take a gospel of love to whites filled with hate." Whereas so much of his energies in Mendenhall had centered on blacks and providing means for their spiritual and physical well-being, he looked now toward "a ministry of reconciliation" that would transcend racial boundaries. [14]

In a period of physical and emotional convalescence following the beatings in Brandon, Perkins began to sketch out a new strategy molded around the three Rs: *relocation* into a needy community, "turning statistics into neighbors"; *reconciliation* across racial, social, cultural, and economic barriers; *redistribution* of resources equitably, not through welfare or handouts, but by training the poor in vocational and management skills. [15] But if Perkins was prepared to take on the issue of racism and reconciliation, he was not ready to return to Mendenhall. On the advice of his doctor, he moved to Jackson.

As in Mendenhall, forty miles to the southeast, the range of programs begun by Perkins in the state capital is impressive. Anchored in West Jackson, Voice of Calvary Ministries lies at the interstices of three neighborhoods, just a few blocks from the Jackson State University campus. Perkins recognized the importance of establishing an evangelical presence and seeking some kind of stability in these transitional neighborhoods, an objective that continues to the present.

Don Howie, director of study programs for the organization, informed me that each of the three neighborhoods requires a different strategy to keep it from degenerating. In West Jackson itself, once an all-white neighborhood and now biracial, Voice of Calvary wants to see the balance and character of the area maintained, to stem the "white flight" that has convulsed other neighborhoods. The Lynch Street community, historically black, is probably the poorest area of the city. Here, during my visit, not a block from one of Jackson's main arteries, roosters behind ramshackle houses heralded the morning. This community lost much of its stability when the court-mandated desegregation of other areas, particularly the suburbs, made it possible for black professionals to live elsewhere. "Here we perform a kind of triage," Howie said. "We're trying first to develop some young black leaders in the community, but it's difficult to identify them. Eventually, we hope to do more in the way of reclamation: buy run-down houses, renovate, and rent them." Georgetown, the third neighborhood, is also in transition—poor, but not so squalid as Lynch Street. As we toured these streets, Howie, formerly the pastor of a white, suburban church, pointed to one house after another that the organization had purchased, renovated, and then rented. They have even managed to sell some of the dwellings after fixing them up. "Ownership is the ideal situation," he said, "both for the individual family and for the neighborhood."[16]

Other programs in Jackson resemble those in Mendenhall. The Voice of Calvary Family Health Center offers low-cost health care.

Harambee Youth Ministries tutors young people of the community in the Bible and in classroom skills. Thriftco, a cooperative that began on the front porch of the organization's Fellowship House, now has two outlets in Jackson and over two thousand members. The International Study Center, run by Voice of Calvary, trains people to launch out with initiatives similar to Voice of Calvary's, both in the United States and in places like Haiti and South Africa. The John M. Perkins Christian Community Development Institute draws college students and summer interns who combine classroom study with some form of on-the-job experience.

While I was in Mississippi, a group of eight students from Messiah College, an evangelical college in Pennsylvania, were participating in the study program. In exchange for four hours of credit during the college's winter term, these students, all of them middle-class whites, sat through a week of lectures on racism, the history of blacks in America, and various evangelical strategies for helping the poor. Lecturers spoke about such notions as individual, institutional, and corporate racism, the systematic exclusion of blacks from economic opportunities. The students were told that convenience stores—Circle K, Seven-Eleven—prey on the poor by locating in ghettos; their high prices for groceries (generally unavailable elsewhere) take money out of the community, and the marketing of ready-to-eat foods, candies, and soft drinks discourages proper nutrition. Students also learned that forty-four percent of blacks in Mississippi live below the poverty level, fifty-five percent of Mississippi blacks aged sixteen or over are unemployed, less than fifteen percent have graduated from high school, three-fourths of black rural homes in Mississippi lack plumbing facilities, and sixty-nine percent of the state's prison population is black.[17]

The students from Messiah also reviewed the biblical warrants for seeking justice, the jeremiads of the Hebrew prophets and the teachings of Jesus. During the second and third weeks the students would assist in some program or project—the thrift store, the youth program, renovation of housing—but at the conclusion of the first week, they were invited to consider the ways in which America's polarized racial situation and inequitable economic conditions had affected their own attitudes and their perceptions of blacks. They were asked to understand the sense of hopelessness and the simmering rage in black ghettos.

Most of the students acknowledged that they hadn't considered these issues prior to their arrival in Mississippi. Several admitted that they had signed up for the course because it allowed them to evade the language requirement at Messiah (apparently, a "cross-cultural experience" satisfies the requirement). As Lemuel Tucker, president of Voice of Calvary, told me later, one of the purposes of bringing such students to Jackson was to "shake them up" a bit, help them to understand the racial situation in America from the other side of the fence. "I want to unsettle them, get them to rethink some of their assumptions, and then motivate them to work toward reconciliation," he said.

The force of this message lies not in rhetoric but in example. Voice of Calvary Fellowship in Jackson evolved hand in hand with Voice of Calvary Ministries, the umbrella organization for the various programs Perkins established. The Fellowship, an evangelical church, addressed the desire on the part of Perkins and many staff members for Christian worship that would be both evangelical and interracial. "Eleven A.M. Sunday morning," people around Voice of Calvary often say, "is America's most segregated hour." And nowhere more so than in Jackson. The Calvary Baptist Church, just blocks away from Voice of Calvary offices, is a huge, imposing structure that, with fences around its playground and high brick walls, resembles a fortress more than a church. Caught amidst changing neighborhoods, Calvary Baptist, a white church, finds itself surrounded by a predominantly black population, and yet, I was told, any black who tried to enter on Sunday morning would be turned away. Voice of Calvary Fellowship, on the other hand, takes pride in its multiracial character. "We've learn to enjoy, to celebrate our differences," Don Howie explained. "One of the things we've noticed is that black and white music is so different. We sing the same songs, but we sing them differently." He smiled. "Sometimes before we sing a particular hymn or chorus, the leader will say, 'We're going to sing this 'the white way' or 'the black way,' '" signaling a different tempo or cadence.

In the years since he returned to Mississippi in 1960, John Perkins has met with a kind of vindication. On February 7, 1980, ten years to the day after his beating in the Rankin County jail, the governor of Mississippi honored Perkins as the state's outstanding religious leader of the year. The organizations in Jackson and Mendenhall are healthy and growing and have spawned satellite projects in places like Perkins's native New Hebron. Volunteers come from all over the nation.

But if Perkins, now organizing a similar ministry in southern California, looked for monuments to his persistence, he doubtless would see beyond the buildings and programs and real estate in Jackson or Mendenhall. From the beginning, Perkins recognized the importance of developing leaders within the black community, and in so doing he perpetuated a long tradition.[18] Historically, the church has functioned as the primary agency for social change among blacks, in part because, since the days of slavery, it was the only social institution controlled by blacks. For more than two centuries black religion has provided the breeding ground for black leaders: Richard Allen, founder of the African Methodist Episcopal Church; Denmark Vesey, leader of a slave conspiracy in Charleston; Nat Turner, a preacher and visionary who led a slave insurrection in Southampton County, Virginia; black women such as Jarena Lee, Zilpha Elaw, and Sojourner Truth; and, in the twentieth century, Benjamin Hooks, Adam Clayton Powell, Malcolm X, and Martin Luther King, Jr., among many others. Even today, many black politicians are ordained and maintain close ties with the congregations that nurtured them.

"I think people development is the most important concept in the Christian faith," Perkins told me. "I feel very good about the black leaders that have emerged in Mendenhall and Jackson. Things will go on in Mendenhall for fifty years. Things will go on in Jackson for fifty years. (After fifty years, anything can go wrong.) I judge everything by community development, when indigenous people rise up to assume leadership roles."[19]

Dolphus Weary, now president of the Mendenhall organization, and Artis Fletcher, pastor of Mendenhall Bible Church, are both products of Perkins's efforts there. So is Melvin Anderson. Over the objections of his grandmother, who feared she might lose her job as a domestic in Mendenhall if her white employers learned that her grandson was involved with Perkins's group, Anderson kept stealing away to Voice of Calvary functions. He now heads People's Development, the non-profit housing ministry in Jackson, taking charge of the various renovation projects, looking out for real-estate properties, supervising volunteer workers. "Someone," he told me earnestly at lunch one day, "has to do this. It *has* to be done, otherwise these neighborhoods will be lost, fall into decay."

The Reverend Joseph Parker, affiliated with Voice of Calvary for much of the past decade, must also be numbered among Perkins's protégés. An ordained minister in the African Methodist Episcopal Church, he recently accepted a call to the Greater Bethel A.M.E. Church in Mound Bayou, northwest of Jackson in the Mississippi Delta region. This historically black town of three thousand lies amidst the worst poverty in the United States, in a region with the highest infant mortality rate in the nation. The last of four cotton gins in town closed a couple of years ago. The median per capita income, Parker told me, ranges between $3,000 and $4,000 a year.

I asked Parker to point to his successes over the past year in Mound Bayou. Usually if you lob a question like that in the general direction of an evangelical minister, you have to brace yourself for a flurry of statistics about conversions, the missionary budget, augmentations to church membership rolls, or the dramatic increase in Sunday morning attendance. He might also regale you with the latest plans for a building program. When I asked Parker about his work, however, he replied, "Well, we have a new business coming into town." He paused. "We may also have a dry-cleaning plant soon."[20]

Parker allowed that most white evangelicals would find such an appraisal bewildering. For them, Christianity cares little about social concerns or matters of justice. Mired in middle-class respectability, they cannot see that being black and poor in America breeds a resentment against the entrenched interests of white Christians, who purvey only a pale reflection of the gospel, what Perkins calls a "Jesus Saves—keep smiling" evangelism.[21] The whole gospel, according to folks affiliated with Voice of Calvary, demands working

toward justice and basic economic opportunity for the dis-
advantaged.

It is a mark of the cultural chasm between white and black evangelicalism that these ideas are viewed askance by most white evangelicals, whose worship tends to be relatively controlled and
"respectable," and whose politics gravitate toward conservative Re-
publicanism. Black religion itself, with its emotion and frenzy, often
strikes white evangelicals as alien and suspicious. Moreover, words
like "justice" and "economic opportunity," when applied to the poor,
smack of liberalism and imply a threat to the social and economic
order that, on the whole, has treated whites kindly. Such rhetoric
also sounds vaguely like the Social Gospel practiced by Protestant
liberals at the turn of the century, which sought the redemption of
sinful social institutions—predatory monopolies, unscrupulous landlords, unbridled capitalism—that kept the urban poor enslaved in
poverty. Evangelicals overwhelmingly opposed the Social Gospel,
preferring instead to emphasize the need for individual conversions
rather than the overhaul of society. John Perkins is certainly no
radical, but he and the people associated with the organizations he
founded have sought to educate fellow Christians about the plight
of the poor and to enlist their help in meliorating the conditions
that perpetuate black poverty.

How do white evangelicals respond to such overtures? I put the
question to Dolphus Weary, head of the Mendenhall organization,
and later to Lemuel Tucker, president of Voice of Calvary in Jackson.
Weary contended that most evangelicals have yet to develop a strategy for dealing with the poor. But it's an issue, he said, that must
be addressed if they mean to take seriously the precepts of Christianity. Tucker believes that evangelicals "are unprepared for justice. They've placed too much stock in some of the arcane issues of
theology and defending their notions of orthodoxy and not enough
emphasis on the basic issues of human dignity and justice."

Perkins himself sees progress, evidence that evangelicals are taking more seriously the social demands of the gospel. "I think programs like Voice of Calvary and Mendenhall Ministries offer real
models of evangelism and social responsibility," he said. I asked
him if he had encountered resistance from fellow evangelicals to his

socially grounded Christianity. "In the early days, yes," he said, "but there's been an evolution. Now we're seen as something of an example, as pioneers. Once evangelicals found issues that they could be active on—issues like abortion and pornography—they began exerting more influence in the social arena. But they have not been very active on issues that affect the poor. The very fact that they began to be active on social issues, however, meant that they could no longer fault people like us for being involved in social action. Once the Moral Majority was organized, social action became acceptable among evangelicals." Still, Perkins, who serves on the boards of various evangelical organizations, cannot get evangelicals interested in sanctions against South Africa, which is seen, again, as a "liberal" cause. He believes that prosperity theology—the God-will-make-you-rich-and-happy notions propagated by such televangelists as Robert Schuller, Kenneth Copeland, and Jim and Tammy Bakker—has blinded many evangelicals to the needs of the poor. "This prosperity stuff is deadly," he said.[22]

In small measures, perhaps, the message was seeping through. The students from Messiah College still weren't sure what the acronym NAACP stood for, but after a week of lectures and a visit to Joseph Parker's church in Mound Bayou, some of them began to wonder whether, in some subconscious way, they too had been affected by racism and even now harbored certain assumptions or prejudices about blacks. "What's hit me the hardest," one woman volunteered, "is the notion that we might be prejudiced in certain ways and not even realize it. It's something we absorb from the broader culture, from television and commercials and Saturday morning cartoons. It's not something we decide. It's very subtle." Most still weren't convinced they were racist in any palpable way, but at least they were asking the question. Some acknowledged that they had felt uncomfortable in Parker's all-black church, that it was easier for them at the church dinner following the morning service to sit together rather than disperse throughout the fellowship hall. That experience, they said, taught them what it felt like to be a minority. One woman said that *Roots*, which they had seen on videotape that week, "made me feel extremely guilty—that we white people are scum for enslaving blacks."

Did others feel any personal responsiblity for the plight of blacks in this country? No, most still did not. But one man said, "Yes, I think we are responsible in that we are born into the system. If we're not vigorously attacking the system and trying to change it, we're a part of it, because we are white and benefiting from it." Another student added: "We hadn't really noticed the injustices before, but now that we see them we bear a responsibility. By failing to challenge the system, we become part of it, and we're culpable."

NOTES

1. "Ross Barnett, Segregationist, Dies; Governor of Mississippi in 1960s," *New York Times*, 7 November 1987.

2. From *Eyes on the Prize*, six-part television documentary, episode 2: "Fighting Back, 1957–1962."

3. John Perkins, *Let Justice Roll Down: John Perkins Tells His Own Story* (Ventura, Cal.: Regal Books, 1976), p. 25. Much of the ensuing account of Perkins's life relies on this book.

4. Ibid., p. 72.

5. Perkins, in fact, views his mission work as a response, or at least an alternative, to the tenets of the Nation of Islam. See John Perkins, "Mendenhall Model Answers the Black Muslims," *Christianity Today*, 30 January 1976, pp. 8–13.

6. After Perkins shifted his attentions to Jackson in the mid-1970s, the programs in Mendenhall took the name Mendenhall Ministries.

7. For a brief sketch of Perkins's life, see Will Norton, Jr., "John Perkins, the Stature of a Servant," *Christianity Today*, 1 January 1982, pp. 18–19.

8. John Perkins, telephone interview, North Pasadena, Cal., 8 June 1987.

9. Milton C. Sernett, ed., *Afro-American Religious History: A Documentary Witness* (Durham, N.C.: Duke University Press, 1985), p. 310.

10. Ibid., p. 241.

11. John Perkins, *With Justice for All* (Ventura, Cal.: Regal Books, 1982), p. 98.

12. Ibid.

13. Ibid., p. 99.

14. Ibid., p. 102.

15. Ibid., ch. 9, 14, 18; Lem Tucker, "The Desire of My Heart," *Inter-Varsity* (Summer 1984): 10–13.

16. "We're not teaching people how to live with rats and roaches," D. L. Govan, a member of the pastoral team at Voice of Calvary Fellowship, said, "we're teaching them to live with dignity." Perkins is not at all averse to free enterprise. During an interview in 1982, he said, "I believe in stewardship that is expressed in capital ownership," but he added, "The weakness of our system is that capitalists believe that the church should not speak against capitalism, but only against socialism, communism, and fascism" (Will Norton, Jr., "An Interview with John Perkins, the Prophet," *Christianity Today*, 1 January 1982, p. 20).

17. Statistics from "John M. Perkins Christian Community Development Institute Workshop Manual," pp. 57–60.

18. See Perkins, *With Justice for All*, ch. 7.

19. Perkins interview.

20. Joseph Parker, interview, 18 January 1987.

21. Perkins, *Let Justice Roll Down*, p. 220.

22. Perkins interview.

8

Bible Bazaar

I'VE OFTEN WONDERED what it would be like to bring back the fathers of western culture's most formative inventions to see how their devices have evolved over the generations. Would Alexander Graham Bell recognize credit-card telephones in our airports? In his wildest dreams, could Thomas Edison have imagined the fidelity of a compact disc? Could Guglielmo Marconi have envisioned facsimile machines, instant replay, or diamond-vision scoreboards? Even Henry Ford, I suspect, would be astonished at how thoroughly his invention has shaped American culture: drive-in banks, hardware stores and funeral homes, a sprawling network of roadways, the alacrity with which we turn forests and fields into parking lots.

If Johann Gutenberg, inventor of movable type and publisher of the first Gutenberg Bible in 1456, were around today, I'd want to walk him through the exhibition hall of the Christian Booksellers Association annual convention. There he would find a bewildering array of Bibles: the Living Bible, the Catholic Living Bible, the Christian Life Bible, the People's Parallel Bible, the New English Bible, the Revised English Bible, the Simple English Bible, the Daily Walk Bible, the Picture Bible, the Thompson Chain-

Reference Bible (fifth edition), La Santa Biblia, the New American
Standard Bible, the Disciple's Study Bible, the New International
Version Personal Reference Bible, Dake's Annotated Reference Bi-
ble, the Discovery Bible, the Rainbow Study Bible, the International Children's Bible, the Open Bible, the Good News Bible, the
Prophecy Bible—to name only a few. He would also find Bibles
available on cassette tapes (in several versions and at least twelve
languages) and on computer diskettes (again, in several versions).

Gutenberg's invention made possible this proliferation of Bibles,
but the Protestant Reformers—Martin Luther, John Calvin, Ulrich
Zwingli, William Tyndale, Miles Coverdale, Thomas Cranmer—
first seized on this invention and insisted that Bibles be made available to the masses. Vernacular translations appeared all over northern Europe and England in the sixteenth century. People began to
read the Scriptures for themselves and no longer through the interpretive template of the Roman Catholic Church, which for centuries had relied on the Vulgate, Jerome's Latin translation of the
Bible. *Sola scriptura*, reliance on the Scriptures only, became a
hallmark of the Protestant Reformation. Just as Luther insisted that
Christians had direct access to God through Jesus Christ and not
through the mediation of priests, so too believers, Luther said, could
interpret the Bible for themselves, absent the prejudices of Catholic
theology.

The Scofield Reference Bible and the Ryrie Study Bible in their
various guises—King James Version, New American Standard Version, New International Version—therefore require some explana-
tion. The idea that the Bible should be viewed through a specific
interpretive lens would have been foreign to the generation of Reformers who followed Gutenberg and who used his invention to
propagate the Scriptures, shorn of Roman Catholic glosses, in the
vernacular of the people. In truth, however, despite all the evangelical rhetoric about *sola scriptura* in the twentieth century, most
evangelicals don't trust themselves to interpret the Bible, so they
turn to others—local pastors, mendicant preachers and lecturers,
authors of thousands of books, commentaries, and reference tools—
for interpretive schemes.

American evangelicals, nevertheless, have an almost mystical attachment to the Bible.[1] I recall being told in Sunday school that a Bible should never be placed on the floor; to do so was a sacrilege akin to allowing the American flag to touch the ground. Evangelicals use the term "Word of God" synonomously with "Bible" or "Scripture," a reflection of the conviction that the Bible contains God's revelation to humanity. In 1978, George Gallup found that forty-two percent of Americans believed that "the Bible is the Word of God and is not mistaken in its statements and teachings"; thirty percent professed to read the Bible at least once a week, of whom twelve percent claimed to read the Bible daily.[2] Evangelical preachers liberally pepper their sermons with biblical proof-texts in order to substantiate their arguments. Evangelical theologians take great pains to demonstrate that their doctrines are *biblical* or *scriptural*, even if the exegesis sometimes is a bit tortured. The internecine warfare waged in evangelical circles over the doctrine of biblical inerrancy in recent years reflects the seriousness with which evangelicals view the Bible, asserting that the Bible was utterly flawless in the original autographs (which, of course, are no longer available). These high-pitched battles have become so intense that detractors have accused evangelicals of bibliolatry: elevating the Bible to the status of an idol that is itself worshipped.

Evangelicals heatedly dispute that charge, but in fact they ascribe extraordinary powers to the Scriptures. I suspect that even the most impatient Sunday morning channel-jumper has caught a glimpse of some televangelist thrusting a Bible high into the air, shaking it for dramatic effect, and extolling "the power of God's Holy Word" or waxing rhapsodic about "the precious Word of God." In a way, of course, such veneration is not surprising. The more extreme iconoclastic Protestants stripped the sacraments of all but symbolic meaning, so that today in most evangelical circles, baptism does not confer God's grace; it merely announces a believer's decision to follow Christ. Holy Communion, generally observed no more than once a month in evangelical churches, merely symbolizes the broken body and shed blood of Christ; nothing supernatural occurs, as with the Roman Catholic doctrine of transubstantiation, which holds that the elements *actually become* the body and blood of Christ, even though they retain the outward appearance of bread and wine. In a theology thus denuded of mystery, many evangelicals have vested the Bible with supernatural power. "God's Word will not return unto Him void," evangelicals often say, paraphrasing a passage from Isaiah.[3] And so American evangelicals have spent a great deal of time, money, and energy to propagate the Scriptures here in America and around the world. John Eliot, Puritan missionary to the Indians, translated the Bible into "the Indian language" (Algonquin) in 1661. The formation of the American Bible Society in New York City on May 8, 1816, knit together more than thirty separate Bible societies, all of them dedicated to propagating the Scriptures among various constituencies, regions of the country, or foreign nations; in 1979 alone, the American Bible Society distributed nearly 110 million Bibles (or portions thereof) just in the United States.[4] The Gideons, an organization of lay evangelicals with headquarters in Nashville, Tennessee, supply Bibles to hospitals, military personnel, and hotel rooms with the confidence that the mere reading of the Bible can transform sinners into saints. The Bible, the Gideons say in the introductory pages to their New Testament, "should fill the memory, rule the heart, and guide the feet." "Read it slowly, frequently, and prayerfully," they counsel. "It is a mine of wealth, a paradise of glory, and a river of pleasure. It is given you in life, will be opened at the judgment, and be remembered forever. It involves the highest responsibility, will reward the greatest labor, and will condemn all who trifle with its sacred contents."

If Bible salesmen conjure images of Depression-era shysters rumbling across the Kansas plains in model T Fords, that notion is hopelessly out of date. Bibles are big business. Nothing illustrates that better than the huge exhibition hall of the Christian Booksellers Association convention, a cavernous room full of elaborate, brightly lit displays, some of them reaching high into the air to attract maximum attention. The CBA convention functions as a trade show for more than five thousand Christian bookstores across the country; it is, in fact, one of the largest trade shows in the nation, with more than 350 exhibitors consuming 275,000 square feet of space.[5] Here publishers display their wares and make their pitches to retail store owners and buyers. I saw several sales representatives in polyester suits and bad toupees at the CBA convention who looked as though they'd be just as comfortable kicking tires on a used-car lot as thumping Bibles in an air-conditioned exhibition hall, but on the whole, if this convention is any indication, the Bible business is slick, glitzy, professional, and fiercely competitive, with salesmen—and a few women—to match. Publishers compete vigorously with one another for market share, retail shelf space, and what they call clerk involvement to sell their products. Here at the convention, they offered various incentives to buyers: favorable credit terms, deferred billing, free shipping. Wm. B. Eerdmans Publishing Co. of Grand Rapids, Michigan, gave a Droste chocolate bar to anyone placing an order. Moody Press, a division of Moody Bible Institute in Chicago, offered a Cross pen.

Bibles are big business. Word Inc. of Waco, Texas, which publishes books for the evangelical market, was purchased by ABC several years back. After fending off a number of hostile takeover attempts, Zondervan Publishing House of Grand Rapids, Michigan, which holds the coveted rights to the New International Version of the Bible, had agreed to a friendly takeover by Harper & Row, owned by publishing magnate Rupert Murdoch, just a week prior to the 1988 CBA convention.[6]

Bibles are big business—especially in America among evangelical households, most of which are more likely to stock a dozen Bibles than only one or a couple. How big a business? Figures are hard to come by because such firms as Zondervan and Thomas Nelson Publishers of Nashville remain tight-lipped about their Bible sales. In the course of the convention I heard estimates ranging from $60 million to $200 million a year in the United States alone. No one can say for certain how many kinds of Bibles are available, but one distributor estimated that her company stocked over three thousand different translations and editions.

Bibles are big business.

But how do you keep selling Bibles in an already flooded market? Mike Colacuori, who describes himself as an "official peddler" for Omni Sales in Indiana, Illinois, and Michigan, compared the demand for Bibles to the demand for new cars. People buy Bibles because the old ones wear out, because of the availability of new versions, or maybe because a reader is getting older and wants larger type, he said. "Sometimes people buy Bibles on a whim, for no good reason. Then you have the first-time buyers: new Christians and kids who grew up in the church."

Paul Shepherd and Ida Fitz know the Bible business as well as anyone. Ida Fitz's father-in-law started distributing Bibles to Christian bookstores twenty years ago. Today Riverside Book & Bible House, a family-owned business in Iowa Falls, Iowa, takes in $35 million a year, out of which, they estimate, Bibles account for more than $25 million, making them the largest Bible wholesaler in the world. "When I started in this business with Thomas Nelson thirteen years ago," Shepherd, now an executive at Riverside, said, "we carried only three colors: black, brown, and red." Now consumers choose from a variety of bindings. A few years back, he said, the hottest color was brown. "Now you can't give a brown leather Bible away." This season's big sellers? Taupe, gray, and mauve.

In order to sell more and more Bibles, publishers have devised all sorts of angles: new translations, new typefaces, new colors, new bindings. Thomas Nelson recently unveiled a leather-bound Bible with a snap enclosure and a shoulder strap affixed to the spine; it looks like an elegant handbag. Several years back one publisher purchased the rights to about a dozen syrupy cartoon-like illustrations and interleaved them into one of its translations to market it as the Precious Moments Bible. Another publisher produced a Bible that helps the reader peruse both Old and New Testaments in a single year. The large-print Bible, Shepherd said, has been one of the strongest sellers over the past decade, a reflection of an aging population of Bible readers. "It used to be that the last quarter of the year was our best season," Ida Fitz said, "but now the demand remains high the year round." People buy Bibles for births, confirmations, weddings, graduations, Easter, Christmas—even for returning to school. Florists buy small Bibles to stick into flower arrangements. "Our office windows overlook the warehouse back in Iowa Falls," Fitz said, "and I don't think there's a day that goes by when we don't look at one another as we see Bibles loaded into box after box and ask, 'Where are all those Bibles going?'"

Despite the inroads of large corporations into the Bible business, many people selling Bibles and Christian literature do so, at least in part, out of a sense of mission. "I've chosen to sell Bibles because it directly promotes the gospel," Mike Colaquori told me. "I wanted to be in this industry." Ida Fitz and Paul Shepherd take evident satisfaction in their work, not only because it provides them a good living—it surely does that—but also, they say, because it "gets the message out." Many of the retailers that a distributor like Riverside deals with every day share similar sentiments. In the 1970s, on the heels of the Jesus movement, many of the people who opened Bible bookstores were long on faith and short on finances, with a surfeit of naiveté and very little know-how. Ida Fitz recalls receiving credit applications back from prospective customers with "The Lord will provide" scrawled across the top of the applications.

The entire industry has become a good bit more sophisticated since then—and a good bit more profitable. Christian bookstores do about $2 billion a year in retail sales, a figure that has doubled since 1980 and is expected to reach $3.6 billion by 1990.[7] The Christian Booksellers Association, with offices in Colorado Springs, Colorado, discourages people from entering the business unless they can come up with at least $20,000 in capital. The CBA also publishes *Bookstore Journal* every month, a trade magazine burgeoning with four-color advertisements, and advises bookstore owners on such issues as inventory control, payroll, and retirement plans. At the annual convention, retailers can attend seminars with titles like "Wrapping Up a Sale," "Cost-Effective Advertising for Small Businesses," and "How to Capture a Piece of the Video Market."

At some point (no one is sure exactly when) someone figured out that the patrons of a Christian bookstore will buy more than Bibles. In most such bookstores, Bibles now account for only about ten to twenty percent of sales. In mall stores, the percentage may be as low as five to six percent. The remainder of the receipts come from books, musical recordings, greeting cards, and other accouterments, all of which were abundantly in evidence in the CBA exhibition hall. A sampling of book titles offers a glimpse into the world of evangelical publishing:

How to Listen to God
You Are Somebody: You're Worth More than You Think
What It Means to Be Real
How to Know You're Saved
How to Be the Happy Wife of an Unsaved Husband
The Sacredness of Sex
Dark Secrets of the New Age
Share the New Life with a Jew
The Church Triumphant at the End of the Age
Santa and the Christ Child
How to Be a Good Dad
Maximized Manhood: A Guide to Family Survival
How to Keep Your Kids on Your Team
Keeping Your Teen in Touch With God
Conquering the Fear of Death
The Joy of Feeling Good
How to Be a Christian and Still Enjoy Life

At the booth of Moody Press of Chicago, a large queue formed to receive free promotional copies of a new book entitled *Mormonism, Mama & Me*, signed by an older woman dressed in a gingham "granny" costume with matching bonnet.

At hourly intervals during the convention, a succession of authors and musicians stationed themselves at five different "Personality Booths" throughout the exhibition hall. There they distributed and autographed copies of their latest books or recordings. Every subculture has its own heroes and stars, a phenomenon evident by the long lines that formed at the "Personality Booths" when someone well known to evangelicals appeared. These "names"—Chuck Swindoll, Mike Warnke, John MacArthur, Florence Littauer, a singer named Carman, a pianist named Dino—are virtually unknown outside the evangelical subculture, but here at the convention they attracted throngs of groupies, young and old.

The groupies especially throng around recording artists, and there are plenty to choose from. So-called Christian music ranges from the punk-rock sounds of Youth Choir, Undercover, and Altar Boys to the heavy metal of Stryper, Saint, Messiah Prophet Man, Barren

Cross, Resurrection Band, and Bloodgood. Carman, from what I was able to gather from descriptions of his music, is the evangelical counterpart to Julio Iglesias. Dino's style reminds many of Liberace. Some Christian artists, notably Amy Grant and Sandi Patti, occasionally produce hits that cross over to the secular charts. This "Christian" music—records, cassettes, compact discs, sheet music, orchestral backup tapes—accounts for a growing proportion—nearly twenty percent—of retail sales in Christian bookstores.[8]

The range of goods available at these bookstores, however, extends well beyond Bibles, books, and recordings. If you're serious about studying the Bible, you'll want a highlighter, a marker used to underline important or meaningful passages. If you use your Bible a lot, sooner or later you'll want to pick up a Bible tote of one kind or another. The BAC & Associates booth at the CBA convention offers a variety, ranging in price from $8.95 to $25.95: Deluxe Unlined Covers available in six designs (various doves, crosses, and fish), Premium Lined Covers, Deluxe Unlined Covers with Pockets, Petite Pastels, Tropical Treats (in colors like salmon and powder blue), Fabric Frillies (quilted fabric with lace edges), and top-of-the-line Trifold Bible Covers (leather-like vinyl with a locking clasp and an attache-style handle on the spine). Mountain Meadow Designs, doing business out of Utah, offers several styles in a canvas-like fabric. Bear Mountain Industries of Independence, Missouri, a couple of booths away, is one of many vendors who specialize in quilted Bible totes with embroidery on the outside and lace on the edges, but these totes, according to one saleswoman, are double-faced with several inside pockets for notebooks and pens. The quilted totes from ComforThings in Holyoke, Colorado, feature lace, buttons, flowers, and ribbons in various designs. Horizon Publishers of Bountiful, Utah, offers both quilted and vinyl Bible totes, but they also carry smaller sizes for pocket New Testaments.

Several vendors at the CBA convention were selling Sunday school curriculum materials and church supplies such as candles, light fixtures, song books, vestments, and choir robes. Evangelicalism's involvement with the temperance movement in the nineteenth and early twentieth centuries led to the substitution of grape juice for wine in Holy Communion and to the abandonment of the common cup or chalice for small, individual-sized glasses barely larger than a thimble. Some years back, suppliers began providing disposable plastic communion cups. New Covenant Communion Supply out of Fort Worth, Texas, for instance, advertises "High-Quality Communion Cups That Never Crack, Stick, or Leak!"

Evangelicals have also tapped into the home video market. Videocassettes run the gamut from lectures and biblical expositions by such preachers as Billy Graham, Kenneth Hagin, and R. C. Sproul to a series of "Bear Hugs" animations and dramatized Bible stories for children to videos of feature-length films such as Donald Thompson's apocalyptic series, *A Thief in the Night, A Distant Thunder, Image of the Beast,* and *Prodigal Planet.* A salesman representing Maranatha Campus Ministries International in Gainesville, Florida, was promoting a ninety-minute videocassette entitled "Rock and Roll Search for God," an exposé of the "demonic aspect of rock and roll music," geared to college students. "After seeing this thing," the representative told me, "they either run toward Jesus and accept Him as their savior or they run back to their old sinful lifestyles."

Calendars and greeting cards also sell very well in the evangelical market. A woman from VALdyme Inc. in Roseville, California, was at the CBA promoting a desktop calendar called Vision Planner, which "helps today's Christian Family prioritize their lives for a satisfying balance between physical and spiritual priorities." Some of the features include pages for prayer concerns and "space each day to record an inspirational thought, reminder, or lesson; keeping Christian faith in daily practice."[9] Many evangelicals would much rather purchase "Christian" greeting cards than "secular" ones. "Things that we value in the body of Christ are often cheapened by such things as greeting cards," said Mike Colacuori, the Bible salesman from the Midwest. "I've seen a lot of cards that might not actually be dirty, yet the punch line is something that undermines traditional Christian values. If a Christian goes into business to sell greeting cards, he's performing a legitimate service." Evangelical customers apparently agree, for there has been a proliferation of "Christian" greeting cards (and greeting-card companies) in recent years.

Many companies manufacture pictures, posters, and wall-hangings of various kinds. Good Things Co. of Norman, Oklahoma, offers two posters (framed or unframed), one of them showing the books of the Bible and the other charting the genealogy from Adam and Eve to Jesus. Jeremiah Junction of Manchester, Connecticut, sells counted cross-stitch patterns in various "inspirational" designs. Max Greiner, Jr., a loquacious young artist from Kerrville, Texas, sells variations on his "Christian Butterfly" design, a butterfly with wings in stained glass and a body shaped like a fish, symbolizing Christ (the first letters of "Jesus Christ, Son of God, Savior" spell *ichthus*—the Greek word for fish). "This is the first original symbol in two thousand years of Christian history," Greiner told me. "In October of 1986 I was desperately trying to conceive of a unique jewelry design to give to my wife on her birthday. After two weeks without an idea, I finally said to God, 'I give up; I need a good idea quick, please!' Instantly after this prayer, the image of the upside-down *ichthus* with butterfly wings appeared in my mind's eye. This one simple idea is probably the most profound and timeless design that has ever come to me. It's ironic that I cannot accept the credit, which must go to God."[10]

Some of the items for sale at the convention are seasonal. JESUS IS THE ♥ OF CHRISTMAS and JESUS IS THE REASON FOR THE SEASON festooned a whole panoply of Christmas goods—cards, gift wrap, posters, figurines, coffee mugs. A number of companies have introduced entire lines of books, videotapes, and trinkets aimed at children; some have devised Sesame Street-like characters—Gerbert and Andy Ant—to promote their wares. Several vendors sell key chains, combs, and bumper stickers: JESUS IS MY ROCK AND MY NAME IS ON THE ROLL, WARNING: IN CASE OF RAPTURE THIS CAR WILL BE UNMANNED, and GET RIGHT OR GET LEFT, a reference to the impending rapture and the apocalypse. Some peddled sponges with various sentiments emblazoned on them: TRUST IN THE LORD, GOD CLEANS ME FROM THE INSIDE OUT, KEEP AFLOAT WITH GOD.

So-called Christian tee-shirts were everywhere. A company named Images in the Son, based in Orange Park, Florida, boasted that they have sold three billion shirts. One style showed two flamingos, one of which had its head in a bucket, along with the warning, YOU CAN'T HIDE FROM GOD! Kingdom Shirt Ministries of Edmond, Oklahoma, specializes in shirts that replicate well-known logotypes and advertising slogans with slight variations: JESUS—THE RIGHT CHOICE (AT&T), OVER 80 MILLION SAVED (McDonald's), JESUS CHRIST—HE'S THE REAL THING (Coke), JESUS—THE CHOICE OF THE LAST GENERATION (Pepsi), FOR ALL YOU DO, HIS BLOOD'S FOR YOU (Budweiser).

Tee-shirts are not the only apparel available. I didn't see them at the CBA convention, but someone told me about "Witness Panty Hose," which featured a fish design interwoven into the nylon and a Bible verse around the ankles. Christian World Inc. of Oklahoma City had perhaps the most lavish display at the convention, with French provincial furniture, plush purple carpeting deep enough to pitch you off balance, and fashionably dressed salespeople dripping in gold jewelry and hair-styling mousse. "Our products will always be unique and only the finest quality because we feel that as a Christian company, God expects us to do only the finest," Mark A. Stevens, president of the company, writes in Christian World's elaborate promotional materials. "I know that with your effort we can help to spread our Father's message to the greatest number of people possible." Christian World sells wedding accessories, table and bed linens, stick-up magnets, and "inspirational drinking glasses and mugs."

For $5.99, the World Bible Society sells a cassette called "Heavenly Touch—Spiritually Inspired Phone Messages for Your Phone Answering Device." Someone else offered a cardboard sun shield for the front window of parked cars. The outside reads JESUS IS LORD, and the reverse side says NEED HELP! PLEASE CALL POLICE. Sonshine Graphics of Corona, California, recently introduced "an exciting new product," a package of home security yard signs, home window decals, and car window decals, all in the shape of a shield with the rather intimidating legend: PROTECTED BY SHED-BLOOD SECURITY UNLTD. "Now believers can proclaim their belief in God's protecting hand in a very tangible and visible way," the ad copy reads. "SHED-BLOOD SECURITY UNLTD. offers the consumer the advantage of both discouraging would-be prowlers and an opportunity to witness to neighbors about their security in Christ."[11]

There is a strong conservative political bias permeating the Christian Booksellers Association. The 1988 convention took place during the same week that the Democrats were holding their national convention in Atlanta. The morning after Jesse Jackson's speech at the Democratic gathering, one exhibitor remarked that the Democrats needed a linguist to sort out Jackson's "'dis and 'dat." At one of the flag-bedecked booths at the CBA convention, men in red neckties, white shirts, and blue suits were hawking something called the American Prayer Action Calendar, which, for $6.95, suggests a different prayer concern—pornography, abortion, homosexuality—for every day of the year. "Our idea is to have Christians all across the country praying for the same issues every day," Harry E. Gibbons, author of the calendar, said. Several weeks hence, the readers would be asked to pray for the Republican national convention in New Orleans; this week, however, they were to pray for the Christian Booksellers Association convention. Harvest House Publishers of Eugene, Oregon, were enthusiastic about a new book entitled *George Bush: Man of Integrity*. Another title available to bookstore buyers at the CBA was *A Fighting Chance: The Moral Use of Nuclear Weapons*, which had received lavish praise from several prominent conservatives. Robert Faid, who describes himself as a nuclear engineer and who holds a master's degree in theology from Coatesville Bible College, was at the convention pushing his new book, *Gorbachev! Has the Real Antichrist Come?*, which argues that Mikhail Gorbachev is the Antichrist predicted in the Bible. "Gorbachev meets fourteen of the sixteen prophetic identity clues in the Scriptures," Faid told me confidently. When you assign numbers to the letters in Gorbachev's name, using the Cyrillic alphabet, he said, it comes out to 666, the mark of the beast. Then there is the matter of the birthmark on the Soviet leader's forehead. "When I look at the top of Gorbachev's head, I see a red dragon and over the right eye, there's a tail that hangs, representing stars," Faid said. This, he believes, resembles the description of Satan in the book of Revelation. "If Gorbachev is truly the Antichrist," Faid concludes,

"Satan branded him in his mother's womb."[12] Moreover, Faid said that he had computed the odds against Gorbachev's being the Antichrist; they work out to 710 quadrillion to one (specifically, 710,609,175,188,282,100 to 1).

A number of people I spoke with expressed uneasiness about all the kitsch everywhere in evidence in the exhibition hall and the materialism implicit in its popularity. "It's almost a misnomer to call this the Christian Booksellers Association," Ida Fitz of Riverside Book & Bible House told me. "So much of the business transacted here is in gifts or what some people call 'holy hardware'; comparatively little has to do with books." So far, Riverside has stayed out of the gift business, although Fitz allowed that her company has already contemplated expansion into that area. "There's more markup in gifts," she said. "That's why bookstores like to move that merchandise."

Other long-term observers sense a real tragedy in the commercialism and the carnival atmosphere at the CBA. Jon Pott, editor-in-chief of Wm. B. Eerdmans in Grand Rapids, sees a trend away from quality literature and an increased traffic in self-help books and various trinkets. "This may be the last time I stay for the whole convention," he said quietly as he surveyed the exhibition floor. "I find it utterly demoralizing." When I asked Luci Shaw, a poet and head of Harold Shaw Publishers in Wheaton, Illinois, for her impressions of the Christian Booksellers Association, she looked down and shook her head. "Yesterday afternoon I got so fed up with the whole thing that I went home to my hotel and cried for two hours." She cited the quest for fame and fortune on the part of both authors and publishers. Within the world of evangelical publishing, she said, "authors become celebrities very fast, and money and power are so corrosive." Shaw, herself a product of the evangelical subculture, is clearly disillusioned. She is now an Episcopalian and has considered distancing her publishing house from the evangelical market. "But I can't do that," she said in a tone of resignation. "I have to make a living."

If Johann Gutenberg managed to make it this far on our tour of the CBA exhibition, I'd want to make one last stop, at the elaborate booth of Tyndale House Publishers, Wheaton, Illinois, publishers of the enormously profitable Living Bible, which has sold over thirty-five million copies since its release in 1970. Gutenberg might faintly recognize the fellow in ersatz Elizabethan costume standing atop a carpeted soapbox hawking Tyndale House's newest product, the Life Application Bible, which retails for $34.95 in cloth binding or $49.95 in bonded leather. This chap purported to be William Tyndale himself, the sixteenth-century translator of the Bible. During "Tyndale's" soliloquy, the publisher's sales representatives distributed small parchment-like folders to the gathering of onlookers. At the conclusion of his pitch, "Tyndale" instructed the crowd to break the seal and look inside for an illustration of the Life Application Bible, which provides not only the Scripture passages themselves, but also a "Life Application Note" to enlarge upon the message of the Scriptures. At the top of the parchment was a passage from the Living Bible:

> For neither you nor anyone else can serve two masters. You will hate one and show loyalty to the other, or else the other way around— you will be enthusiastic about one and despise the other. You cannot serve both God and money.[13]

The "Life Application Note" followed:

> Money has the power to take God's place in your life. It can become your master. How can you tell if you are a slave to money? (1) Do you worry about it frequently? (2) Do you give up doing what you should do or would like to do in order to make more money? (3) Do you spend a great deal of time caring for your possessions? (4) Is it hard for you to give money away? (5) Are you in debt?
>
> Money is a hard master and a deceptive one. Money promises power and control, but it often cannot deliver. Great fortunes can be made—and lost—overnight, and no amount of money can provide health, happiness, or eternal life. How much better to let God be your master. His servants have peace of mind and security both now and forever.

The sales representatives milling around the booth seemed pleased with the response. Tyndale had another winner.

Bibles are big business.

NOTES

1. For an excellent treatment of the various—and contradictory—ways in which Americans have used the Bible throughout history, see Nathan O. Hatch and Mark A. Noll, eds., *The Bible in America: Essays in Cultural History* (New York: Oxford University Press, 1982).

2. Walter A. Elwell, "Belief and the Bible: A Crisis of Authority?" *Christianity Today*, 21 March 1980, pp. 20–23.

3. Isa. 55:11.

4. Mark A. Noll, *et al.*, eds., *Eerdmans' Handbook to Christianity in America* (Grand Rapids: Wm. B. Eerdmans, 1983), p. 488.

5. George W. Cornell, "Christian Book Business Booms," Rockford (Ill.) *Register Star*, 24 July 1988, p. 8C (this story was picked up from the Associated Press).

6. In 1987 Zondervan had a net income of $859,000 on sales of $105.8 million; see "Murdoch Buys Bible Printer," *New York Newsday*, 14 July 1988, p. 49 (this story was picked up from Reuters).

7. Cornell, "Christian Book Business Booms," p. 8C.

8. Ibid.

9. Quotations taken from VALdyme promotional literature.

10. Quotations from a conversation with Max Greiner, Jr., and from his promotional literature.

11. From the ad copy of Sonshine Graphics's advertisement in *Bookstore Journal* (July 1988): 16.

12. Art Levine, "The Devil in Gorbachev," *Washington Post*, 5 June 1988, pp. C1, C4. Faid says that the biblical reference to Satan as a red dragon with a trail of stars is Rev. 12:3–4.

13. Luke 16:13 (TLB).

9

Episcopal Indians

ACCORDING TO DAKOTA LEGEND, a young Indian woman and her child refused to accompany her tribe as they fled south before the advance of white soldiers. When some of her people later returned to the camp to find her, they discovered that she and the child on her back had turned to stone. That stone, called Standing Rock, has been held in reverence by the Sioux for generations, and today it rests on a pedestal in Fort Yates, North Dakota, overlooking, in the words of a nearby plaque, "the waters and the empire once held by the mighty Sioux Nation."

When Jesus commanded His disciples to preach the gospel "to the ends of the earth,"[1] He might have had in mind places like Fort Yates, North Dakota. Fort Yates may not be the end of the earth, but, as the old saw goes, you can see it from here. I was here to see what evangelical impulses persist within the Episcopal Church, a denomination not generally associated with evangelicalism, and also to assess the extent to which Christian missions engage in a kind of cultural imperialism, an insistence that converts adopt the missionaries' culture along with their religion. In the nineteenth century, mainline denominations—Congregationalists, Baptists,

Methodists, Presbyterians, Roman Catholics—organized missions among the Indians, but most of them have since lost interest in the enterprise, even though they maintain a residual presence on reservations throughout the West. Here at Fort Yates in the Standing Rock Indian Reservation, a handful of Episcopalians are struggling to retain a foothold and to temper some of the cultural imperialism that has characterized Christian mission efforts in the past.

The waters of the Missouri River no longer flow at Standing Rock's feet; the United States Army Corps of Engineers saw to that some years back when they built a dam at Pierre, South Dakota. The river running past Fort Yates and the Standing Rock Indian Reservation became Lake Oahe, a huge expanse of water that swallowed up much of the land along the Missouri, clogged adjoining wells with silt, and left the carcasses of countless trees pointing their dead, whitened branches above the water in a kind of eerie and desolate beauty.

Lake Oahe provides irrigation, flood control, and recreation, but the waters no longer flow, and that offends Father Innocent Good House, a Sioux Indian and rector of St. Luke's Episcopal Church in Fort Yates. "An Indian believes that the waters of a river should flow," he said. The damming of the Missouri, he believes, underscores a difference between Indian and Christian religions and their views of the world. Whereas Indians believe in fashioning their lives in harmony with nature, Christians too often have interpreted the biblical injunction to have dominion over the earth as license to alter the created order, to tamper with its rhythms and control its unpredictabilities.

But Good House, a quiet, taciturn man of sixty-eight, is more interested in the parallels between Christianity and Indian religions and in convincing his fellow Sioux of the compatibility of those traditions. Over the course of several days, he pointed out those parallels. Both religions have sacraments. Both are monotheistic—Indians believe in the Great Spirit, the creator, while the Judeo-Christian tradition honors Yahweh, the creator. The Indian naming ceremony, when an Indian child of about twelve years receives an ancestral name, resembles christening or confirmation or the Jewish bar mitzvah. The rite of purification resembles baptism. In the course of a vision quest, an Indian goes up to a hill for four days of prayer, seeking spiritual guidance, an exercise not unlike Jesus's wanderings in the wilderness for forty days. Good House finds affinities even in social patterns. The extended kinship ties among Indians is similar to the fellowship of believers or the communion of the saints that characterizes the Church. Just as the early Christians of the New Testament held goods in common and provided for one another's well-being, Indians for centuries have practiced a kind of welfare system that, informally and by common consent, provides for the sick, infirm, and elderly. The Church has looked to elders for spiritual guidance and counsel; Indians venerate their elders, because they are closer to death and, hence, closer to God, and because they have amassed wisdom in the course of a lifetime.

It would be easy, I suppose, to dismiss these sentiments as mere puffery, the kind of inclusive posturing that liberal Episcopalians have elevated to an art form in recent decades. Episcopalians have never been noted for theological rigidity, after all, much less for evangelistic fervor, although there are a number of charismatic Episcopal parishes in the United States. But Innocent Good House carries about him a sincerity and earnestness—even a quiet passion—about both his faith and his heritage. He can speak in one breath about the importance of bringing his fellow Sioux to Christ and in the next about the necessity of perpetuating Sioux religious traditions without any sense that the two might be mutually exclusive.

The affinities between Christianity and native religions, however, have not always been apparent to Christians working among the Sioux. "When the missionaries came onto the reservation," Good House said, "they made me a Christian, but they also destroyed my language and my culture." The task of making Christians of the Indians was made easier, ironically, by the parallels between the two belief systems, parallels obvious to many of the Indians, even if the missionaries chose to ignore them.

Spanish missionaries—the Jesuits and, later, the Franciscans— began proselytizing the natives of the New World early in the sixteenth century. Conversion of the Indians provided a major rationale for colonization during the seventeenth century, as English Puritans, Dutch Calvinists, and French Jesuits sought to transform "savages" into Christians. In almost all cases, contact with the missionaries spelled disaster for Indian cultures. Exposure to alien diseases and viruses often decimated native populations.[2] In other instances, missionaries effectively disarmed the Indians, leaving them vulnerable to the attacks of other Indians or unscrupulous whites. Almost invariably, missionaries chose to ignore the commonalities between Christianity and Indian religions and demanded that their converts abjure all participation in native rituals. "The greatest problem of the missionary," Father Fermín F. Lausuén, head of Spanish missions in California, wrote in 1801, "was how to transform a savage race such as these into a society that is human, Christian, civil, and industrious."[3] Missionaries would go to almost any ends to convert the Indians—whom they regarded as barbaric, heathen, and godless—and to make them docile and even "white."[4]

John Eliot's mission among the Indians of seventeenth-century New England provides a good example. Eliot, a Puritan, took great pains to learn the Algonquin language and, by all accounts, genuinely cared for the Indians and sincerely sought their conversion. He demanded, however, that his charges give up their hunting-and-gathering way of life and segregated them into fourteen "Praying Towns." There he taught them to grow crops, required that they cut their hair, and even schooled them in the vagaries of Ramist logic, a system of thought propounded by a European philosopher that would tax the intellectual faculties of any theologian. Although they had converted to Christianity, these Red Puritans remained segregated in Praying Towns and were never fully accepted by the larger Puritan community. When the Indian rebellion known as King Philip's War broke out in 1675, prompted by the steady encroachment of the Puritans onto Indian lands, Puritan magistrates (over Eliot's objections) drove the converted Indians out of their settlements and onto Deer Island in Boston Harbor, where, without adequate provisions, many of them perished in the bleak winter of 1675–1676.[5]

In the nineteenth century, the United States government, armed with superior weapons and the doctrine of manifest destiny, subjugated the Indians militarily and herded them onto reservations. The Homestead Act of 1862 encouraged white settlement in erstwhile Indian territories. Christian missionaries from the East then began their efforts in earnest, often cooperating with federal agencies. Christianity became not merely another, purportedly superior, religion, but also a means for domesticating the Indians and schooling them in the superior ways of white culture. During my stay in Fort Yates, one of Good House's parishioners showed me a button issued in the 1800s by the U.S. Indian Department that she had found nearby in what was once the Dakota Territory. The design depicts an Indian and a plow, with sun and rain overhead. The surrounding motto reads, "God Helps Them Who Help Themselves," that familiar Christian bromide often attributed, inaccurately, to the Bible.[6]

Protestant missionaries among the Indians proffered their own cultural biases. After translating the Old and New Testaments and various hymnbooks into Dakota, a Sioux dialect, the Reverend Stephen Return Riggs also translated *The Pilgrim's Progress*, that classic of English Puritan spirituality, for the edification of the Sioux. In 1890, Miss Mary Collins and Grindstone, a converted Sioux, broke up a Ghost Dance at Chief Sitting Bull's camp on the Grand River and lured the Indians away to a Christian worship service.

Indian culture and traditions suffered under these assaults. Several people over the course of my visit listed the effects of this dissolution: despair, poverty, unemployment, exogamous marriages, and the breakdown of kinship ties. Indeed, a sense of hopelessness seems almost palpable at Standing Rock Indian Reservation. The signs of poverty abound. The unemployment rate among those sixteen and older is seventy-nine percent.[7] In the absence of jobs and industry, federal assistance provides the major source of income, yet the Sioux feel stifled by government regulations that restrict their use of the land. A once-proud people has been reduced to aimlessness.

Boredom exacts a toll. Bingo has become quite popular here. "There's nothing wrong with bingo itself, I guess," Father Good House told me, "but when people sell everything they have to play bingo, then it's wrong. If you would go into even some of the nicer houses in town here, you would see barely a stick of furniture. They've sold it off to get money for bingo."

The second "B" that plagues the Sioux, especially the young, is booze. "It's a big, big problem here," Good House said, "the number one problem," an assessment shared by virtually everyone I talked with on the reservation. Young Sioux turn to alcohol and often to drugs out of a sense of despair and hopelessness, drinking themselves into stupors that all too frequently turn violent. "Alcohol and drugs are ruining our Indian people," two Sioux women agreed. Several people told me of family members who had died because of the effects of alcohol, resulting either in suicide, automobile accidents, or outright violence. The problem, according to Edna Good House, the rector's wife, is especially acute among veterans. "They leave the reservation and join the army," she said. "The army teaches them how to kill, and when they get back here, resume their drinking, and get into an argument, they pull out a gun and start shooting."

"Look in any Indian cemetery around here," Father Good House added. "You'll see the headstones of people who died in their twenties and thirties."

St. Paul's Episcopal Cemetery, in South Dakota, about thirty-five miles south of Fort Yates, lies on a hill overlooking the village of Little Eagle. The barren, treeless landscape offers no relief from the hot sun and temperatures well in excess of one hundred degrees. Sweet clover, a yellowish wildflower and the only vegetation in sight, covers the hillside and much of the cemetery. A low wire fence surrounds the burial ground; a simple, wooden plank high over the gate identifies the cemetery on one side and, on the other, reads: JESUS SAID, "I AM THE WAY, THE TRUTH, AND THE LIFE". White, weathered crosses, most of them askew, pitched alternately by blistering heat and deadening frost, mark the graves of those who lie beneath the parched, cracked earth:

ORLIE L. LITTLE DOG
1960–1981

KATHERINE KILLS CROW
1959–1975

JOHN CARRION, JR.

1953–1972

CORNELIUS BOBTAIL BEAR

1957–1984

WILLIAM BOBTAIL BEAR

1958–1985

Another graveyard on a nearby rise, the Elk Horn Hill Cemetery, tells a similar story about depredations of alcohol and the perils of youth on the reservation.

Observers have long puzzled over the peculiar Indian vulnerability to liquor. Some posit a physiological weakness that leaves them susceptible, while others blame a lack of discipline. Sociologists cite a familiar litany of conditions—unemployment, boredom, a sense of powerlessness—that leads to despair and then to the bottle. Father Good House, while not dismissing these factors, believes that rampant alcoholism among the Indians arises from a fundamental confusion about who they are, a confusion born of cultural disintegration and this tension between the traditions of Indian culture and the demands of white civilization. "To me, drinking and violence are caused by culture shock," he said, "the result of an uncertain identity."

Good House wants to see the Sioux recover their heritage and traditions, and this weekend, beneath a relentless July sun, the Sioux of Standing Rock are trying to do just that. The Little Eagle powwow began Thursday evening with a gathering of spiritual leaders—ministers and medicine men—and will continue through Sunday. This annual event, observed in towns and villages throughout the reservation on various weekends during the summer, is a kind of extended family reunion, a time to celebrate Sioux traditions, renew acquaintances, and dine on such fare as cornbread, Indian tacos, and barbecued buffalo.

The centerpiece of the festivities this year is the dedication of a memorial to the 260 men and women of the Little Antelope district (the immediate area) who served in the United States armed forces. Throughout the afternooon of speeches and ceremonies, the residents of Little Eagle, who raised over $5,000 to erect the monument, regarded it with evident pride. Interspersed with speeches by local veterans, officers of the South Dakota American Legion, and a representative from Senator Tom Daschle's office, the Sioux conducted various dedicatory rites of their own, including a peace-pipe ceremony and a naming ceremony, performed by Joe Flying Bye.[8] "We seek the power to live upon this earth in a good way," one Sioux said, explaining the significance of the peace pipe. And then he reiterated, almost plaintively: "We still want to live upon this earth. We still want to live in a good way."

That evening, the powwow shifted to an arena outside of town for ceremonial dancing. On this dusty parcel of land covered with a fragile veneer of weeds sits a small, circular grandstand, rather rickety with age. Inside, Indians in a variety of ceremonial garb dance about the arena to the beat of drums and the chant of "singers" whose songs sound (at least to my ears) more like a high-pitched, cacophonous whine than music. The entire scene, though rich in history and tradition, also contains its share of incongruities. The singers—paunchy men seated on lawn chairs and hunched over a bass drum that looks as though it was purloined from a high school band—project into a microphone that amplifies the sound across the arena through large, gray speakers. A warren of concession stands, selling hot dogs, ice cream bars, and Coca-Cola, rings the grandstand. Beyond that, Indians visiting the powwow from greater distances have pitched canvas tents or parked camping trailers and motor homes.

Inside the arena, the dancing continues to the music of successive groups of singers, representing various towns on the reservation. The dancers, most of them young, prance around the arena in steps that range from nimble and elegant to plodding and heavy-footed. By about nine o'clock, the gaits have slowed somewhat, and no one minds when the announcer calls for an intermission, during which Vernon Iron Cloud, a Congregationalist minister from Cannon Ball, conducts a naming ceremony for a young Sioux girl. Indian rites such as this provide the occasion for elaborate gift-giving. After the young girl receives her Indian name, her family carries armloads of gifts into the arena, most of them hand-made star quilts, for distribution to friends and relatives. The patriarch of the family then takes the microphone to offer an elaborate apology that he cannot give more gifts. If we had a little more money, he says, we might be able to do more. As it is, the distribution of three to four dozen quilts takes more than half an hour.

Such gift-giving in itself represents an affirmation of Indian traditions. It cements kinship ties and celebrates interdependence. "No Indian keeps a star quilt that she has made," Edna Good House explained. "She always gives it to someone else. It's the Indian way."

There's no such thing as a rich Indian, several people told me. "A true Indian does not accumulate worldly goods," Father Good House said. "Very seldom will an Indian have an estate go to probate. He simply leaves nothing behind."

After the naming ceremony and the distribution of gifts, the dancing resumes and continues into the early morning hours. A powwow, Father Good House believes, is an important exercise in the conservation of Indian ways, and for Little Eagle, this year's powwow comes at a propitious time. In recent weeks, three young people of the village have died in alcohol-related violence. Some are so desperate for alcohol that they have taken to separating the alcohol out of Lysol, a cleaning disinfectant. (Good House recently conducted the funeral of a young man in Fort Yates who tried to do this, apparently while already intoxicated. He separated it incompletely and died when the chemicals burned his mouth, esophagus, and stomach.) In Little Eagle, Good House told me, "the social problems are escalating—they're killing each other and drinking—because we don't have a stable economy. When there's no work, the social problems escalate. Too often, the Church's efforts have amounted to a band-aid ministry; the problems are getting bigger, and the Church's ministries are getting smaller." Moreover, the economic conditions and the struggle for economic survival, he said, have cut into the attractiveness of the Church.

Virtually everyone agrees that the Sioux have evinced a greater interest in their traditions in recent years. The occupation of Wounded Knee, South Dakota, in 1973 dramatized some of the Indians' grievances against the federal government in particular and white civilization in general. Since then, more and more Indians, many of them young people, have tried to regain touch with Indian culture.[9] Many have embarked on vision quests. Courses in reservation schools teach Indian history. Boys take an interest in Indian rites and ceremonies. Girls are learning to quilt, make earrings, and bead with a loom. I spoke with several women who regret having failed to learn to "speak Indian" from their grandmothers, who had spoken nothing else. Alice Jewett, a middle-aged women and mother of three, can make a star quilt in three days. "I want to learn to make moccasins," she said, adding, however, with a note of sadness, that Indian traditions are "slowly fading out." She counsels her children to learn Sioux and to "marry their own kind." But they don't, she said in a tone of resignation.

Father Good House had warned me that I would encounter a spectrum of opinions regarding the compatibility of Sioux traditions and Christianity. He has noticed in recent years a waning of interest in the Church among the youth in proportion to the resurgence of interest in native traditions. "The search for roots," he said, "is often painful and slow, yet it's important." I met several strict traditionalists who adhere only to Indian religious rites and who reject Christian traditions altogether. Two women, one from White Horse and the other from Wakpala, South Dakota, saw no contradiction between Indian religions and Christianity. These women, both of them Episcopalians, participated enthusiastically in the Little Eagle powwow. They acknowledged, however, that most churches are not so tolerant. The pentecostals, they said, call Indian traditions "devil worship," the "devil's doings," and accuse participants of "dancing for themselves." "They run down the peace pipe," Alice Jewett said. The Catholics, after decades of resistance, are starting to blend traditions, but the Mormons and Jehovah's Witnesses, relative newcomers to the reservation, denounce the practitioners of Indian ceremonies as "sinners." The Mormons came into Wakpala, Beverly Howard said, and "messed up a lot of church members"; the Witnesses, she added, "mix us up." Both women agreed that the Mormons, the Jehovah's Witnesses, and even pentecostal groups prey on the confusion Indians feel about the legitimacy of their traditions.

Just a few blocks from the powwow, one of Little Eagle's streets dissolves rather unceremoniously into a gravel parking lot surrounded on three sides by mobile homes. Straight ahead, one trailer sits behind piles of scrap lumber. To the right, a second white trailer sports a makeshift wooden entryway shaped like an A. On the left, looking slightly more dignified, a larger mobile home serves as the present church building for the Little Eagle Holiness Church. I caught up with the Reverend John Bush, pastor of this church, late on Saturday evening. The sounds of the powwow across town drifted by, and yet this dusty parking lot bustled with activity. Bush himself, a somewhat rakish looking fellow in denims, western shirt, and a straw cowboy hat, appeared to be working with several others on some kind of construction or clean-up project, and it quickly became clear that he had little interest in the goings-on across town.

The next afternoon I sat down with Bush, his wife, DeVonna, and three of their friends who were visiting from Green Grass, South Dakota. John and DeVonna Bush, both Ogallala Sioux Indians from the Pine Ridge Indian Reservation in South Dakota, became Christians under the ministry of Wesleyan Methodist missionaries. They decided to become missionaries themselves, attended Northwest Indian Bible School in Albertson, Montana, and came to Little Eagle to begin a holiness church in 1981.

I asked Bush how many of his congregation had participated in the powwow that weekend. "Probably all of them," he said, a bit uneasily. When I asked if he objected to their participation, Bush became evasive. "God has to deal with each person individually," he said. "People will continue to do things until God shows them differently. Each person has to have his heart open to God."[10]

How did he feel about the compatibility of Indian traditions and Christianity? "You can't mix Indian religion and Christianity," Bush said. "A long time ago Indian religions were all right—before Christianity; after that, there was a new way, through Christ. Now there's a better life, a better way." Marie Fiddler, one of the friends from Green Grass, said that her ancestors had engaged in Indian religious rituals before the missionaries came, but "once the church came, they put those Indian traditional practices aside. At that time there was no Bible. That's why them people lived that way."

DeVonna Bush recalled an encounter with Indian traditionalists when she was a teenager. "They look down on you if you're a Christian and accuse you of following a white man's religion. I was called a traitor by a medicine man." For a time she tried to reconcile Christianity with her people's traditions. "It took me a while to realize it was wrong to mix the two," she said. Her husband reiterated that a true Christian "can't mix the Bible and traditions," which he characterized as heathen and pagan.

When I rehearsed for them the parallels between Christianity and Indian religions that Father Good House had pointed out to me, they were singularly unimpressed. Episcopalians on the reservation, I said, see nothing evil or sinful about incorporating native rituals into their worship services, that in fact those native rituals represent an affirmation for Indians of who they are. Yes, they are Christians, but they are more than that. They have an ethnic identity as Indians as well.

"When the medicine men pray," Marie Fiddler responded after a pause, "they pray to someone between earth and heaven and not to God." But wouldn't they insist they were praying to the Great Spirit, which might simply be another name for God? "We have to have a standard, and the Bible provides that standard," Bush said. "When the Bible came in, it showed them that Jesus was the only sacrifice. After that, the peace pipe didn't have any place in worship. We're not here to change the way they live. We're here to tell them that there is a better way through Jesus."

Several times in our conversation, Bush cited the Sioux Sun Dance ceremony as an example of the paganism inherent in Indian religions. A Sioux who wants to perform the Sun Dance ritual will seek out someone who has performed the ritual himself. The candidate then undergoes an extended period of instruction and preparation, lasting up to a year. The dance itself, held during the moon of the ripening chokecherries, lasts several days, during which time the candidate dances for long intervals and neither eats nor drinks. A circular arbor of poles covered with leafy boughs surrounds the dance site, and a sacred lodge, where the candidate receives his final instructions, is constructed slightly to the east. A forked cottonwood tree, located in the center of the dance arbor, serves as the Sun Dance pole.

At dawn on the final day, mentor and candidate greet the sun and pray for strength. A peace pipe is passed to all assembled for the ceremony, amidst the smell of burning sweet grass, a purifying incense. After further ritual preparations and dances, the candidate's skin is pierced just below the shoulder and a skewer inserted like a hatpin. A rawhide thong then attaches the skewer to the top of the cottonwood Sun Dance pole. Once secured, the Sun Dance proper begins, amidst the songs and encouragements of fellow tribesmen. The candidate dances slowly at first, gazing constantly at the sun, and then the tempo gradually quickens as the dancer, borne along by hunger, thirst, pain, and fatigue, receives his vision. The ceremony concludes only when the candidate's gyrations succeed in tearing the skewer free from his flesh.[11]

Bush dismisses all this as paganism and quite unworthy of anyone who considers himself a Christian. Father Good House, who has never witnessed a Sun Dance, confesses to some discomfiture about the ceremony, but he believes that the intimations of sacrifice for the good of the community and even the self-inflicted torture recall Christ's sufferings and crucifixion.

The 1982 hymnal of the Episcopal Church contains a hymn adapted from a Dakota Indian chant:

> Many and great, O God, are thy works,
> maker of earth and sky;
> thy hands have set the heavens with stars;
> thy fingers spread the mountains and plains.
> Lo, at thy word the waters were formed;
> deep seas obey thy voice.[12]

The congregation at St. Luke's in Fort Yates didn't sing that hymn the morning of my visit, but there were other reminders of the compatibility of Christianity and Indian traditions. A God's eye hangs above the lectern; an Indian ceremonial staff hangs over the board that announces the morning hymns; an Indian star quilt behind the altar reminds parishioners of the God whose realm extends to the four corners of the earth.

Innocent Good House's homily noted that a misguided search for meaning sometimes leads to cults, sometimes to alcoholism. "We need a commitment to God," he said, "to stand against the plagues of alcohol and drugs." Railing against a faith that makes no demands of the faithful, he said that Christians of our day have reduced the cost of discipleship to rummage-sale prices. He emphasized to his parishioners the importance of personal devotions and evangelizing their friends for Christ.

The Prayers of the People that morning included petitions for the sick, the imprisoned, and those troubled with alcohol. Father Good House uses every opportunity at his disposal to warn against the evils of liquor. When an Indian lives beyond age fifty-nine, he told me several days earlier, he is regarded as an elder in the Sioux kinship system and is accorded certain privileges, including the right to be heard. Whenever Good House conducts the funeral service for a young victim of alcohol, he counsels the survivors to avoid a similar fate. "Of course I preach on the resurrection," he said, "but I also emphasize that we who remain are the ones who have to do something about this problem." A poster in the narthex of St. Luke's depicts two Indian women with tears running down their faces, against the background of a liquor bottle. "Alcohol is not only harmful to your health," the legend reads, "but to the ones you love too!"

Father Good House sees some signs of hope, however tentative, among his people. For many years, he was the only Indian rector on the reservation, until Father Harold Eagle Bull took the parish at Cannon Ball, twenty miles north of Fort Yates. He cited various programs, funded by the diocese of North Dakota, aimed at young people. "These people are beginning to learn something about God the creator," he said. Some of the younger Sioux, Good House believes, are also beginning to attach a stigma to drunkenness. Many Indians are trying to recover their traditions, and still others, though far fewer in number, have responded to his vision of a faith broad and inclusive enough to embrace their hereditary culture.

But the obstacles persist. Only about two dozen parishioners had shown up for the Sunday service. The original mainline denominations that evangelized the Indians have largely lost interest in Indian missions, giving way to groups like Jehovah's Witnesses, Bush's holiness church, and the well-financed Mormons, who condemn native religions and lure many of the best students off the reservation to be educated in Mormon schools. As the proliferation of these churches on the reservation suggests, the hard-nosed refusal to countenance Indian traditions is clearly more successful than Good House's belabored attempts to reconcile Christianity with native rituals. Some of that success doubtless derives both from a lingering sense of the inferiority of Indian culture and from an unambiguous call to renounce all native traditions.

Father Good House's efforts at reconciliation also suffer from the lack of institutional support. The Episcopalians have virtually abandoned mission work among the Indians in favor of more contemporary concerns such as the ordination of women, gay rights, and liberation theology that, ironically enough, advocates the struggle of the poor in Latin America against oppressive social institutions. That irony deepens if Innocent Good House is correct in his assertion that Christian missionaries, including Episcopalians, contributed to the cultural disintegration that lies at the heart of the social problems now confronting the Sioux.

The cultural imperialism of nineteenth-century missions and the destruction of native culture have indeed left indelible scars. Father Good House's evangelistic efforts on the reservation have met with some deep-seated resentment toward Christianity. "I don't think many of the Sioux have forgiven the Church for what it has done to us," he said quietly. "I think that some sort of public reconciliation should be one of the priorities of evangelism among the Indians." Edna Good House, a member of the board of trustees of Standing Rock College in Fort Yates, told of divisions that have afflicted the community in recent years, bitter disagreements that led to the establishment of a second high school in the town. "The community is divided," she said, "because we don't hear the gospel." She also said that when her husband retires in two years there will be no one to take over the church in Fort Yates. "That person would have to be in seminary now," she said, "but he would have to pay his own way. The people here have no money."

As I prepared to leave Fort Yates, Edna Good House, in the best Indian tradition, insisted on lading me with gifts: two quilted pillows and an Indian star quilt. "An Indian never says 'goodbye,' " she said, "only 'see you later.' We have no word for 'goodbye.' "

"The Sioux language has no curse words, either," Father Good House added. "It's a beautiful, beautiful language," he said wistfully.

Since the waters of Lake Oahe rose two decades ago, only a single road, a narrow isthmus, connects Fort Yates with the rest of Standing Rock Indian Reservation. On the way out of town I passed the original gravesite of Sitting Bull, General Custer's nemesis at Little Big Horn, who died in the 1890s while defending the Sioux Ghost Dance. At Highway 1806 I turned right and headed north along the once-flowing waters of the Missouri.

NOTES

1. Acts 1:8 (NIV).

2. By some estimations, the Indian population of central Mexico declined from twenty-five million in 1519 to just over one million in 1605; see Charles Gibson, *Spain in America* (New York: Harper & Row, 1966), p. 63.

3. Jay P. Dolan, *The American Catholic Experience: A History from Colonial Times to the Present* (Garden City, N.Y.: Doubleday, 1985), p. 24.

4. This is the general conclusion of Henry Warner Bowden in *American Indians and Christian Missions: Studies in Cultural Conflict* (Chicago: University of Chicago Press, 1981). His argument is considerably more nuanced than what I've summarized here, but he finds generally that the stronger and more stable the native culture, the better those Indians withstood the assaults of Christian missionaries.

5. See Neal Salisbury, "Red Puritans: The 'Praying Indians' of Massachusetts Bay and John Eliot," *William and Mary Quarterly*, 3rd ser., XXXI (1974): 27–54.

6. I am grateful to Virginia Luger of Fort Yates for pointing this out to me.

7. This was the unemployment rate as of January 1987. I am grateful to the staff of Senator Daniel Patrick Moynihan (New York) for supplying me with this information.

8. Despite his representation at the dedication, Daschle has opposed efforts in the U.S. Senate to restore 1.3 million of the 7.3 million acres that the U.S. government wrested from the Sioux in 1877.

9. See, for example, Robert S. Ellwood and Harry B. Partin, *Religious and Spiritual Groups in Modern America*, 2d ed. (Englewood Cliffs, N.J.: Prentice-Hall, 1988), pp. 168–70.

10. John and DeVonna Bush interview, 26 July 1987.

11. For a fuller description of the Sioux Sun Dance, see Royal B. Hassrick, *The Sioux: Life and Customs of a Warrior Society* (Norman: University of Oklahoma Press, 1964), pp. 239–47; see also Bowden, *American Indians and Christian Missions*, pp. 215–20.

12. From *The Hymnal 1982*, © 1985 The Church Pension Fund. Used by permission.

10

Camp Meeting

FOR SOME MONTHS I had been looking for a Southern camp meeting to get a flavor of old-time religion. There are plenty to choose from in America today, from Alabama to Oregon, Florida to California; one directory, published by Asbury College in Kentucky, listed 114 camp meetings for 1987, but even this list was by no means exhaustive.[1] Then one day a brochure arrived in the mail. "Enjoy a Southern Vacation in a Spiritual Atmosphere," it said, sounding more like an invitation to a cruise than a revival. The theme of this year's conference was "Free Indeed," which could mean almost anything from a kind of right-wing, patriotic freedom to freedom from sin—or a combination of the two. Camp Freedom advertised itself as "wholesomely interdenominational," but I had little else to go on before my arrival in St. Petersburg, Florida.

The rising bell at Camp Freedom chimes at six-thirty. When I pulled into the campground shortly thereafter, it was still dark. By seven o'clock the faithful had gathered in the chapel (known here as a tabernacle) for Morning Prayer. Brother Bedsaul Agee, a large, portly man with a booming voice, took charge of the meeting and introduced Brother Rissinger, frail and infirm, to deliver the morning meditation. Rissinger's Bible shook noticeably as he spoke about his concern for the "falling away from holiness principles" among the people of God.

Holiness. A large sign over the platform behind Rissinger read HOLINESS UNTO THE LORD. The people who run Camp Freedom come out of the holiness tradition, a movement emanating from John Wesley's conviction that the biblical injunction "Be ye perfect" should be taken literally and that complete freedom from sin was possible in this life.[2] Wesley's belief in "entire sanctification" became popular in the nineteenth century, especially in Methodist circles. The holiness movement emphasized the centrality of sanctification or the "second blessing" of the Holy Spirit, which followed the experience of conversion. The second blessing eradicated "inbred sin," perfected the will, and thereby rendered the believer free from sin. By the close of the nineteenth century, however, the Methodist hierarchy had grown chary about the enthusiasm and emotion that attended holiness gatherings, so many of the people drawn to holiness beliefs broke away from Methodism (and other denominations) to form holiness churches, such as the Church of the Nazarene and the Pilgrim Holiness Church. Other denominations also retain strong ties to the holiness movement, including the Wesleyan Church, the Bible Methodists, the Brethren in Christ, the Salvation Army, and the Church of God (Anderson, Indiana), among others. Those in the holiness tradition emphasize the gifts of the Spirit, including divine healing, and their worship tends to be lively and enthusiastic.

Brother Rissinger, I am certain, was once a lively and enthusiastic preacher, and even now there are flashes of his former fire when he inveighs against the holiness people who dare to attend church only on Sunday mornings and not on Sunday evenings and during the week. "Time is getting short," he warned, "there is not much time anymore." As evangelical preachers are wont to do, Rissinger talked about his own religious experiences. "The Lord sanctified me in 1945," he said. "The feeling was wonderful. I've never had the same feeling since." He compared the Christian life to a pond and said that if there is no overflow to the pond, it becomes stagnant and covered with scum. "I truly don't like to see all that scum on top," he said. "We need to get rid of the scum. The world is looking to us for spiritual refreshment. That life of yours should be continually flowing. Let your life overflow."

When Rissinger sat down, Bedsaul Agee took charge once again and thanked "the dear brother" for his meditation. He then invited the congregation forward for prayer, whereupon everyone gathered near the platform, knelt, and began praying aloud—simultaneously. The effect was a cacophonous murmur accented by an excited emphasis from time to time that punctuated the din. "Amen!" "Oh, Father!" "Praise the Lord!" "Burn within our hearts and stir us, Lord!" "Praise Jesus!" "Hallelujah!" "Father, we want a blessing. We want to feel it. Give it to us, God. *Glo*-ry to Jesus!"

The overall effect was a long, plaintive wail. At various moments, a head rose and a handkerchief wiped a tear before the head bowed again to resume praying. "Burn within our hearts and stir us, Lord!" "Amen!" "Praise Jesus!" "Heal the sick." "Help us Lord, in a special way to get the victory done!" "Heal the sick." "Oh, Jesus, Jesus!" "Help us, Lord!" "We love thy truth. We love this book!" one man said, raising his Bible. "Fill us today!" "May our souls be blessed. May we be comforted." "Amen!"

After about fifteen minutes, the collective murmur rose to a crescendo, full of noise and excitation, like a long-distance runner expending a final burst of energy in a chug toward the finish line. The praying continued for another ten minutes, but one by one members of the congregation rose from their knees, adjusted eyeglasses, and waited in silence for the eight o'clock breakfast bell.

The gathering was all white and quite elderly—I didn't see anyone who looked under fifty—but I was still puzzled about the group's denominational ties. Nearly all of the women wore white bonnets on their heads, the sort of covering that most of us associate with the Amish. A few of the men had long beards. Some of them wore suits and neckties, others wore suits and dress shirts buttoned to the neck, but no ties.

At the close of the prayer meeting, a man who introduced himself as Larry Strouse came up to me and said, "I don't believe I've seen you here before. Are you a Christian?" By now, toward the end of my travels, I should have been prepared for the question, because

I had faced it so often. It was, I had decided long ago, just another way of asking, "Who are you? Can I trust you?" As we stood in line at the dining hall, Strouse began to address some of my questions about Camp Freedom.

Most of the people there came from the Great Lakes region: Pennsylvania, Michigan, Indiana, Ohio, Minnesota, Ontario. Many were Wesleyan Methodists or Brethren in Christ. A lot of the folks at Camp Freedom, Strouse told me, had grown up as Mennonites or Amish but had abandoned those churches after their experience of sanctification. Strouse, dressed in a sportcoat and tie, leaned toward me and lowered his voice. "There's no salvation in them there customs and traditions," he said. "Most of them Amish people aren't even saved." Many of those who had been born again, like the ones at Camp Freedom, maintained their traditional dress, even though they had been excommunicated by their fellow Mennonites and Amish.

At breakfast, I sat across the table from Jacob and Ada Sollenberger, beekeepers from Franklin County, Pennsylvania. With only the slightest prompting, they told me their life stories. Both grew up in the Old Order River Brethren, a religious group begun in the eighteenth century by Jacob Engle and so named because most of his followers lived along the Susquehanna River in Pennsylvania and because of their insistence on baptism by trine (threefold) immersion in a flowing river. Ada Sollenberger, a warm, lovely women of seventy-five, and Jacob, her bearded husband, seventy-one years old and a bit quieter than his wife but no less genial, were dressed as though they had just stepped off the set of *Witness*, Hollywood's 1985 motion picture about the Amish. "The Bible teaches modesty and simplicity," Mrs. Sollenberger explained. "Romans 8 tells us to present our bodies as a living sacrifice to the Lord, and First Corinthians instructs the women to keep their heads covered."

Despite her upbringing, Ada Sollenberger said, "I didn't start to serve the Lord until I was twenty-six years old. I had a real experience with God," she said. "Before that I dressed quite fashionable. I could show you pictures." A couple of years after her conversion, she met Jacob at a River Brethren love feast in Jacob's parents' home. They were married after a short courtship; forty-seven years

later they clearly remain devoted to one another and openly affec-
tionate. "God did not get me a husband until I got my life turned
around," Ada said, placing her arm around Jacob's shoulders.

Even though they were both born-again Christians when they
married, their second blessings didn't come until later. "When the
Lord took our second child," Ada said, "I was just broken. But then
the Lord touched me and I was filled with the Holy Spirit. This
was in 1944." Shortly thereafter, she continued, "Jacob had his big
experience with the Lord."

"I had church pride," Jacob interjected, meaning a kind of religious arrogance. "But then I was filled with the Holy Ghost."

"It happened at home in bed," Mrs. Sollenberger added, without
a trace of guile or irony. "The Lord filled him up with glory. We
knew we had found something wonderful."

Because the River Brethren did not believe in the second blessing,
the Sollenbergers gravitated toward the Brethren in Christ in 1951;
"putting on the uniform" of plain-style dress was a conscious decision
that accompanied their joining the Brethren in Christ. The Brethren
had a dress code in those days, although they have since abandoned
it. The Sollenbergers have retained the old rigor and even seemed,
at various times in our conversations, a bit defensive about it. "When
you see a policemen or a soldier or a nurse in uniform," Ada said,
"you know who that person is and what they stand for. The same
should be true with Christians. The Bible says, 'Come out from
among them and be ye separate.' " While it is true, Jacob added,
that " 'man looks on the outward appearances and God looks on the
heart,' the outward appearance is the only basis that other people
have for judging what's *in* the heart."[3]

Although all holiness people certainly do not insist on plain-style
dress, moral strictures and behavioral taboos are common, even
though they have eased somewhat in recent years. Dancing, card-
playing, alcohol, motion pictures, and "worldly" music are all viewed
askance in holiness circles. They are entertainments of the devil
that lure the unwitting into sin, debauchery, and prurience. Women
must never cut their hair because it is given as a covering, a conviction that accounted for all the buns and "doorknobs" I saw at
Camp Freedom.[4] Holiness scruples forbid the wearing of cosmetics

or jewelry. Dress should be modest at all times, as I was quickly reminded after I slipped away for a run during my first day at Camp Freedom. When I returned, an elder of the camp hurriedly pulled me aside, put his hand on my shoulder, and gently but quite emphatically informed me that the camp "has a rule about not wearing shorts on the campground."

The tradition of camp meetings in America reaches back to the late eighteenth century, and they became a fixture of religious life in the South during the Second Great Awakening of the early nineteenth century. The Second Awakening, a widespread revival that convulsed three theaters of the new nation—New England, western New York, and the Cumberland Valley—tamed some of the rowdiness of frontier life. Indeed, there was plenty to tame, especially in the South. One in three brides was pregnant, according to some estimates. Alcohol consumption was prodigious and (literally) staggering, due in part to the cheap and plentiful supply of grain. Inebriation led to abuse of wives and children, neglect of the fields, and outright violence. Americans of the early republic drank on the average of five gallons of ninety-proof alcohol a year, more than triple today's consumption. Children and even infants were given liquor, and drinking began with breakfast and continued before, during, and after meals. Water was thought to have no nutritional value; indeed, according to some wags, it was good only for navigation. Even Benjamin Franklin opined that if God had intended man to drink water, He would not have given him an elbow capable of raising a wine glass.[5]

Camp meetings of the early nineteenth century brought religion to the frontiers and changed some of those habits. Word circulated among the frontier settlers about the time and location of a camp meeting, and entire families loaded into wagons and gathered at the appointed place for preaching and revival—as well as for some surreptitious drinking and carousing. The camp meeting functioned as a huge social occasion, bringing together people from widely dispersed settlements in a large region, but it also schooled them in enthusiastic, evangelical religion. In perhaps the most famous camp meeting of the Second Great Awakening, approximately twenty-five thousand settlers gathered at Cane Ridge in Kentucky in August 1801. Many souls were saved at gatherings like Cane Ridge—although cynics have argued that even more were conceived—and these revivals were marked by what contemporaries called spiritual "exercises." The barking exercise, for example, was quite common; people who came under the influence of the Holy Spirit barked uncontrollably. Others were afflicted with the "jerks," when their bodies contorted involuntarily. Others danced or laughed or fell to the ground under the influence of the Spirit, and some accounts tell of heads rotating 360 degrees.

The camp meeting became a fixture of American religion in the nineteenth century; by mid-century, in fact, various manuals appeared with instructions about how to conduct a successful camp-meeting revival.[6] It was important to locate the meeting near a creek or river so that water would be available. Those attending the meeting camped around the edges of a clearing, where the meetings took place. The days were highly structured, beginning each morning with family prayer at five o'clock and concluding late at night with the evening service, where most of the conversions took place. In between, the day was filled with several prayer meetings, a morning and an afternoon service, and a time during which the laity could seek spiritual guidance from the many clergy in attendance.[7]

Camp meetings were not confined to the South. Amidst the urbanization of the latter part of the nineteenth century, places like Ocean Grove, New Jersey, and Oak Bluffs, Massachusetts, provided physical and spiritual renewal for the weary industrial worker. The camp meeting itself became institutionalized; permanent campsites with wooden pavilions replaced the open fields.[8] Camp meetings endure in the twentieth century, although the substance varies greatly. The Indian River Camp Meeting in South Carolina is really a huge, extended family reunion, an event so large and important that politicians, even senators, regularly drop by. There is no longer much religious fervor to such gatherings, at least by the standards of Camp Freedom and other holiness camp meetings tucked away in the hills of West Virginia or the backcountry of North Carolina or hard by the Gulf of Mexico in Florida.

Camp Freedom itself is rather inauspicious. It lies on a modest acreage across Fifty-fourth Avenue from the Sons of Italy lodge. The permanent sign for the campground reads:

> **CAMP**
>
> **FREEDOM**
>
> 6980–54TH AVE. N.
>
> YOU ARE WELCOME!
>
> DELIVERANCE FROM SIN
>
> IN CHRIST

A special sign announced the camp meeting, lasting twelve days, from late January into early February: COME—BE BLESSED BY OLD TIME GOSPEL PREACHING AND SINGING.

Palm trees and citrus trees line the edges of the property. There are a few permanent cinder-block buildings on the campground, including the dining hall, various offices, and motel rooms. Most of the area, however, is set aside for camper trailers. By almost any standard, the accommodations are modest. The grounds themselves are rather unremarkable and certainly not secluded. Traffic roars by only one hundred yards away from the tabernacle, a white, very plain, cinder-block building which is clearly the centerpiece of the campground. The tabernacle seats two or three hundred people on homemade wooden benches that only recently have been upholstered. The ceiling is low, supported by pine rafters. Two parallel strings of florescent bulbs provide the lighting. A huge platform dominates the front of the auditorium, flanked on the left by a ten-by-fifteen-foot room with a sign on the door that reads "Men's Prayer Room." The "Ladies' Prayer Room" is on the right. Between them, running in front of the platform, is a two-foot-high wooden altar rail that sits on a patch of carpeting placed there for the comfort of those who come to kneel at the altar.[9]

Because holiness groups believe in the gifts of the Holy Spirit, divine healing is often a part of their gatherings, although, unlike pentecostals, they generally frown on speaking in tongues. I heard a good deal of shouting and ecstatic utterances during my visit to Camp Freedom, but nothing that could be confused with speaking in tongues. The directors of the camp meeting scheduled only one service of healing but decided to offer it early in the revival so that the sick and infirm might be able to enjoy what one preacher called "the fullness of healing" for the remainder of the camp meeting.

At the beginning of the Friday afternoon healing service, called "Christ's Miracle Moments" in the brochure, Brother John Rosenberry, one of the many clergymen at the camp, stepped to the pulpit and announced, "I feel healing in this atmosphere this afternoon." Bedsaul Agee gave the sermon. "Our God is able to meet our needs," he said. "I had a hand with three withered fingers, and the flesh was restored on those in two days, and the doctor said he never saw anything like it in all his days. Of course he didn't. It was a supernatural miracle of God!" Agee promised healing and even "deliverance from evil spirits" to the faithful. He then invited them to come forward to the altar rail for healing. "How about you this afternoon," he said, "do you think God has a miracle for you?"

Simon Lehman, director of the camp meeting, then came to the pulpit to expand the offer to those who were not present at the service. Two ushers passed out white paper cocktail napkins to people in the congregation who wanted to request prayer for "a beloved friend or relative." Lehman instructed them to write the name and the affliction of the absent loved one on the napkin. The ushers collected the napkins, and Lehman then invited members of the congregation who sought healing to walk forward to be anointed with oil, in the manner prescribed in James 5. "There's room at the cross for you," Lehman said. "Jesus loves you. He wants to touch you."

I had noticed an air of expectation throughout the campground that morning in anticipation of the healing service. "I said to Jacob this morning," Ada Sollenberger told me, "that I really didn't need healing today, unless the Lord wanted to help me with my weight. The Lord has blessed us with six children, and I've never gotten my weight back down to where I wanted." Ada Sollenberger did not walk forward, but Jacob did, along with many others in the congregation. They were met at the front by the clergy, in teams of two, who knelt beside each individual, quizzed him or her about the affliction, and, placing their hands on his or her shoulders, prayed for healing. The tabernacle reverberated with plaintive moanings and shouts of deliverance mixed with stern admonitions to "rebuke the power of evil" and "heal this affliction in the power of Jesus's name." After each prayer, the clergy pulled out small vials of oil from their coat pockets and dabbed a tiny bit of oil on the forehead of each supplicant. When the clergy finished with those who had come forward for healing, they divided up the stack of cocktail napkins and essentially repeated the same process, touching the oil to the napkins.

Despite its obvious peculiarities, the entire service was conducted with decorum and dignity, not the frenzied, carnival atmosphere that I'd witnessed at the Capstone Cathedral in Phoenix. After the prayers, Lehman asked the clergy to spread the cocktail napkins across the length of the altar rail; he then instructed the members of the congregation who had requested healing for others to pick up the napkins and send them to the afflicted loved ones. He asked, finally, for testimonies of healing from the congregation. None was forthcoming, so Lehman hedged. "Now there may be some who don't *feel* healed yet," he said. "Don't go by feeling. Go by the Word of God. Go by faith that you are healed in the name of Jesus."

Just as there was no shortage of services at Camp Freedom (three a day, in addition to the sundry prayer meetings), so too there were plenty of preachers—about a dozen, including those who dropped by for guest appearances. Most of them were quite skilled. Their stentorian voices alternated between shouts and whispers. Their fists pounded the pulpit. They offered graphic descriptions of the perils of worldliness and sin. And they kept the attention of their audiences, who responded with "amens" and tears and wailing and shouted affirmations.

One visitor, Brother Paul Martin, president of Penn View Bible Institute, a small holiness school in Pennsylvania, echoed the general suspicion of worldliness and of learning that is fairly common in holiness circles. "We get so wrapped up in psychology and general psych and other psychs that we're all psyched up," he said derisively.

Martin bragged that Penn View was a "conservative holiness Bible school, a Bible institute with a camp-meeting atmosphere," and that "the students who leave us know they're saved and that they're sanctified before they go out and face the world. There's a world out there that's dying and going to hell," Martin said. "We need to reach them. We need to be bold for Jesus Christ."

Indeed, one of the recurrent themes in the preaching at Camp Freedom was the need to eschew "worldliness" and separate from the world. "Wouldn't it be wonderful if our grandchildren, our great-grandchildren, if it could be said of them, 'They are totally separated, they don't have the diseases of the rest of the world'?" Bedsaul Agee intoned. "We are strangers and pilgrims here. We are not a part of this society. We belong to the heavenly throng, and we ought to act like it while we're here. We ought to live like it and enjoy the blessings thereof."

"*In* the world but not *of* the world" is a favorite aphorism among holiness people (and evangelicals generally). It helps if you can identify those who are worldly, those who stand outside the ken of righteousness, not only for the ostensible purpose of bringing them into the fold, but also because it vindicates your own standing as someone special in God's eyes. After one of the services, Philip Compton from South Carolina, eighty-two years old and a regular at Camp Freedom, cornered me. "Do you love Jesus?" he asked. "I love Jesus. You know why I love Jesus? I love Jesus because He first loved me." Compton, a bald man with a weathered face and a large hearing aid behind each ear, walked around the campground with a handful of books. I had noticed him huddled at various times with other people, thumping the books like a used-car salesman kicking tires. He pulled out a paperback he had written and published himself entitled *Give the Family Something Better*. "I'm against pornography and abortion," he announced. "And *abortion* is the right word for it. You know why?" He looked at me earnestly. "Because you oughtta shun abor-shun."

At the conclusion of another service, the preacher in charge of the meeting invited responses or testimonies from the congregation. An older, white-haired woman near the front rose to her feet and unleashed a long harangue about worldliness and her anxieties about the the younger generation. "Oh, my Lord," she wailed, her voice rising and falling for dramatic effect, "my concern is have I prayed enough. This morning at ten minutes to three, I wondered why I was awakened, so I began to pray, and I asked God to take care of the one that needed it the most because I don't always know why I am awakened. But I'm so glad. If the Lord has to give me pain in my arm to get me awakened early in the morning and talk to Him, I'll take the pain." Her voice became shrill and insistent. "I have been burdened for our young people. Friday and Saturday nights I pray more than ever for some mother's child out on the streets and nobody to pray for them. My heart is burdened for our young people. I'd just love to take them all in."

At the Saturday afternoon service, the people of Camp Freedom got a look at some exemplary young people from Hobe Sound Bible College, a holiness school across the state. The men were dressed in ties, white shirts, and three-piece suits. The women wore plain, very modest dresses and no makeup or jewelry, except for wristwatches. In keeping with holiness scruples, the women had very long hair wrapped into buns either on top or in back of their heads.[10]

But if the students from Hobe Sound represented all that was virtuous and lovely in the eyes of those at Camp Freedom, there were always reminders of the perils of worldliness. That night, as the congregation gathered for the evening service, the man seated next to me, who had taken an interest in my research, pointed to an attractive, blonde woman in her mid-thirties. She was dressed fashionably, her shoulder-length hair pulled back in a pony tail. She wore makeup and gold jewelry, a string of pearls and high heels. She would have attracted attention almost anywhere, but against the very bland pastiche of Camp Freedom, she drew the eyes of the congregation like steel shavings to a magnet. "See that girl there," my informant said. "She was brought up strict, but she reversed." This woman, the daughter of one of the preachers at the conference, was a pharmacist back in New Jersey. She was also divorced and had, in the words of the man next to me, "fallen away from the Lord." There was a lesson in all this, of course. "That's what happens when you go the way of the world."

The service in the tabernacle that evening opened with a lively song whose chorus went:

> He brought me out of the miry clay.
> He set my feet on the rock to stay.
> He puts a song in my heart today,
> A song of praise. Hallelujah!

Such rejoicing is all the more powerful when juxtaposed with a reminder of the depredations of the world, the miry clay of sin. Brother John Rosenberry obliged. "Our hearts go out to the world in which we live," he prayed. "The world of teenagers, of kids out on the street who need Jesus. They're suffering terrible things in New York and San Francisco and Calcutta. We need to bring Jesus to the world."

There is a kind of protocol that governs behavior at holiness or pentecostal gatherings. In some churches, worshippers lift both arms high into the air, palms up, to indicate that they are affected by the Holy Spirit, or, more precisely, to indicate a broken, obedient will, receptive to the Holy Spirit. At Camp Freedom, protocol dictates a brief, discreet wave of one arm. When some element of a prayer or a song or a sermon strikes a chord, members of the congregation simply lift a hand and wave it quickly, in the manner of a second-grader trying to catch the eye of her teacher. The congregation also responds with amens and shouting, especially in the presence of a skilled preacher.

Brother H. E. Schmul from Salem, Ohio, widely regarded as the best orator at the camp meeting, stepped to the pulpit. His theme tonight was repentance, or the lack of it. He bemoaned the fact that he saw little difference between Christians and "the world" and wondered if that similarity had something to do with the prevalence of "health or wealth or prosperity gospel," the notion, immensely popular in many evangelical circles, that God wants to make you rich. Too much of the preaching today, Schmul said, "does not disturb the sin" in people's lives, "their adultery or their immorality or their fornication or their cheating or their lying or whatever."

Schmul himself would not be guilty of such reticence. Sin, he said, "is a moral corruption that will result in final separation from God." Schmul became more and more impassioned as the audience shouted him on. "It's a madness. It's a madness that, 'regardless of the consequences I have to do it. I have to shoot it. I have to drink it. I have to smoke it. I have to have it. I have to have him. I have to have her.' It's a madness. People rush into this regardless of the consequences." He paused and lowered his voice. "One thing that is happening is good, even though it's bad. I'm talking about AIDS," he said. Schmul dismissed the various education programs directed against the spread of AIDS. "The real answer is a change in the hearts of men," he said. "God's way of all purity, of all chastity, is the way. God's plan is the *only* way! Amen." The AIDS epidemic, Schmul suggested, was having a salutary effect. "Some people are backing up on this homosexual thing. Some of the gays that had to have sex the homosexual way are changing their minds after seeing their buddies drop off or fall over like flies. When they're sure that a person who has AIDS is going to go down the tubes and go out into eternity—they're really beginning to change their minds a little," he said with evident satisfaction.

Only the blood of Jesus Christ will cure sin, Schmul continued. "No man, no man, *no* man ever sins purely out of weakness but lets himself go in his weakness to do as he wills." Here Schmul touched on a matter of perennial controversy within Protestant circles: the extent to which an individual is responsible for his or her salvation. Citing the New Testament writings of St. Paul, Martin Luther and John Calvin had insisted that we all inherit Adam's sin and that only the grace of God, mediated through Jesus Christ, delivers us from the condemnation we so richly deserve. We can do *nothing*, they insisted, to earn our salvation; God, in His inscrutable wisdom and mercy, has chosen to rescue us from the squalor of our sinfulness, *regardless* of our merit.

In an age inebriated with self-determinism, Lutheran or Calvinist theology does not sit well. It seems narrow and fatalistic. But such naysaying misses the point. Luther had been profoundly troubled about the state of his soul. He couldn't escape a sense of his own unworthiness and his insouciance toward God. Was he saved or damned? Had he prayed enough? Had he received the Eucharist often enough? Had he sinned since his last confession? The slightest lapse, he believed, meant perdition.

Luther's confessor finally advised him to study Paul's letters to the Romans and the Galatians in the New Testament. There Luther "rediscovered the gospel" that liberated him from the works-righteousness of medieval Catholicism and from the burden of earning his salvation. We are saved by grace through faith in Jesus Christ, Luther concluded, not by dint of our own efforts, which fail pitifully before a holy and righteous God. Good works, then, are not a condition of salvation; rather, they follow in the life of the believer as a natural response to grace.

In many Protestant circles, however, Luther's breakthrough, which John Calvin codified and systematized in the *Institutes of the Christian Religion*, has been compromised by a theological strain generally known as Arminianism, named for Jacobus Arminius, a Dutch theologian of the early seventeenth century, who restored human agency to the doctrine of salvation. Anyone can choose to follow Christ; by the same token, anyone can lose his or her salvation by falling back into sin. There is no such thing as "eternal security." While this theological recidivism obfuscated the Reformation's insistence that the grace of God alone provided deliverance from sin, Arminian theology (also known as Wesleyanism, for John Wesley) caught on in America. Its emphasis on human agency worked well in the revival meetings on the frontier. Preachers sought to persuade and cajole sinners into the kingdom—salvation, after all, was simply a matter of choosing God over Satan, good over evil—and the self-determination implicit in Arminiam or Wesleyan theology appealed to Americans of the new nation who had recently taken control of their political destiny.

Arminianism long ago eclipsed Calvinism in American Protestantism. Camp-meeting evangelists and Methodist circuit riders carried it to the frontiers, and it persists to the present among holiness people, who believe that their salvation hinges on their probity and their ability to eschew evil. For Brother Schmul, then, conscious or deliberate sin is not, as Calvinists insist, a consequence of our fallen nature; it is a matter of our volition and specific transgressions of sundry moral codes, and the responsibility to resist temptation lies with the individual. Moral lapses are deadly. "I don't believe there are Christian men who are going to be taken up in the rapture from the arms of a harlot," Schmul preached. "I don't believe they're going to put a hole in the ceiling of these various dives and saloons around the country where the saints can move out of those places when Jesus comes. I don't believe that. The Bible doesn't teach that. There's no grounds for it in the Word of God." The congregation responded with hearty amens. Even those who carry grudges in their hearts, Schmul said, "are going to the same hell along with the harlots and the prostitutes and the drunkards and the swearers and the ne'er-do-wells."

True repentance, Schmul said, meant leaving the old sinful life behind. "There is no cheap grace," he concluded. "There is no cheap salvation. Saving faith is impossible without repentance and obedience and renunciation."

What was all this rhetoric about "worldliness" that pervaded the preaching at Camp Freedom? Unlike Calvinism, which holds that the elect of God attain salvation regardless of merit and cannot resist God's grace, the Wesleyan tradition views salvation as a matter of volition—we must *choose* to forsake our sinfulness and follow Christ. "We don't go to heaven to become saints," Edsel Trauten, one of the preachers at Camp Freedom, said. "We become saints to go to heaven." We must prove ourselves worthy of salvation on earth before we can hope to receive a reward in heaven. Brother Schmul said that a believer's identification with Christ "will lead you against the world, against the flesh, against the devil; it will lead you to opposition; it will lead you to persecution; it will lead you to fiery trials; it will lead you to a place of contradiction with the world." He then warned of the consequences of equivocation. "If you are seeking an accommodation with the world," he said, "then, friends, you are fooling yourself, and you are toying with your eternal destiny. We are not citizens of this world; we are citizens of another country." Life on earth, then, is a constant struggle to root out sinfulness and show oneself worthy of salvation; sanctification, or the "second blessing" of the Holy Spirit, cleanses sin, but there is no "eternal security" in the Wesleyan tradition. Just as we come to

God of our own volition, so too we can lose our salvation by lapsing into sin.

Indeed, sin cannot be taken lightly in Wesleyan theology. "My friend," one of the preachers shouted, "if you're really converted, you're going out of the sin business, you say goodbye to the world." The repeated, insistent warnings against the depredations of the world, then, are more than mere rhetorical flourishes. The destiny of one's very soul is at stake. The moral and behavioral strictures shield the believer from sin and temptation and keep him or her on the narrow road to heaven. "We know you're all trying to get to heaven," Brother Lehman told one of the gatherings. "Some of you aren't ready yet, but we'll try to get you ready."

All of this issues in an underlying, though largely unspoken, anxiety. The people at Camp Freedom sing the old Protestant hymn, "Blessed assurance, Jesus is mine / Oh, what a foretaste of glory divine!" but I encountered precious little assurance beneath the fragile veneer of confidence.

One afternoon, I struck up a conversation with "Roger," a youthful-looking gentleman in his late sixties.[11] Roger lives and works in Indiana most of the year, but he arranges his vacation time so he can be in St. Petersburg for the camp meeting every winter. He asked if I had toured the campground, and in the course of our walk he related the story of his life. "The Lord sure helped me," he began. "He saved me from a life of sin when I was seventeen. I lied and cheated; I would steal. But you can't find joy in serving the devil. You can find pleasure, but it's only for a season. Jesus is the only one that satisfies. He is the *only* one."

After his conversion, Roger felt obligated to make restitution for all of his youthful misdeeds. "I went back to five-and-dimes and grocery stores and so many places to apologize to storekeepers for the things I'd stolen. I'd do work for them to make it up. I even went back to schoolteachers to apologize for cheating on tests and assignments. I'd been to twelve different schools in twelve years, so that took some time and effort, but I did it." Roger credited his mother with being a godly influence in his life. "I surely had a wonderful mother," he said. "My mother never had a haircut in her life, never wore jewelry or cosmetics. I'm sure glad the Lord saved me from a life of sin."

By this time, I had heard countless conversion narratives at Camp Freedom, and nothing in Roger's account struck me as unusual. After a pause, however, he continued. "I want to tell you something else. May I?" he asked. "When I was growing up, I was always kind of a sissy. I found myself attracted to boys rather than girls." He hesitated. "I'm a homosexual." He spat out the words in disgust. Roger had some sexual encounters with older men when he was a teenager, but after his conversion at age seventeen he promptly broke off all such relationships. Coping with his sexual urges thereafter without giving in to temptation, he said, was hell. In addition, he faced suspicion and ridicule from his peers. During World War II, he recalled, "people constantly would ask me why I wasn't in Europe fighting for my country."

"I remained celibate for thirty-seven years," he continued, "but then I felt myself falling into temptation." His voice became intense, almost fierce. "I was lean in my soul at that time, and I would pray, 'Lord, help me get my mind on you.'" Despite those prayers, however, Roger lapsed into sin, a year-long relationship with a younger man. "It still haunts me," he recalled. "It's a blot on my life. I finally came to the point where I said, 'Lord, it's either you or the world.'"

As Roger continued his story, he struck me suddenly as a tragic figure, a man haunted by what he considered a wanton transgression deep in his past. I tried to imagine the self-hatred he felt, the sense of vileness that shadowed him constantly. Indeed, there was a sadness to many of the people I had met at Camp Freedom. Even as they spoke of the sweetness of Jesus and their deliverance from sin decades earlier, I detected an underlying uneasiness, an uncertainty about the fate of their souls. The need to keep a strict moral accounting for one's life reminded me of Martin Luther's anxieties about whether or not he had sinned since his last confession, thereby imperiling his immortal soul. The insistent proclamations and the triumphal hymns about deliverance from sin at Camp Freedom sounded tinny to me, an exercise in self-persuasion. The seductive darkness of the "world" for most of us—and even, I suspect, for more than a few at Camp Freedom—lies not in the taverns and bordellos and movie theaters but much closer to home, in the recesses of the heart. It's easier, though, and a good deal more comforting, to insist that the enemy is outside rather than inside. You need to shore up your defenses and patrol the ramparts to keep the adversary at bay.

For Roger, however, the enemy had penetrated the fortress, and even these many years later he couldn't be certain about the effects of that contamination. His intensity had abated now, and he spoke in measured tones. He alternated between expressing his own deep sorrow and repeating the bromides of sermons he had heard for half a century. "To know the Lord is life eternal, but to know the world is nothing," he said. "My biggest regret is that I cannot say that I've been faithful to my Lord for a full fifty years; instead, I fell back into sin thirty-seven years after I had given my heart to God."

He paused, dabbed the corners of his eyes with a handkerchief, then looked away into the distance. "Sin is not worth it," he said, "because that one little sin may keep you out of heaven."

NOTES

1. *The Camp Meeting Challenge* 10 (Spring 1987): [2–7].
2. Matt. 5:48.
3. The references here are, respectively, 2 Cor. 6:17 and 1 Sam. 16:7.
4. This scruple derives from 1 Cor. 11:15.
5. See W. J. Rorabaugh, *The Alcoholic Republic: An American Tradition* (New York: Oxford University Press, 1979) regarding alcohol consumption in the early nineteenth century.
6. The most popular camp-meeting manual of the nineteenth century was B. W. Gorham, *Camp Meeting Manual: A Practical Book for the Camp Ground* (Boston, 1854).
7. Most of this information comes from Dickson D. Bruce, Jr., *And They All Sang Hallelujah: Plain-Folk Camp-Meeting Religion, 1800–1845* (Knoxville: University of Tennessee Press, 1974).

8. See Randall H. Balmer, "From Frontier Phenomenon to Victorian Institution: The Methodist Camp Meeting in Ocean Grove, New Jersey," *Methodist History* 25 (April 1987): 194–200.

9. This "altar" nomenclature, which is quite common in evangelical churches, raises an interesting issue. Although evangelical preachers make "altar calls" and invite the true believers to "lay their all on the altar," there is, technically, no altar in the vast majority of evangelical churches. An *altar*, of course, is a place of sacrifice; in Roman Catholic churches, it is the place where the "sacrifice of the Mass" is performed, when the bread and wine of Holy Communion *actually become* the body and blood of Christ, even though they retain the outward appearance of bread and wine. The "sacramental" theology of most evangelicals, however, is *memorialist*—that is, the elements of Holy Communion serve merely to remind us of the death of Christ; there is no objective partaking of grace, as Catholics and others believe, nor is there, properly, an altar where the eucharistic rite is performed. Evangelicals have instead spiritualized the notion of altar to mean, roughly, the surrender of the individual to the will of God. They persist in using the terminology of the altar, however.

10. These scruples about feminine attire derive, in part, from 1 Tim. 2:9–10.

11. I have altered some of the details of this story in order to disguise the identity of the person involved.

11

Oregon Jeremiad

OREGON'S HIGHWAY 66 meanders west out of Ashland, hugging the sides of mountains on its way toward Klamath Falls. At Greensprings Summit, elevation forty-five hundred feet, the road levels off a bit, then begins a gentle descent and winds past Tubb Springs, a small roadside state park. The late afternoon sunshine coming through the pines dapples the macadam road. A logging truck rolls by, heading the other direction toward the sawmill down in the valley.

Just past a fire ranger station and beyond the twenty-two mile marker, a small green sign announces "Lincoln." Several shingled buildings come into view, behind them a few cows and chickens and horses, a mill pond, an abandoned sawmill of corrugated steel, and a bark burner, rusted and listing slightly, looking like an inebriated, oversized teepee. A sign in front of one of the roadside structures reads: THE OREGON EXTENSION OF TRINITY COLLEGE. To the left, on a gentle rise opposite the larger buildings, five houses and five cabins nestle among tall pines. Wood-smoke curls out of the chimneys in early November, the fragrance mixing pleasantly with the scent of pines in the thin mountain air.

The whole panorama, framed by larger mountains in the distance, is arresting. Surely even John Henry, a hard-nosed businessman of the 1920s, must have thought so. Henry constructed this logging camp, but, in a fit of pique at Franklin Roosevelt's New Deal, decided to close up shop in the 1930s. The property then devolved upon a succession of owners, and by the 1960s and early 1970s, having withstood various communitarian experiments, the buildings had fallen into disrepair.

Enter Douglas Frank and Thomas (Sam) Alvord. Frank and Alvord came upon Lincoln in 1974, near the conclusion of a western tour that had taken them through Montana and Idaho in search of land. They represented a small group of people from Illinois who wanted to establish an alternative education program for college students.

By the summer of 1975, Lincoln bustled with activity. Five faculty members, most of whom had been associated in some way with Trinity College, an evangelical liberal-arts school in Deerfield, Illinois, moved with their families into the houses on the property.[1] Teams of volunteers evicted the goats and squatters who had occupied the cabins. They carted away truckloads of garbage, patched the plumbing, installed kitchens, repaired fences, and painted the cabins. One of the large buildings became the library, which also serves as study area, lecture hall, and social meeting-place for the community. By Labor Day, twenty-two students took up residence in the cabins and prepared for four months of rigorous interdisciplinary study.

For Frank and Alvord, the Oregon Extension grew out of years of friendship and endless hours in front of campfires in the wilderness talking and dreaming about the future. In the 1960s they, together with Jim Titus, Frank's brother-in-law, directed Camp Sandy Hill for Boys in Maryland. After Frank became a professor of history at Trinity College, he, Alvord, and Titus formed Trek Inc., a not-for-profit organization that took small groups of teenagers (some of them wards of the court) for ten-day canoeing excursions into the Boundary Waters Wilderness of northern Minnesota.

The "Trek Curriculum," though not overtly evangelical or confessional, sought to teach values and instill a sense of responsibility in its young charges. "Think before you act," they were admonished.

"Remember that every action has a consequence."[2] Those lessons, of course, took on a special urgency in the wilderness, days away from emergency help and suburban amenities, where an errant match or a food pack left at the side of a portage trail could spell catastrophe.

Back at Trinity College, Frank quickly became one of the most popular members of a young, energetic faculty who, under the protection of an indulgent dean, encouraged their students to think critically, to examine their faith and ask questions of themselves and their superiors. Frank's outward appearance doubtless contributed to his popularity and to the mystique that came to surround him. Here was a man of impeccable evangelical credentials—reared in a missionary household, a graduate of Wheaton College—who sported long hair, granny glasses, a beard, and dressed in denims and work shirts. But if his appearance excited the curiosity of young, impressionable fundamentalists, most of them from conservative homes, his classes got them thinking. An advocate of the Socratic method— education, he once told me, is the art of asking the right questions— Frank turned his quick wit and his restless intellect loose on several generations of students. In United States history, he started them questioning some cherished shibboleths about America's past and prompted them to consider some of the darker corners of American history: America's treatment of Indians and blacks, he suggested, belied its putative Christian origins; the consumer culture that so dominates American life, he pointed out, exacted a price from the less fortunate and the Third World. In a course on contemporary world affairs, students from conservative Republican households began questioning for the first time the morality of America's involvement in Vietnam.

After several failed attempts to find a church in the Deerfield area that maintained a critical distance from suburban, middle-class values, Frank, Alvord, and others organized a "house church," a group of evangelicals who met for worship in each other's homes. Here, amidst a ferment of ideas and personalities, they began to concoct plans for a college semester in the wilderness, an enterprise that would combine their love for the outdoors with their appetite for ideas.

As it took shape in the autumn of 1975, the Oregon Extension, this community of scholars at Lincoln, offered a curriculum that invited students to examine twentieth-century ideas, values, and norms from an evangelical perspective. Each of the four month-long segments of the semester (Modern Visions of Society, Science and Technology in the Modern World, Modern Visions of Humanity, Religion and the Human Condition) opened with a week of introductory lectures, extensive common readings, and group discussions. Over the next two weeks, students chose topics germane to the particular segment and, under the direction of a faculty member, prepared papers or some other project that reflected their reading and thinking on those topics. At the end of the third week the community gathered to listen to various findings, an occasion for interaction and discussion. During the fourth week, students and faculty took off on some sort of outing—backpacking in Yosemite, climbing Mount Shasta, spending several days in San Francisco or on the Oregon coast—during which time, under informal circumstances, they continued to discuss ideas, to rehash what they'd read and what it meant.

The formal structure of the semester has changed little since the program began in 1975, although the content of the readings and the nature of the discussions have evolved somewhat. When I knew the program in its early years, the faculty evinced a suspicion of institutions generally, especially evangelical institutions, a vague uneasiness about the Church in general and evangelicalism in particular. This suspicion, in some degree a product of the iconoclastic tenor of the times, reflected a sense that evangelicalism had slipped its theological moorings—that it had lost its prophetic voice and thereby had rendered itself irrelevant to thinking Christians. The folks at Oregon wanted not so much to engage the evangelical subculture about its shortcomings as to harangue it or, perhaps worse, simply ignore it.

I caught up with Doug Frank in San Francisco in the fall of 1986, eleven years after the Oregon program began. For two days we walked the streets, visited bookstores in Palo Alto and Berkeley, and talked. I then traveled back to Oregon with Frank and his students to observe life at Lincoln.

Early in our conversations, Frank recounted for me a chapel service he had attended during a recent visit to an evangelical college. The sermon that morning, delivered by the college's president, used the New Testament, in Frank's judgment, to "baptize" American consumerism and extol the virtues of prosperity theology, the notion that God is itching to fulfill the material desires of every Christian. The president, preaching on a text from the third chapter of Paul's epistle to the Philippians, implied that his recently acquired sports car was God's reward for his work and faithfulness. Because of his financial status, moreover, his wife could now indulge her taste for imported antiques. God never intended for us to be poor or deprived, he argued, echoing the bromide so popular in contemporary evangelicalism. God wants us to live full and happy lives.

The preacher ignored key portions of the text entirely. In verse 10, Paul writes that those who seek to know Christ must partake in the "fellowship of His sufferings," but the sermon mentioned nothing about suffering; instead, it seemed to promise the good life to anyone who wanted it. Nor did the preacher bother to mention the cross of Christ, which is at the center of the chapter and, indeed, the whole epistle. "It was a classic case," Frank said, "of distorting a passage to make it palatable to middle-class kids who want to go out into the corporate world and rise to the top for Jesus."

The issue of how evangelicals have misunderstood and, at times, deliberately misused the Bible has plagued Frank for years. Only after coming to terms with our inherent sinfulness, he argues, can we know the full embrace of God's love and forgiveness, the unspeakable gift of God's grace. But grace too often is neglected in evangelical circles, where there is a tendency to dwell on the law of judgment rather than the gospel of God's grace. "All I hear within the evangelical subculture these days is the law, one version of the law or another; they're all competing. They're all determined to make us feel guilty and give us burdens too heavy to bear." Frank sees the consequences of exalting law over gospel in the evangelical students who come to study with him in Oregon. "Our kids show it," he said, "and they hate it. Our students come to us with the burden of being a Christian on their backs. They're bent over with it." Some of them have dispensed with their faith completely. Others try hard to maintain the pious lifestyle they were told to live, but they feel burdened with it. "It's the law," Frank said. "Paul is right in his Epistle to the Romans: The law kills. It's supposed to drive us to the grace of Christ, but evangelicals wield it as a weapon against one another and against their enemies, and it drives people away from Christ."

In Frank's opinion, this emphasis on the law and its exclusionary tendencies encourages evangelicals to draw lines and to make judgments about the spiritual condition of others, to impose a kind of dualism on the world. "We put ourselves on the good side of that line and figure out who's on the bad, so we can take our shots across the line and justify ourselves." Frank believes that the Bible teaches that only Christ can justify. "That's why the doctrine of justification in the Bible is so beautiful," he explained, "because God does it for us. When *we* do it, we always have enemies; you can't justify yourself without making an enemy."

The temptation to moralize, Frank contends, afflicts all of evangelicalism, both left and right. Right-wing fundamentalists such as Jerry Falwell, Pat Robertson, and Tim LaHaye have garnered media attention in recent years with their excoriations of sinfulness in American society, but there is also a less visible evangelical left wing, the best example of which is the Sojourners Community in Washington, D.C., publishers of *Sojourners* magazine. This group had its genesis at Trinity Evangelical Divinity School in Deerfield (which shares a campus with Trinity College). *Sojourners* consistently decries the arms race, American intervention in Central America, and espouses other generally liberal political views on the basis of an evangelical understanding of the gospel. While Frank finds himself in general sympathy with its political views, he sees the same moralistic tendencies in *Sojourners* that he sees in Falwell, a heavy weight of judgment that extends even to the magazine's graphics. "That's a consequence of their evangelical theology," he said. "It's not that we shouldn't say things are wrong, but moralism has to do with lines, with pointing fingers. It doesn't make an analysis of evil that's 360 degrees, that says 'we're all culpable, we're all encompassed within the same human determinisms.' And therefore, that type of moralism doesn't very often acknowledge its own com-

plicity. Moralism assumes autonomous human beings who are free
to make autonomous decisions about right and wrong, and even
when it notices that people don't often do that, that people generally
choose the wrong over the right, it still assumes that those decisions
can be made. Therefore, there's a burdensome feel to moralistic
analysis. It's the law. It's finger-pointing."

In refusing to acknowledge our own fallenness before God, Frank
says, we fall prey to self-righteousness and pride and even hatred.
"If you buy into a kind of logical, rationalistic, legalistic evanglical-
ism, you can't get past that. So I'm not sure you can really love,
because you're constantly drawing lines, making judgments about
others, and your love becomes condescension. It's conditional, and
it's reaching down to the other, reaching across the line to the evil
one. It's not embracing one who is within the same circle of sinfulness as you are. I think Paul, the apostle, draws a circle around
all of us and says, 'we're *all* sinners.' "

What Frank calls rationalistic evangelicalism doesn't admit of that
possibility. It draws rigid lines separating good from evil. One of
the most persistent refrains in evangelical sermons is the contrast
between Christianity and the world. "I'm to the point now when I
know I'm in the presence of bad theology when I hear that line
being drawn," Frank said. "I'm not in the presence of the gospel.

"What distinguishes a Christian from a non-Christian is confession, that we confess who we are, that we fall within that 360-degree
circle of sinfulness. There's a certain freedom in that, in acknowledging our humanity, our sinfulness before God and recognizing
that Christ alone restores us to a relationship with God. That ability
to confess, to acknowledge my fallenness, it seems to me, is a wonderful gift. I cannot with any justification walk down Castro Street
and think of myself as better than the gay couples who walk by arm
in arm. I cannot do that. I'm one with them in some respects, and
if I thought about it for about twenty seconds, I could think of some
ways in which I am just like them."

Rationalistic evangelicalism lies at the root of these moralistic
impulses. Rationalistic theology, which Frank traces to Enlightenment influences, strips the Bible of its dynamic character. "Evangelicals start with an inerrant Bible, which says that the Scriptures

are without error in the original autographs—which, by the way, we don't have. *Inerrancy* is a rationalistic term; it doesn't talk about a living Word. Evangelicals, it seems, need a Bible that can be nicely categorized, outlined, systematically organized, doctrinally elaborated, and all that stuff, so they can have all their 'i's dotted and 't's crossed. It places some kind of guarantee on our theology. It's necessary somehow to give credibility to the fact that we have abstracted a theological system away from the Bible and then presented it as the truth. But that whole process kills the living truth somehow."

The evangelical fondness for proof-texts, seizing on a specific Bible verse to shore up every argument, follows from this rationalistic bent. "We have a verse for everything. That's part of the rationalism. We treat the Bible as a series of numbers having little or no relationship to one another. We take a number here and a number there and plug them into our little grid."

There is, as Frank points out, an irony in all this. Evangelicals were under attack by rationalists—by Darwinism and the canons of the Enlightenment—at the turn of the century. Rather than continuing to insist on the importance of faith, however, evangelicals bought into a rationalistic epistemology entirely. As a consequence, the evangelical subculture today is peppered with groups organized to prove the existence of God, to supply evidences for miracles, proofs for the resurrection, and even to propagate something called "scientific creationism," which seeks to vindicate the Genesis account of creation. "Rationalism is a tight logical system," Frank says. "You're either right or you're wrong. If your logic works out, then you're right. You win. And I think evangelical logic-choppers buy into that because it gives them a sense of certainty. It adds up. If the logic adds up to your conclusion, you need to brook no opposition. It's really a tool of violence.

"The Pharisees in the New Testament are a good example of that. They're the most moral people in the Bible, and yet they're the ones who kill Jesus. The Pharisees become almost the centerpiece of the New Testament as a paradigm of fallen humanity, and yet these are the most moral, most religious people in the first century. They even use their absolute morality against Jesus. They come to

Jesus and say, 'Hmm, let's see now. By the terms of our absolute morality, you have just broken the Sabbath.' So we have human beings using absolute morality to do violence against God, even as they insist that God is the author of their morality. These are moral people. They're not bastards any more than we are. Absolute morality makes legalists. So in that context morality becomes a tool of violence. The gospel says we're all bastards, but God loves us anyway. The moralist says, 'Maybe you're a bastard, and I *used* to be one.' That's a betrayal of the gospel, the good news of our salvation through Christ. The Bible teaches that Jesus saves us in spite of ourselves."

Clearly, what animates Frank is what he calls "the life of the mind." He reads voraciously and widely, even obsessively—fiction, theology, sociology, psychology, economics, history—and he loves talking about ideas. A book is seldom out of reach. He is himself relentlessly rational, and so his criticism of evangelical "logic-choppers" sometimes cuts close to home. But he is not one-dimensional. He enjoys music and good food (we made more than one pilgrimage in San Francisco in search of the perfect sourdough bread). He seems to gather strength and sustenance from the wilderness, and occasionally he will take a break from study to split wood for the houses and cabins at Lincoln. He regularly leavens his conversations with a gentle humor, which he often turns on himself in a self-deprecating way that suggests that, however earnest he may appear at times, he prefers not to take himself too seriously.

Life at the Oregon Extension revolves around intellectual pursuits, and, in that way, Lincoln represents an extension of Frank's own eclectic interests. Although Frank, graying now as he approaches his mid-forties, seems uncomfortable about assuming leadership, the other faculty seem tacitly to acknowledge that much of the spirit, energy, and direction of the Oregon Extension comes from him. Not that everyone else is just a bit player; indeed, one of the striking characteristics of the place is its sense of collegiality, of shared purpose. The faculty as well as the entire college program tend to ignore the boundaries of traditional academic disciplines. During my visit, Sam Alvord, who holds several advanced degrees in English, lectured on Jacques Ellul, a French sociologist. Jim Titus, Lincoln's resident biologist, has recently shown an interest in Martin Luther and Reformation theology. John Linton, who joined the faculty in 1980, reads everything from astrophysics to Old Testament, the field in which he earned his doctorate.

The result is a kind of cauldron of ideas, regularly seasoned with new insights and constantly stirred and restirred in discussion, whether structured discussions in the classroom or informal conversations on a wilderness trail or over coffee at the Mountain View Inn down the road. Because the faculty and students read many of the same books, there is a common intellectual genealogy that shapes their thought. Frank first read and lectured on Jacques Ellul in the autumn of 1975, the year the Oregon Extension opened. "I had a sense that Ellul was on to something," Frank recalled. Ellul, a Christian, sees the modern believer as caught in a dialectic, torn between two commands: "do something" and "whatever you are doing means nothing." Ellul's reading of the Bible and his understanding of the human condition lead him to be suspicious of political change and human institutions generally, and that suspicion allows the Christian a certain detachment, an indifference to the success of his or her actions. Changes in the world, Ellul believes, are often cosmetic. The real lostness, boundness, captivity of the human condition has not changed; we've just changed the outward appearance of our masters. Humans are captive to a whole variety of determinisms—sociological, economic, biological. Paradoxically, according to Ellul, the beginning of freedom is the acknowledgement of our unfreedom, an awareness of the determinisms that bind us and circumscribe our lives. Real freedom is an experience that can occur only by the grace of God and in the presence of the revelation of God in Jesus Christ.

Ernest Becker, a cultural anthropologist, also has had a formative influence on the people at Lincoln. In *Escape from Evil*, Becker argues that all evil and misery in the world can be traced to man's fear of death and his attempts to make himself immortal. Man devises all sorts of constructs to convince himself that he will live forever, and he invests himself in heroic figures who define the enemy and then symbolically slay that enemy. People project their

own puny selves onto the hero and feel as if they're full of power
and righteousness. This allows them to avoid facing their own mortality. Evangelicals, Frank says, have consistently rendered their
allegiance to such heroic figures, various charismatic, pugnacious
leaders like Billy Sunday and Jimmy Swaggart who take on and
conquer the enemy, and who in so doing vindicate the power and
righteousness of their followers.

Other intellectual influences on Frank and the Oregon program
include social critics such as Wendell Berry and Philip Slater, sociologists like Peter Berger and Max Weber. In recent years, they
have been reading the theology of William Stringfellow, Vernard
Eller, Martin Luther, Søren Kierkegaard, and Karl Barth.

That pantheon of theologians certainly places the people at Oregon outside the mainstream of evangelical thought, whose taste in
theology frequently runs more toward Carl F. H. Henry, Chuck
Swindoll, and Robert Schuller. Indeed, it is difficult to escape the
impression that the geographical isolation of Lincoln, for all its bucol-
ic delights, has bred an intellectual isolation as well. Frank and his
colleagues sometimes resemble prophetic curmudgeons, dressed in
sackcloth and ashes and crying doom, primarily for one another's
benefit. In the early years of the Oregon Extension, they regularly
brought in outside lecturers, but that practice has waned. "We're
finding fewer and fewer people who speak our language," Frank
conceded, "who address the kinds of issues we care about."

Frank thinks the arrival in 1980 of John Linton, a Bible scholar,
goaded the folks at Lincoln to return to the Bible with renewed
seriousness and fresh understanding, absent the biases of their fundamentalist upbringings. "Linton has taught me to read all the ethical tables in the Bible—particularly the passages where Paul says
do this, do that, don't do this, don't do that—the way Karl Barth
read them," Frank said. "Barth believes that the imperative is always
imbedded in the indicative. He points out that there's always a
statement before and after those ethical tables that we don't actually
do those things we're supposed to, and yet God forgives us. We are
saved, now and forever, despite our shortcomings. Barth says that
it's in the context of knowing the embrace of God that we can carry

out these things. That gives a very different feel to the ethical tables than what I was taught growing up."

The evangelical weakness for moralizing, however, gives these ethical tables exaggerated importance. "There are relatively few of these tables," Frank notes. "It's just that we evangelicals have pulled them all out and memorized them and made our kids memorize them. We're drawn to them like a magnet." Frank sees this evangelical reliance on rigid, legalistic morality as a symptom of adolescence, and he has thought for some time about evangelicalism as a type of sustained adolescence. No stage of life is more prone to hero worship than adolescence. An adolescent is strongly influenced by group conformity and the expectations of other people; it's a stage in which self-consciousness is at its height. "I see the evangelicals' penchant for gazing inward to assess their own spirituality as a heightened form of self-consciousness," he said. "They're constantly comparing themselves to the standards of spiritual behavior they've established and asking 'How am I doing?' and 'Am I good enough?' and 'How do I appear to others?' " Spiritual appearances are very important to evangelicals, just as an adolescent spends a lot of time in front of the mirror.

Adolescence is also a period of rebellion, a search for individuality, identifying yourself in opposition to authority—feeling on the one hand that you have to submit to authority and on the other hand chafing under it and wishing you could be your own boss. "My instinct is that evangelicals don't love God very much, that they relate to God the way a child or an adolescent relates to an authority figure," Frank said. "So there's often a lot of fear in their motivation, and there's mistrust of who God is. And I think there's also a lot of anger, but it's all suppressed because, of course, you can't be angry with God any more than an adolescent is supposed to be angry with his parents."

The Lincoln Christian Church meets in the pine-paneled cookhouse early on Sunday mornings. People from both the Oregon Extension and the surrounding mountain community gather for worship just as the sun clears the surrounding mountain ridges and chases off the white, wispy clouds that shroud the tops of the pine trees. The morning chill lingers, however. Like everything else here, worship at the Lincoln Christian Church is casual, not all that far removed from the house-church days back in Deerfield; the people here have little patience with ritual or formality of any kind. Patsy Alvord plays the piano, and the congregation—students, faculty, mountain folk, and children, lots of children—sings with exuberance. Sam Alvord, wearing corduroy pants and a crew-neck sweater, rises to welcome the worshippers. Looking across the congregation of thirty or so seated before him, he acknowledges the return of some who have been away for several weeks and then welcomes a former student, an alumnus of the Oregon Extension from its early years. "You haven't changed much," Alvord tells him. "It's good to see you again." He then asks if there are announcements, prayer requests, or items of thanksgiving. Several ask prayer for family members or neighbors. Someone says, "I'd like to thank whoever it is who gets up early on Sunday mornings to start a fire in the stove so it's nice and warm for church." After a pause, Howard Claassen, a retired physicist from Wheaton College who has built a home there on the mountain, says quietly but with evident satisfaction, "I'll consider myself thanked."

In addition to his teaching responsibilities and other tasks around Lincoln, Alvord, known sometimes as Marryin' Sam for all the weddings he has performed for former students and community folk, has taken on the role of unofficial pastor of Lincoln Christian Church. There is a genial ease to the proceedings, an informality that extends from the welcome to the prayers to Alvord's brief homily, which concludes the meeting.

In some respects, as befits a community centered around learning, the Sunday Bible study that follows the worship service is more important than the service itself. After a twenty-minute break, John Linton shambles into the room. Linton is the picture of perpetual dishevelment, and he takes a lot of good-natured ribbing from his colleagues. Dressed in denims, hiking boots, a flannel shirt, and a pea-green army coat, he seems to have a steaming mug of coffee fused permanently to his right fist. He wears a brown woolen stocking hat pulled down over his longish, straight hair. ("I think he puts that hat on about the first of November," Frank commented, "and doesn't take it off again until sometime in April.") Linton, however, with the earnestness with which he approaches the Bible, has added a whole new dimension to the community at Lincoln. In Frank's words, "Linton's gotten us into the Bible." Linton himself, with characteristic understatement, says, "I have the fond hope that the Bible might mean something."

It's easy, Frank thinks, for evangelicals to dismiss the Bible, even though they give lip service to its importance and constantly argue its inerrancy. "It's so obvious to me now that when you take a book like the Bible, declare it inerrant, and extract everything from it and put it all into a nice, neat little system and tell your kids what they're supposed to believe, the book becomes dead. I remember when I was maybe thirty saying something like—I'm embarrassed to tell about it even now—saying something like, 'Well, what's so difficult to know about the Bible? It says we're supposed to love each other, so let's just get busy and do it!' That's a very pious way of saying 'This is just a book that has an idea in it that God wants us to understand and try to work out in our lives,' as if we were autonomous people who could just start doing that, as if we didn't have to hear on a daily basis who we are and who God is in contradistinction to ourselves.

"So what Linton does is he's brought the book alive for us. Through him, we're hearing the Word being spoken afresh. Sometimes he takes a passage of Scripture that we, growing up in evangelical households, have heard all of our lives and he'll put an inflection on a word and we'll see it in a whole new light. It's exciting stuff."

Linton pulls up a chair in the middle of the room and announces that this morning's study centers around Hebrews 6, a passage that has long bedeviled evangelicals because it seems to admit of the possibility that a believer might lose his or her salvation. After reading the chapter, Linton asks, "Did you hear anything as this chapter was read that you wanted to get into?" There follows a series of questions which Linton acknowledges with only a sentence or two, but he is merely collecting the thoughts and comments of the group, almost relishing their confusion.

Linton leans back in his chair. "Here's what I think is going on. The writer is talking about contrition or penance, not as a one-time occurrence, but that all of life should be an act of contrition. Here's how I would want to interpret this. When the Bible speaks of enlightenment, both here and in the first chapter of John, it makes it clear that the true light which enlightens every man is Jesus. He comes unto His own, and His own reject Him. That's a sad story, unbelievably sad. But as many as received Him, He gave to them the authority to be the children of God. You can't then invent all sorts of things in the Christian life to try to get enlightened. That's a key move, because we're forever trying to devise programs to get enlightened, to make us more spiritual, as though Jesus hadn't already enlightened us.

"The writer of Hebrews says that such enlightenment lies beyond our power. We don't have this freedom in ourselves; it is God's gift. And can we be certain that God has given it to us? Yes, of course; He's sworn once to Abraham and another time when he said, 'thou art a priest according to the order of Melchizedek forever.' The traditional, fundamentalist way of reading this passage engenders doubts about whether or not our salvation is secure, but that's not what the writer is saying at all."

As the discussion continues, Linton grows more and more animated; the caffeine apparently has kicked in. "Now if you're following this even roughly, you're probably wondering what this Melchizedek business has to do with this. What is it about Melchizedek and Jesus being a priest after the order of Melchizedek? What does it mean that Jesus is a priest forever, and how is that a rebuke to people who are trying to make a new foundation?"

"He's doing it for them," someone answers.

"He's doing it how often for them?"

"All the time."

"That's right. Somehow, Jesus is serving you as priest in a way that you can't get around. So don't start a new foundation based on your own righteousness or contrition. You've got a high priest in Jesus who lasts forever and ever and ever. You know who makes repentance for you? Jesus makes repentance for you. He repents. You think that you're repenting? Well, yeah, that's a good thing.

You ought to do that. But don't confuse it with the repentance that's done by the priest, Jesus, who mediates between your sinfulness and God's holiness. Jesus is doing that forever!"

Linton's approach to the Bible has influenced everyone at Lincoln. "Linton has an almost mystical attachment to the Bible," Frank said. "There may be something to that."

That evening in his living room, I remarked to Frank that I didn't think he would willingly have called himself an evangelical ten years ago. He said no, probably not—certainly not with any enthusiasm. Even now, he sometimes refers to evangelicals as "they" and at other times as "we," an ambivalence born, it seems, not so much of rebellion as of sadness at the ways evangelicals have misused the gospel. "But I've come to see that I *am* an evangelical," he insisted. "It's part of who I am, my history. At some psychological level, I'm thoroughly in the camp. There was a point ten years ago when I was trying to get free of the subculture. Now I feel like I'm almost being forced out of it, not by people but by a kind of despair."

Frank spoke in slow, measured phrases. A chilly autumn breeze swept in through the screen door. "I'm increasingly gripped by the tragedy of the subculture, by the harm it does to its people, especially its kids. It's becoming more and more clear to me that the subculture is based on lies and denials. It doesn't understand the gospel. What is this good news that we're supposed to be so excited about? Evangelicals don't have a clue, it seems to me. It's appearing to me more and more as a real tragedy. This group of people, and I among them for a long time, that felt as if it was the guarantor of orthodoxy in America and even the world, is blind. Its very gospel is secularized; it has bought into a rationalistic, secular epistemology. It's become more interested in morality than grace, and in that way it's just like any other subculture. Every subculture is interested in morality. We're no better than the Mormons; in fact, in terms of morality, we're not as good as the Mormons. The Mormons outdo us. If that's what the gospel is all about, then they're to be emulated. But they don't understand the gospel, either. We think we do.

"It just seems like a tragedy to me, all these people going through these motions and all these big churches, and all our kids seem like they're more and more lost. More and more of our students have little or no interest in God or hate God altogether. They think of Him as a being who gives them rules but doesn't love them."

But Frank's theology, let alone his temperament, will not allow him to succumb to despair. His newly recovered sense of identity as an evangelical has led to engagement with other evangelicals, an almost messianic effort to save evangelicalism from itself, even though he recognizes the danger of falling into the very moralistic trap he argues against. "I suspect that, so often, even the way I talk about a theology that doesn't draw lines resorts to line-drawing in spite of itself," he acknowledged, "by saying the way you read the Bible is wrong." Frank's book, *Less Than Conquerors: How Evangelicals Entered the Twentieth Century*, explores the ways in which evangelicals betrayed the gospel in the face of various cultural pressures around the turn of the century.[3] He argues that fundamentalists went wrong after the turn of the century when they became enslaved by a contrived, legalistic ethical system—a set of behavioral strictures and taboos—which effectively institutionalized their penchant for line-drawing. They also embraced dispensational premillennialism, which identified evangelicals themselves as the only moral people left in the world. Dispensationalism, as put forward by John Nelson Darby, C. I. Scofield, Dwight Moody, and others, was based on the premise that the world was getting worse and worse. Dispensationalists smugly insisted that they knew what others, whom they labeled non-Christians, did not—namely, a plan for the ages, as revealed in the recondite passages of Scripture, that identified evangelicals as the righteous remnant and, therefore, privy to God's secrets. Frank's book interleaves history with theology, sociology, and cultural analysis, an interdisciplinary approach that clearly reflects his intellectual tastes.

He has also lectured at various evangelical colleges around the country, and on August 23, 1986, he addressed the faculty of Wheaton College, the bastion of evangelicalism where he earned his bachelor's degree twenty-three years earlier. Frank spoke of the brokenness and pain that he has witnessed among so many adolescent evangelicals, a sense of alienation from a God who demands all sorts of moral and behavioral concessions from them—the God of their parents' making, who is more interested in exacting tribute than bestowing His grace. He noted that these students, products of a consumer culture that values appearance above all else, have become very adept at hiding the pain they feel behind well-scrubbed facades of happiness and piety and self-assurance.

I asked Frank to distill the argument of his next book, a work now in progress. "Evangelicals have lost sight of the good news of the gospel," he said, "the possibility that in Jesus we see God's suffering for all of us. He turns our sin and violence against Him to our good and declares His mercy—unlimited, free mercy—to all of us. We can now live in a kind of thankfulness and freedom, accepting that mercy.

"That's such good news to me. It just sounds like such good news to me. I can declare that good news. My job isn't to go out and say to someone, 'Unless you repent, you shall surely die, and I shall not,' or something like that, but rather, 'You and I are both really messed up, and God declares that He loves us both and continues to forgive us day by day and shows His mercy infinitely and eternally to us, regardless of our merit.'

"When have evangelicals ever taken seriously the statement of Jesus on the cross, 'Father, forgive them, for they don't know what they're doing'? We don't take that seriously. We say, 'Father, we'll forgive those who know what they are doing, who say that they're sinners and repent.' It's conditional. But Jesus says about even His killers, who are *not* repentant—they're not weeping and wailing and gnashing their teeth; they're probably jeering and cheering—but Jesus says, 'Forgive them, they don't know what they're doing.' That's very good news, that somehow, way over our heads, in ways we are not even free half the time to admit or understand or explain, Jesus is forgiving us. That's real good news to me. I don't think evangelicals understand that concept. Evangelicals so often are the bearers of bad news: 'Unless you repent, you shall surely die.' That's true, but that's not the whole story. And if you *do* repent, evangelicals insist, then you've got to get your whole life organized and start jumping through these hoops and being a good Christian. At any time, you could fall out of fellowship with God. You've got to show yourself to be better than the rest of the world so you can be a witness for Christ. That keeps us from doing what Jesus did, which is hang around with sinners and drunks. We don't do that.

"I want this next book to stop evangelicals dead in their tracks. I would love to do that." The crusty prophet has emerged again. He hesitated, laughed at his own pretensions, and then continued. "I would love to see the whole evangelical subculture in this country raising its hands in praise to God and saying, 'We are sorry bastards, but God is merciful.' Wouldn't that be wonderful? There'd be a revival! That would be so refreshing. 'We are sorry bastards. Lord, have mercy.' "

NOTES

1. Since my visit, the Oregon Extension has become affiliated with Houghton College, a Wesleyan school in western New York rather than Trinity College. A new president at Trinity College, eager to placate some of the more insistent fundamentalists within Trinity's supporting denomination, the Evangelical Free Church of America, severed the college's ties with the Oregon program.

2. From "A Proposal for a Trek Curriculum," photocopy.

3. Douglas W. Frank, *Less Than Conquerors: How Evangelicals Entered the Twentieth Century* (Grand Rapids: Wm. B. Eerdmans, 1986).

Epilogue

MY INTERLOCUTOR has been gazing out the window. He turns now, clears his throat, and regards me across the desk.

"You seemed to let that Frank character speak for you in the last chapter," he says. I allow that, well, yes, perhaps I did. What I admire about Frank, I explain, is his ability to maintain a distance from all the ephemera of American evangelicalism without discarding his faith. It's my impression, moreover, that most people reared in the evangelical subculture either embrace it altogether or abandon it altogether. Either option strikes me as disingenuous, an easy way around a tradition that is at once rich in theological insights and mired in contradictions.

A prominent historian of American religion is fond of describing evangelicalism in America as a mosaic, a metaphor intended to convey a sense of its multiplicity, diversity, and complexity. While I sympathize with the sentiment behind such a description, American evangelicalism as mosaic is an image that I've never found compelling. It belies, I think, the folk appeal of evangelicalism, its grass roots character. For me, a mosaic conjures European patronage rather than American piety. If you study a mosaic from a distance, moreover, an overall design comes into focus.

Discerning any single pattern in American evangelicalism is difficult at best. Beyond general—but by no means unanimous—agreement on personal conversion, the importance of Scripture, and the expectation of an apocalypse, evangelicals contend with one another over the rigor of those beliefs and the appropriate expressions of piety. Splitting theological hairs over such recondite doctrines as premillennialism or the gifts of the Spirit or the exact mode of biblical inspiration has become something of a sport in evangelical circles, but one that is played with ferocious earnestness. The slightest deviation from the position that one or another group stakes out as "orthodox" provides the occasion for expulsion or schism.

Belief has always been important to evangelicals. "*Believe* on the Lord Jesus Christ, and thou shalt be saved," the Authorized Version admonishes.[1] Evangelicals regularly repeat that refrain, and, lacking hierarchical structures or liturgical rubrics, evangelicalism in America is held together in large measure by its insistence that followers subscribe to a set of doctrines, however variously they might be defined from one evangelical congregation to the next. That in itself, I think, sets evangelicalism somewhat apart from other religious traditions in America. Jews in America (as elsewhere) are bound by their common identity as a separate people. Roman Catholics acknowledge a common authority, even though of late they have not followed the dictates of that hierarchy. Methodists rely on a strong organizational structure; for many Lutherans, there is a kind of vestigial ethnicity that unites the various groups. Episcopalians historically have been latitudinarian in their theology, but what distinguishes them is their worship, their shared liturgy as prescribed in the Book of Common Prayer. The history of mainline Presbyterianism over the past century can be read as a retreat from confessionalism, so that what holds Presbyterians together is polity, the impulse to do everything "decently and in order." Denied ordinations and heresy trials among Presbyterians in recent decades have been challenged successfully on *procedural* grounds, not on the basis of whether or not the principal affirms the right doctrines.

These are generalizations, to be sure, but one of the reasons that belief is so important to evangelicals may be that they cannot claim any of these other "adhesives" as the basis for whatever cohesion exists among them. Evangelicals unite instead behind a charismatic leader, a common spiritual experience, or a set of doctrines—and, more than likely, some combination of the three. Convictions are essential to that mixture. We live in a skeptical, post-Enlightenment age where belief has become unfashionable; the liberal and ecumenical trends in Protestant theology, furthermore, have blurred doctrinal differences in the name of unity, toleration, and inclusiveness. But while many theologians and denominational leaders plunged headlong into the ecumenical current, a large number of their communicants stayed on the riverbank.[2] People need boundaries in their lives, a sense of limits, a feeling for what is appropriate and inappropriate, right and wrong, true and heretical.

Evangelicalism provides that. For a growing number of Americans, it offers an unambiguous morality in an age of moral and ethical uncertainty. It offers theological surety in a culture that is not yet ready to divest itself entirely of its belief in God. For many people in the waning decades of the twentieth century who recognize that science and technology has not been the promised savior of civilization, belief is more comfortable than unbelief, faith is preferable to doubt.

Despite the evangelicals' general insistence on belief, however, they cannot agree on any one configuration of doctrines. And so, parodoxically, their doctrinal precisionism has produced the incredibly diverse evangelical subculture in America: fundamentalists, pentecostals, charismatics, Wesleyans, Nazarenes, Assemblies of God, Church of God, Church of the Open Bible, fifty-some stripes of Baptists, not to mention independent, non-affiliated congregations that go by names like Evangelical Chapel or Community Bible Church. All of them fall (more or less willingly) under the rubric of evangelicalism.

Were I to designate a metaphor for this rather unwieldy evangelical subculture, I'd find the image of a patchwork quilt more satisfying than a mosaic. A quilt, especially one produced at a quilting bee, is folk art rather than fine art; it requires the work of many hands, each of which contributes its own "signature" to the project.

Its beauty, moreover, lies precisely in its variegated texture and even, sometimes, in the absence of an overall pattern. Unlike a mosaic, it is also quintessentially American.

Evangelicalism itself, I think, is quintessentially American. Religious disestablishment—the absence of a state church—gave rise in the United States to a kind of free market of religion. Various denominations and individual congregations compete with one another for popular followings, thereby lending an unmistakably populist cast to religion in America. Evangelicals have always fared well in this competition. Their preachers have mastered the art of oral discourse, especially persuasive rhetoric, in a nation of talkers, among a people who pick up a telephone rather than write a letter, who enjoy the static-borne banter of CB radios, who are addicted to talk of all kinds, including the prattle of commercials and talk shows on radio and television. Evangelical preaching and worship, casual and nonliturgical, comes across well in the open fields of the eighteenth century or over the airwaves of the twentieth.[3] Indeed, the informality of evangelical worship reflects the larger culture. We Americans prize informality, witness our impulse to address others, even fresh acquaintances, by their first names. Other countries mint coins or strike medals to commemorate important occasions; in America we silk-screen a few dozen tee-shirts: TANGLEWOOD 50, THE INDY 500, RAGBRAI XVI, HANDS ACROSS AMERICA, SUPER-BOWL XXI.

America is also a media culture—more particularly, a television culture. Television is the great validator. Appearing on television (for whatever reason) makes you *someone*; without it, as any also-ran politician can attest, you are no one going nowhere. The televangelists understand that, I think. They understand Americans' fixation with celebrity, and they recognize the popular appeal of casual, informal worship and expert preaching, especially when it purports to champion "traditional values" in an age that seems to have lost its moral moorings.

The weakness for celebrity, the affinities between evangelicalism and the medium of television, and the tendency of evangelicals to gravitate to charismatic leaders, leave the subculture vulnerable to self-aggrandizement and egomania. "Nobody wants to play rhythm guitar behind Jesus," as the Oak Ridge Boys say, "everybody wants to be the lead singer in the band."[4] But there are other ways in which American culture and the evangelical subculture have fed off each other. Prosperity theology, which amounts to a baptism of American materialism and consumerism, is all the rage in evangelical circles these days, as I discovered in my travels. Jesus will save your soul and your marriage, make you happy, heal your body, and even make you rich. Who wouldn't look twice at that offer? Even if you drop a twenty in the collection plate every Sunday, it's still cheaper than a therapist. Surely such a message has an obvious appeal to the middle-class aspirations of many American evangelicals, but I had been unprepared for how thoroughly the God-will-make-you-rich-and-happy pablum has pervaded evangelicalism, especially among people who pride themselves on biblical literalism. Whatever happened to the scandal of the gospel, to Jesus's invitation to forsake everything—family and fishing boats, beachhouses and BMWs—to follow Him?

Returning to the subculture after several years' hiatus, moreover, I was astounded at how the media, especially television, have permeated evangelical worship. Soloists and musical ensembles gyrate to "canned" orchestra music from cassette tapes played over elaborate sound systems. Applause regularly punctuated Sunday morning services almost everywhere I went, as though each congregation was a studio audience. God apparently likes applause, a fact that had eluded me as I grew up within the evangelical subculture.

Television, furthermore, only exaggerates the evangelical weakness for charismatic leaders and the cult of personality. Lacking an overarching organization, distinctive polity, authority structure, or liturgical rubric, evangelicals generally galvanize around a personality who articulates—and even defines—the faith of his followers according to his own idiosyncratic reading of the Bible. Indeed, what an evangelical leader does—be he Jimmy Swaggart or Robert Schuller or Neal Frisby or Jack Wyrtzen—is to construct a reality for his followers. Word of Life Island in the Adirondacks, Dallas Theological Seminary, the Capstone Cathedral in Phoenix, Camp Freedom in Florida, and even Donald Thompson's films are all socially constructed universes, full of symbols and invested with meaning.[5] In Phoenix, Neal Frisby has contrived a world of divine healing and deliverance in which Frisby himself, the Rainbow Prophet and former alcoholic, provides a symbol of hope for people who clearly do not share in the good life of this world. The Capstone Cathedral, replete with prophetic and dispensational symbolism, offers a retreat from that outside world.

Other structured realities may be less bizarre, but they also offer a retreat and regular commerce with others who share similar views of the world. The peculiar and highly regimented theology of Dallas Theological Seminary is at odds with the prevailing currents of the broader society, and yet there in the heart of Texas a group of white male seminarians dressed in yuppie suits can gather around a table in the student center to discuss the nuances of their eschatology without fear of challenge, or they can chortle about a professor's masterful, ugly put-down of a female student. The structured reality of Voice of Calvary in Mississippi represents a nobler vision, to be sure—one of racial harmony and social justice—but it is no less illusory, no less incongruous with the larger world. In the contrived universe of Jack Wyrtzen's ninety-acre island, the girls are modest, the boys chaste, and everyone is a "Christian" (or soon will be). Douglas Frank's community, cradled in the Cascade Mountains, is also quite insular, try as he will to ensure that theirs is a geographical isolation and not an intellectual one. In the celluloid world of Donald Thompson's films, righteousness prevails over godlessness, and the meek finally inherit the earth, albeit after an apocalyptic struggle.

In the larger universe, of course, the meek do *not* inherit the earth any more than teenagers wear bathing togs that reach beyond their fingertips or a majority of Americans subscribe to dispensationalism. All of these socially constructed realities, then, offer an alternate, idealized view of the world, a place of retreat and escape, no less than the utopian communities that dotted the American landscape in the nineteenth century. Indeed, the entire evangelical subculture itself is a socially constructed reality, a place of retreat built primarily after the Scopes Trial of 1925, when fundamentalists became convinced that the larger American culture had abandoned them. Nestled safely within the subculture for most of the twentieth century, evangelicals smugly contrasted their world with the outside world in a kind of orgy of dualistic rhetoric: good *versus* evil, sacred *versus* secular, righteous *versus* unrighteous, saved *versus* damned. Evangelicals felt secure within the cocoon of this contrived universe of churches, summer camps, Bible institutes, colleges, and seminaries. Only in the mid-to-late 1970s, when a conservative mood swing looked congenial and when politicians promised, in effect, to impose the ethos of the evangelical subculture on *all* of American society, did evangelicals begin to venture outside the cocoon.

Since undertaking this project, I have been asked countless times for my opinions about the future of evangelicalism in America. The question invariably comes from nonevangelicals who have little appreciation for the history of evangelicalism and who clearly are skittish about the influence of fundamentalists in politics. Although I am more comfortable as a historian than as a prognosticator, I generally respond that we can look for some mitigation of fundamentalist ardor in the coming years—it's difficult, after all, to sustain religious fervor for a long period of time, and even more difficult to pass that piety along to the next generation—but that evangelicals will continue to make their presence felt in American culture, just as they have (more or less visibly) throughout American history.

If my peregrinations taught me nothing else, they showed me that the evangelical subculture is broad and deep in the United States, and it is sustained by numberless institutions—churches, missions, camp meetings, publishing houses, colleges, seminaries, Christian schools, Bible camps—that often escape the notice of the casual observer. This network of institutions provided the foundation for the evangelical return to the public arena in recent years.

Evangelicalism will also persist, I think, because of its timeless appeal. It promises intimacy with God, a support community, an unambiguous morality, and answers to the riddles of eternity. It offers eternal life, and nothing frightens us mortals more than death. The evangelical theology of conversion and assurances of a reward in heaven appeal to Americans, who have always nurtured the illusion that they control their own destinies. Many evangelical preachers have added still other enticements: the promise of deliverance from sickness, suffering, and pain, and, more recently, the prospect of material prosperity.

Evangelicalism simply will not go away. In the 1920s H. L. Mencken, no friend of evangelicals, remarked that if you tossed an egg out of a Pullman window almost anywhere in the country, you would hit a fundamentalist. Pullman cars are obsolete in America today. Fundamentalists are still around.

No pilgrim returns from his journey unchanged. Myself, I shall long remember the energy and self-assurance of Donald Thompson, the resilient faith of Jacob and Ada Sollenberger, and the quiet determination of Innocent Good House, fighting to reconcile his faith with his heritage, straining to see signs of hope among his beleaguered people. I recall Neal Frisby, the Rainbow Prophet of Revelation, as a pathetic figure, although I am confident he would refuse my sympathy. I shall also remember Frisby's followers who, night after night, bring their sad, broken lives to Jesus. If Douglas Frank is right, however, we all have sad, broken lives, and all our self-righteous moralizing serves only as an artifice to shield us from that awful truth. I recognize myself in the adolescent struggles of Amy Durkin, Candy Schroeder, and Carl Watkins. I wonder where their pilgrimages will lead. Will they stumble by the way or somehow, through persistence or fate or even the grace of God, claim the faith of their parents as their own? I won't soon forget the dolorous strains of "Seek Ye First the Kingdom of God" in Santa Ana, California, the triumphalism of "Mine Eyes Have Seen the Glory" in Concord, New Hampshire, or singing "We Shall Overcome" on the anniversary of Martin Luther King's birth with the folks of Mound Bayou, Mississippi, who still have so much to overcome.

I think I heard the gospel in those hymns. I heard the gospel at various discrete moments in my travels and certainly in Douglas Frank's sad yet insistent quarrel—a lover's quarrel, really—with evangelicalism. Those small epiphanies affected me, evoking as they did the religion of my childhood. That the evangelical gospel can still be heard at all above the din of what passes for evangelicalism in America today is miracle enough, perhaps, to capture the attention of even the most jaded observer. What it all means I'm not yet sure, but I now find it less easy to dismiss the preposterous evangelical claims about a God of amazing grace who, despite our bumbling and nonsense and hoary theological schemes, saves us from ourselves.

No pilgrim, after all, returns from his journey unchanged.

NOTES

1. Acts 16:31 (KJV), italics mine.

2. This is the conclusion—that mainline churches are losing members because of their inchoate theology—of Wade Clark Roof and William McKinney, *American Mainline Religion: Its Changing Shape and Future* (New Brunswick, N.J.: Rutgers University Press, 1987).

3. I owe this idea of America as a nation of talkers to Harry Stout.

4. The refrain from "Rhythm Guitar," by T. A. Hill.

5. On the social construction of reality, see Peter L. Berger and Thomas Luckmann, *The Social Construction of Reality: A Treatise in the Sociology of Knowledge* (Garden City, N.Y.: Doubleday & Co., 1966).

INDEX